THE PHANTOM GRINGO BOAT

THE PHANTOM GRINGO BOAT

Shamanic Discourse and Development in Panama

STEPHANIE C. KANE

SMITHSONIAN INSTITUTION PRESS

WASHINGTON AND LONDON

Copy Editor: Craig Noll
Production Editor: Duke Johns
Designer: Kathleen Sims

Library of Congress Cataloging-in-Publication Data
Kane, Stephanie C.
    The phantom gringo boat : shamanic discourse and development in Panama /
Stephanie C. Kane.
    p. cm.
    Includes bibliographical references and index.
    ISBN 1-56098-361-2 (alk. paper). — ISBN 1-56098-360-4 (pbk. : alk. paper)
    1. Emberá Indians — Social conditions. 2. Emberá Indians — Government
relations. 3. Emberá Indians — Politics and government. 4. Rural development —
Panama — Darién (Province). 5. Human ecology — Political aspects — Panama —
Darién (Province). 6. Darién (Panama : Province) — Politics and government.
7. Darién (Panama : Province) — Social conditions. I. Title.
F2270.2.E43K36   1994
972.87'4004982 — dc20   93-45976

British Library Cataloguing-in-Publication Data is available

Manufactured in the United States of America
01 00 99 98 97 96   5 4 3 2

The photographs appearing in this book were taken by the author unless otherwise noted in
the captions. For permission to reproduce illustrations appearing in this book, please correspond directly with the owners of the works. The Smithsonian Institution Press does not
retain reproduction rights for these illustrations individually, or maintain a file of addresses
for photo sources.

The jacket/cover design is based on a drawing by anonymous Waunan artist(s).

To my mother's mother, Pearl Sirota,
and my father's father, Louis Kane
To Pa, the Emberá spirit of thunder and lightning
And to Ira Buchler, wherever he may be

Contents

Preface

The perspective represented most strongly here is that of the Emberá of Darién, an indigenous lowland tropical forest people with whom the author lived and worked intensively between 1984 and 1985. Indeed, this book is the first book-length ethnographic work on the Emberá of Darién, who are also known as the Chocó, a popular name that is taken from the Department of Chocó in Colombia, where many thousands of Emberá live. Included in the Chocó ascription are the Waunan (= Nonamá), a sister linguistic group of the Emberá, who live closely among them. Two other closely related indigenous groups are the Catio and Chamí.

Emberá (Chocó) Language and Text

Emberá and *Waunan* are thus the names of (1) two cultural groups commonly known as Chocó and (2) their languages, the principal feature that distinguishes them. Their languages are related (there is almost 50 percent agreement of cognate roots) but mutually unintelligible (Loewen 1963a, 1963b). In his dissertation, Loewen (1958:1) identifies twelve dialects of "Chocó": three Waunan and nine Emberá, on the basis of phonological, morphological, and lexical features associated with particular local areas in the Chocó River basin of Colombia. Whether Emberá and Waunan are of the Chibchan, Carib, or a third independent linguistic stock is yet unclear (Rivet 1943–44; Greenberg 1956; Steward and Faron 1959; Loewen 1963a, 1963b; Loukotka 1968:255–58; Key 1979). See Reichel-Dolmatoff 1945 for a bibliography of early linguistic work on the Chocó.

According to an agreement with the Emberá teachers, I use the alphabet developed by them in collaboration with Professor Rafael Gamallo for the bilingual program of Darién at the University of Panama. The accompanying phoneme chart is taken from their preliminary document.

Phoneme Chart of Emberá

Vowels

	Front	Central	Back
High	i	ɨ	u
Low	e	a	o

Note: Every vowel can occur nasalized, indicated in my transcription with umlaut (ï, ë, ɨ̈, etc.). Accent marks follow rules for Spanish stress: unless marked otherwise, words ending in a vowel or in *n* or *s* are accented on the next-to-last syllable; those ending in other letters, on the last syllable.

Consonants

		Labial	Dental	Palatal	Velar
Stops	voiceless	p	t	ch	k
	voiced	b	d	dz	g
	fortis	b′	d′		
Continuants	voiceless		s		j
	voiced		z		
Nasals		m	n	ñ	
Liquids		w	l	y	
Vibrants	simple		r		
	complex		rr		

Source: Organización de Profesionales Emberá 1984:chap. 5, pp. 4–5.

Transcription Key

The texts presented are rough translations from Emberá to Spanish to English, or from Spanish to English. They represent different levels of accuracy, depending on whether or not they were transcribed word for word from a tape recording, whether they were written down in translation as the person was speaking, or whether they were written in translation from memory. The key to transcription is the following:

T	transcription from tape recording
−T	transcription without tape recording
E	original in Emberá
S	original in Spanish.

According to this key, T/E, for example, indicates that the transcription is from a tape-recorded Emberá text; −T/S indicates that there is no tape recording and that the original speech was in Spanish.

Also, in a few places within transcriptions I include a translator's note [TN] in brackets, indicating comments made to me during translation of a text.

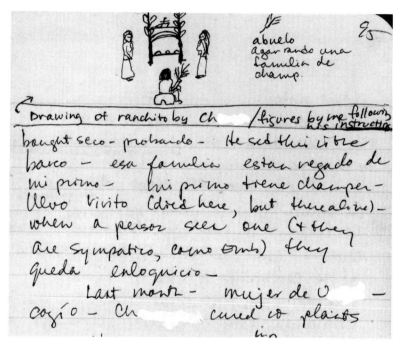

Figure 1. Field notes with sketch of Grandfather's ritual by Valentín and author.

Acknowledgments

Ten years have passed between the time this research project began and the completion of this manuscript. During those years I met scores of people who enriched my life. I thank you all. Here I mention only those most directly involved in my research and writing.

I thank the Emberá for the gifts of companionship and knowledge. Thanks to First Cacique Isidro Guainora for his confidence in my goodwill. Thanks to the storytellers, shamans, artists, and historians, whom I leave unnamed in the interests of preserving confidentiality.

I thank the non-Emberá Panamanians, North Americans, and Spaniards who eased my way through Panama. In Yaviza, thanks to the Garcías; the staff of RENARE, SNEM, COPFA, and MIDA; the curates and missionaries. In Panama City, thanks to Pedro Luis Prados and Marcela Camargo of the National Institute of Culture (INAC); the Política Indigenista; the now-defunct Forces of Defense; the Wattens and the Gorgas Memorial Laboratory; the Hughes and the Cartographic School of Fort Clayton; Olga Linares and the Smithsonian Tropical Research Institute; Francisco Herrera, Peter Herlihy, and Ana Montalvan.

I thank the Organization of American States and the Institute of Latin American Studies of the University of Texas at Austin for research grants.

I thank Ira Buchler, chair of my dissertation committee, for his guidance, friendship, and mythical discernment. Thanks to all the Texas folks: Joel Sherzer and Tony Woodbury for training in the transcription of indigenous language texts; José Limón and Amy Burce for their interest in my experiments with writing and representation.

I thank Michael Taussig for continuing to open up the discursive possibilities of scholarship.

I thank Pauline Greenhill, Vera Mark, and Michael F. Brown for their careful reading of an earlier draft of this manuscript. Thanks also to Mary Crain, Kristin Koptiuch, David McMurray, Theresa Mason, Phil Parnell, and Janet Roesler for perceptive comments on drafts of selected chapters. Thanks to Daniel Goodwin of the Smithsonian Institution Press, without whose encouragement this book may not have been written.

I thank the artists whose work enlivens these pages: Jane Benson and Lincoln Stoller for their photographs; Eli Goitein for his drawings; and Kevin Montague for printing photographs.

I thank the Kanes, the Michlers, the Savages, the Stuarts, Gayle Burbank, and Kenneth Cohen for giving me love, refreshment, and a sense of place during my years as an itinerant professional.

Special thanks to the women of my dissertation group, with whom I discovered the fabulous combination of intellectual exchange and enduring friendship: Joan Gross, Kristin Koptiuch, Vera Mark, Theresa Mason, and Janet Roesler.

Introduction

The Emberá are part of a culture area that may be characterized by the surreal dimension of its discourse and image-making. The post-Conquest conjuncture of Indian, black, and Spanish—a history of violence and strange alliance—imbues reality here with a magical cast. In a semiotics of the unnatural, the fantastic and incongruous images of the surreal remain out of keeping with the social ordinary, reminding of the cruel possibilities of disruption that have so often destroyed the continuity of everyday life in this part of the world. In this sense, the surreal is an awareness of historical extremes, a reminder of civilization's barbarities, and a source of power that expands the possibilities of discourse and evades control of outsiders. The magical real is a form of cultural resistance that is trained to history. While surreal images and survival knowledge circulate among the three races (as they call themselves), overlapping and blurring the boundaries between them, the way that each race uses image and knowledge creates their distinctive forms of cultural politics. Geographically, the culture area corresponds to the tropical forests extending, in patches now, from the Darién of Panama through the Chocó and Putumayo of Columbia and into Ecuador. Following Taussig (1980, 1987) and Whitten (1985), this ethnography grapples with the contradictory ways of apprehending the developing world that arises out of this historical conjuncture.

Although there have been no previous full-length ethnographies written of the Emberá of Darién, there is a long history of Euramerican writing that describes their culture and ecology. A number of bibliographies can orient the reader more fully to the regions of Darién and Chocó. These include Shook, Lines, and Olien 1965, Pardo 1981, and Weber and Alvarado 1984. Descriptions of nineteenth-century Darién are provided by Reclus (1972), an engineer investigating the possibility of the first interoceanic canal. The series of articles published between 1950 and 1980 by the Panamanian anthropologist Reina Torrés de (Iannello) Arauz are the best descriptions we have of previllage Emberá subsistence and symbolic practices in Darién. Faron's (1961, 1962) summer on the Chico River of Darién produced a valuable study of previllage kinship. Geographers and botanists have also contributed to our knowledge of the cultural ecology of the Emberá and Waunan of Darién; see, for example, Covich and Nickerson 1966, Bennett 1968, Duke 1970, 1986, Paganini 1970, and Herlihy 1985, 1986, whose dissertation research documented the shift from dispersed to concentrated village settlements. The Panamanian historian Francisco Herrera (1971) has written about the new politics accompanying the early phase of village formation. And I have also written a series of articles on different aspects of Emberá social life since village formation (Kane 1986a, 1986b, 1988, 1989, 1990, 1992). For comprehensive studies of regional development, see Organization of American States 1978, 1984 and Mendez 1979. Ethnographic, ethnohistorical, and geographic literature on the Emberá and Waunan of the Chocó includes Reichel-Dolmatoff 1960, 1962; Wassén and Holmer 1963; Peñaherrera De Costales and Costales Samaniego 1968; Kennedy 1972; Gordon 1957; Castrillón 1982; Pardo 1984, 1987a, 1987b, 1992; Stipek 1976; and Vasco 1985. For in-depth ethnographic studies of the blacks of the Chocó, the same group who are neighbors of the Emberá in Darién today, see Price 1955, West 1957, Pavy 1967, and Whitten 1974.

As part of this multiracial culture area, the Emberá and Waunan of Darién orient most strongly to the east and south, over the low mountains that separate Panama from Colombia. At the same time, however, they are newly integrated members of the Panamanian nation-state. In this arena, they assume a political identity and economic struggle that engages with the other indigenous groups of Panama, including the Kunas, Guamíes, Teribes, and Bokotas (Torrés de Arauz 1980; Bort and Helms 1983). While the culture area oriented toward Colombia is bound together by history and the popular imagery of the magical real, participation in the nation-state, although drawing strategically on the notion of culture, relies more heavily on a discourse of ethnic politics and development. The tension between these two orientations is an underlying theme of this ethnography.

The book is composed of shifting scenes, spliced according to theme. It sets the rhythms of everyday activities against the structures of kinship, capital, myth, and military force. Through analysis of event and habit, the kind of phenomena that would be consistent with what the Emberá refer to as the Emberá Way, I sketch the dimensions of social life that pertain to ecology, economy, politics, health, and memory. Meaning condenses around images, words, embodiments, quantifications, and secrets. In tellings gleaned from the everyday, the implicitness and ineffability of social knowledge is explored (cf. Taussig 1987:4, 287–88, 367). Shaded with lines of difference, perspective, and translation (this author's among others), the range and complexity of "the personal" is evoked.

Each chapter is organized around a set of interpretive dilemmas that highlight the way in which myth and magic are integral aspects of social life. The basic assumption underlying this interpretive theme is that empirical knowledge is always partial and partially imaginary. The phantom gringo boat, a metaphor for development, makes its first elusive appearance in Chapter 1. In this chapter, I brief the reader on the ecopolitics of regional development and articulate my intentions and methods. The next five chapters serve to familiarize the reader with Emberá practices, concerns, and mythical principles. Juxtaposing descriptions of everyday life with texts of myth and local history, Chapter 2 invites the reader to contemplate the particular discontinuities that characterize Emberá life in the late twentieth century. Around these juxtapositions circles the imaginary figure of the Indian, a negotiated fantasy that traces the ramifying paths of foreign intrusion in the context of Conquest, colonialism, and flood. The chapter begins with a telling of two contrasting events (hunting iguana and participating in a political congress) that focus on the perspective of a traditional male elder, who for reasons of education, language, and lifestyle, feels out of place in the congress. Chapter 2 also includes a social history of his family's garden, told from the perspective of his eldest daughter and focusing on the resourceful way that she incorporates capitalist codes for assigning value into indigenous land rights discourse.

Chapter 3 shifts into the Easter holiday mode, showing how celebration and taboo regulate the links between culture and ecology. Focusing particularly on sexual taboo, a basic principle of Emberá cosmology is elaborated—namely, that the potential for danger and creation is intensified by the tendency of human transformation (as that which might be experienced by people engaged in sexual intercourse) to attract other co-occurring transformations. In Chapter 4, death is the perspective from which social life is viewed. Beginning with a visit to a burial ground that is the home of a recently murdered patriarch, the village's first settler, the text moves through everyday life (e.g., gathering food with women in the forest) to suggest the ways in which the living orient their actions and relationships in respect to one whose live body is absent. The thematic focus of the chapter is the dynamic interface between the dead and the living, expressed in the way that the patriarch's kin see and hear his ghost in the landscape, in dream, and in hallucination, and how they return again and again to the unknown details of the unsolved murder case. Using an interpretive technique that depends on the remarkable consistency in which Emberá go about their daily lives, his kin are able to use odd, misplaced locations of the body and found objects as clues.

Chapter 5 documents the construction of a canoe, showing how this quintessentially masculine endeavor depends on the collective effort of both sexes and discussing how social and historical changes have affected the construction and use of the canoe with respect to gender and generation. The events described include the ethnographer's discovery of "double vision," that is, the opening of analysis to the magical as well as material dimensions of transforming a tree into a canoe. Chapter 6 presents four series of events that were precipitated by mysterious misfortune (sudden disappearance of a relative, an inexplicable sign of animal mutilation, a nightmare, and a case of spirit possession). Analysis focuses on how the shamanic mode of interpretation is used by nonspecialists, outside of any formal ritual context, to explain and resolve situations in which the facts are basically unknowable.

The final three chapters, while continuing to draw from events and tellings, reach for another level of synthesis. Chapter 7 discusses how state interventions in Darién depend on concepts of human being that are fundamental to Emberá beliefs and practices. Using four texts that range between imaginary and real, the chapter attempts to describe the framework by which Emberá figure themselves as human beings in the universe, a framework I call the scale of sentient beings. This universe encodes the global political economy within its scope. Central to its construction are the quandaries of agency and scale that result from the local experience of invisible yet impinging forces, such as the transnational forces that motivate development. By focusing on the reconfiguration of racial boundaries at a time of historical transition, I explore the ways in which the state changes the meanings of existing cultural difference. In this analysis of race and the emergence of new tendencies toward racism, the interconnected-ness of gender oppression is also considered. Chapter 8 discusses shamanic ritual as a means to deal with the contradictions and misfortunes of the times. It includes a transcript of a ritual I attended in which the shaman talks about the relation between shamanic and Euramerican allopathic medical practice. Analyzing the position and reputation of three shamans, I discuss shamanic power in relation to social and political context. The ninth and final chapter analyzes women's contradictory position in cosmo-logical and political economic terms, showing how women's everyday ac-tivities provide the foundation for not only Emberá culture but also the local development of the modern nation-state. It grapples with the way "tradition" figures in the struggle to control resources, a struggle in which landownership and household autonomy are particularly at issue. The question here is not one of authenticity but, rather, of how this thing called tradition is invoked differently by representatives of state power (including some scholars) and by those, like indigenous women, who are margin-alized by state power. Finally, the chapter assumes an Emberá perspective on global politics, including an allegorical version of the U.S. invasion of Panama. Viewed from Emberá frames of reference, the book tries to shake Euramerican conventions that place themselves — and the discourse of global politics — so firmly in the "real."

Abbreviations

COPFA	La Comisión Panama–Estados Unidos para la Prevención de Fiebre Aftosa / Panama–United States Commission for the Prevention of Hoof-and-Mouth Disease
INAC	Instituto Nacional de Cultura / National Institute of Culture
MIDA	Ministeria de Desarrollo Agropecuario de Panama / Ministry for Agriculture and Cattle/Swine Development
PRD	Partido Revolucionario Democrático / Democratic Revolutionary Party
RENARE	Dirección de Recursos Naturales Renovables / Administration of Natural Renewable Resources
SNEM	Servicio Nacional de Eradicación Malaria / National Service for Eradication of Malaria

Chronology

Date	Events in Panama (cf. Weeks and Gunson 1991:xiii–xviii)	Fieldwork
1979	Panama Canal treaties go into effect, and Canal Zone officially ceases to exist.	
1981	Torrijos dies in unexplained plane crash.	
1983	National Guard is reorganized and named Panama Defense Forces	
July	Manuel Antonio Noriega becomes commander of Panama Defense Forces.	Preliminary fieldwork in Panama City and Cueva.

1984

May — PRD candidate Nicolás Ardito Barletta narrowly defeats Arnulfo Arias Madrid in fraudulent elections.

August — Fieldwork year in Panama City, Yaviza, Tamarinbó, Palo Blanco, and Cueva begins.

October — Barletta sworn in as president.

1985 — Pan-American Highway completed to Yaviza.

July — Fieldwork year ends.

September — Dr. Hugo Spadafora, former vice-minister of health, is assassinated.

1987

June 7 — Colonel Días Herrera accuses Noriega of rigging the 1984 elections and murdering Dr. Spadafora.

June 26 — U.S. Senate approves resolution calling for Noriega to step down.

1988

February 5 — U.S. attorneys announce Noriega's indictment on drug trafficking charges.

March — U.S. government freezes Panama's assets abroad. Failed coup attempt against Noriega.

1989

October 3 Failed coup attempt against
Noriega.

December Noriega's ad hoc assembly ap-
points him head of state with
unlimited powers. The United
States invades with 26,000
troops and installs Guillermo
Endara as president.

1990

January 3 Noriega surrenders to U.S.
forces.

January 4 Noriega arraigned in Miami on
drug charges.

January 25 President Bush promises $1
billion aid.

September 10 Largest-ever cocaine seizure in
Panama — two tons.

THE PHANTOM GRINGO BOAT

one

Contours of Social Space

The shimmering colors and diesel fumes of the phantom gringo boat beckon to the Emberá Indian shaman and his two young grandsons. Following the motor's whine into the mist, the old man becomes ill, mute. Recognizing the challenge of illusion, he summons his will and his spirit familiars to engage in battle with the otherworld beings who lure him. The consequences of the power he gains in the ensuing struggle are persistent and mixed. (See pp. 167–68.)

Voice

Hearing the story from the grandsons, now old men themselves, the ethnographer finds in it an allegory for development. Promises that come from unknown territory and cannot be ignored draw the Emberá onward, only to recede again into the mist before they can be realized. So seem the grand schemes for Panamanian development in the 1970s and 1980s, in which the narrow stretch of Darién forest east of the canal and west of the Colombian border, and the Emberá people who live within it, are key. Encouraged by promises of participatory democracy and a semiautonomous forest reserve, and finding themselves increasingly locked in by the boundaries of nation-states, ramifying transport routes, and multiplying multiethnic populations, the majority of Emberá abandon the tactics of retreat and dispersion that they have relied upon since the Conquest. In a dramatic display of collective action, households are moved from dispersed into concentrated settlements for the first time in written history. The new villages become the regional foci of the Emberá's first political organization linked to the state. Health and education resources are distributed through the villages by the national government.

The indigenous movement into villages first gathers momentum in the 1960s, some years before General Omar Torrijos, who seizes control of the Panamanian National Guard in the 1968 coup, develops a populist platform that focuses on rural development. Torrijos makes the Emberá movement into villages part of this platform. It is backed by funding and expertise from the U.S. government and the Organization of American States. In 1981, Torrijos dies in a mysterious plane crash. His successor, Manuel Noriega, continues to support regional development programs in Darién, including the political mobilization of the Emberá. Noriega is not as successful in walking the line between tyranny and popularity, however. By the early 1990s, when I begin writing this book, withdrawal of U.S. support, the invasion and Noriega's fall, and the post–U.S. invasion ruin lead to the nearly complete collapse of Panama's governmental institutions.

In the United States, far from Panama City bombings, I listen to radio reports. I imagine the Emberá listening to the radio out there in the forest, at some distance from the invasion's center but much closer than myself. And I imagine them looking into the distance, watching the promise of village formation fade into the mist, like a phantom. Development is perhaps no more real than the gringo boat that the grandsons tell me in 1985 can in special cases be seen tied up next to one of the village houses in the Chico River, where the grandfather-shaman brought it those many years ago. The footless spirit crew and its headless captain, once captured by the grandfather, are irresponsibly freed from shamanic control in the course of his death. A generation later, their mutilated forms are yet wandering the village outskirts, threatening its youth with maddening spells of confusion. How like the chaos of war, abridged to the proportions of local memory.

The phantom gringo boat crosses the gap between known and unknown, testing the field of forces between cause and effect. A motorized archetype of desire, it pierces the distance, reaching both forward and backward toward the originary powers of Conquest, colonization, and development. Such a force field defies the limits of participant observation, the

Figure 2. River from sky, Darién. Photo by L. Stoller.

ethnographer's basic method. And so I adopt an Emberá remedy for partial knowledge, allowing the possibilities of extraordinary vision to expand the empirical frame of direct experience. Shifting between scientific and poetic registers, I search for currents to carry the intentions of those with whom I speak and to mine the discourse of magic to convey the doubled experience of local and global scale.[1] Across this expanded frame, figures of the gringo make their tracks across Darién's mythical history, and the erstwhile ethnographer recedes from local memory like a phantom.

Darién Ecopolitics

In the Darién, a narrow strip of riverine forest between the Caribbean Sea and the Pacific Ocean, the political economy of the times can be read in the landscape. Because of the regularity and cohesiveness of basic survival practices, it is easy to note the distribution of the two most established social groups in the region—the Emberá Indians (who, with the Waunan, are known as the Chocó) and the blacks (known as Darienitas, Chocoanos, or Libres). Observation of house material, design, and placement, for example, can be used to trace the contours of social space, contours that readily lend themselves to political transformation.

The Emberá build open-walled houses on tall stilts on the tops of natural levees in the mid and upper reaches of the rivers. Traditionally (where tradition is understood as an indigenous response to Conquest and colonialism as much as an active connection to some version of the ancient past), the Emberá place their houses in a dispersed pattern. Looking up from the waterline, passersby in canoes commonly see Emberá houses standing singularly, or in twos and threes, in small forest clearings bordered by fruit trees that disappear and then reappear with the curves in the watercourse. By the mid-1980s, about two decades since the Emberá began to think of village formation as a viable survival strategy, concentrated settlements with anywhere from a handful to nearly a hundred houses are a common sight.

Black agriculturists, who, like the Emberá, depend on cultivated plantains, bananas, rice, and corn and on wild mammals, birds, fish, fruit, and nuts for basic subsistence, nevertheless construct their houses differently. They build riverine houses on the ground, rather than up high, and they close in their walls with reeds, rather than leaving them open. They tend to build on the lower reaches of the rivers, closer to towns like Yaviza. Indeed, most blacks in Darién prefer to be merchants, service providers, and officials in town, where they build houses and stores of milled lumber and cinder block. The blacks have long since established dominance over regional trade and politics, but their control over links to the nation's capital has been weakening with the state's focus on the development of "indigenous peoples"—a category from which, by virtue of their race and African ancestry, blacks are excluded.

The political economy of the times can be read in the river, the "highway of the Emberá." Along the banks, reeds and grasses resistant to the sun's blaze colonize areas that have been repeatedly burned for cultivation. They once were common only downstream. But now that villages are established upriver and agricultural production intensifies, areas of reed and grass increase, replacing forest trees that once shaded travelers. Without the hold of strong tree roots, banks are worn down by yearly floods, and riverbeds become wider and shallower. Along the entire inhabited length of the rivers, except for sections too steep for farming, cool forest has been pushed back from the banks. Only beyond the last village, as the mountainous headwaters approach, does the canopy reach far enough across the water for monkeys to jump from one side to the other.

On the other side of the mountains, in the Chocó of Colombia, which is an extension of the Emberá and black homelands, the forest is also vanishing. But in the vastness of the Colombian side, it is said that the weakness and disinterest of the government and the brutality of drug cartels and guerrilla and paramilitary forces create an atmosphere that is not conducive to everyday life. There the forest vanishes without the hopes for a better life that the Emberá villages of Darién, Panama, are meant to secure. Word of the opportunities travels with kin and brings more people across the international border between Colombia and Panama to reestablish themselves. Fulfilling the migratory potential of their culture, the Emberá move their households and seedlings across the water in the belly of a sculpted tree (canoe) and center it anew on a hearth high above the ground. Using their special knowledge and skill, the Emberá, together with their sister linguistic group the Waunan, manage to survive. But the customary practices of household autonomy, upriver retreat, and limited exchange with neighboring groups, which have served them well since the Conquest, appear to have reached the limits of success. Finding themselves between forest edge and the center of international capital in Panama City, the Emberá people turn to meet the world, choosing leaders to fight for their land and the manna of development.

The Darién has attracted European and American adventurers, miners, lumbermen, and missionaries ever since the Spaniards arrived in the early sixteenth century. In 1913, as Abbot notes in his testament to the "most gigantic engineering undertaking since the dawn of time" — the Panama Canal — it is evident that the isthmus from Darién to Nicaragua "is probably the most thoroughly surveyed bit of wild land in the world" (p. 31). Considering the persistent intensity of foreign interests, it is nigh miraculous that the forest continues to be compatible with indigenous subsistence practices. I don't think the torpidity and denseness of the jungle is sufficient explanation, although it certainly slows things up. I think, rather, it is the fortuitous convergence of Emberá retreat from non-Indian population centers and the international control of regional borders that have allowed the Emberá to continue living in their own distinctive way in Darién. Or perhaps it is more precise to say that these factors have allowed the Emberá to re-create their way of life under increasingly contradictory conditions.

At the turn of the twentieth century, the canal was built, U.S. interests in Panama were sealed, and Panama became independent from Colombia. A new international border was drawn along the mountain range that runs along the easternmost end of the isthmus, dividing the Emberá homeland into the Darién of Panama, Central America, on the one side, and the Chocó of Colombia, South America, on the other. The isolated Darién forest — still the only gap in the Pan-American Highway between Alaska and Tierra del Fuego — became a natural barrier that helps secure the new international border (see Fig. 3).

As the world pushed close around it, the Darién remained relatively protected, becoming a sanctuary for the Emberá, the Waunan, and the diaspora blacks freed from Spanish slavery into this part of what Euramericans call the New World. Building on displacement, both Indians and blacks have maintained racial and cultural differences and have developed a unique regional social structure of reciprocity. Generations of Emberá and Waunan have poled and motored downriver from their traditionally dispersed sites in the upper reaches of Darién's rivers, hauling bananas and plantains to the market towns established by blacks at river confluences. They have traded their produce with the cargo boats and stores owned by black merchants, until recently the only regional links to the outside world. And so they have cohabited the region into the late twentieth century.[2]

The Darién forest might have been lost in the 1960s, when the U.S. Atomic Energy Commission did a study to determine if nuclear excavation of the isthmus for a second interoceanic canal was feasible. The simultaneous funding of a helicopter-scale ethnobotanical survey (Duke 1970, 1986) suggests that U.S.-Panamanian interests were prepared to sacrifice the forest. As it happens, Darién was left as is until the 1970s, when General Torrijos made civic action and delivery of health and education services part of his militaristic-revolutionary vision. The populist, leftist mask Torrijos used to disguise the dictatorial side of his rule opposed the oligarchy and embraced the poor, rural sectors, workers, and students (Scranton 1991:52–53, 56–57).[3] At this time (and probably still today), Darién appeared on national maps as vast empty areas of green with only sparse population centers. Like the conquistadores before him, Torrijos saw it as a rich, uncharted domain, mostly empty except for Indians — and he made plans for them too. Darién was targeted for intensive development, and the Emberá and Waunan found themselves in the center of events.[4]

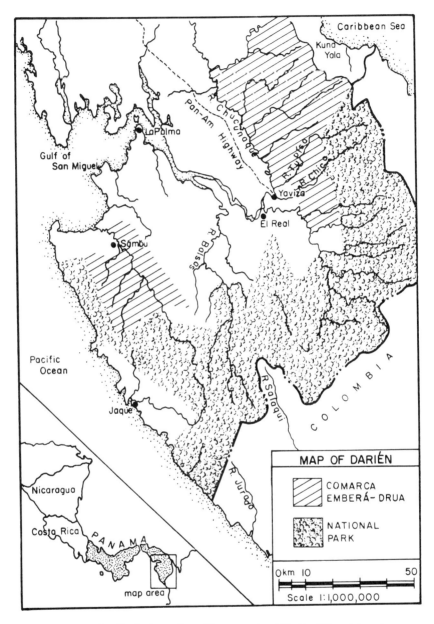

Figure 3. Map of Darién. Redrawn from "Parque nacional Darién: Sitio patrimonio mundial y reserva de la biosfera," unpublished document from MIDA/RENARE (1984).

The focus of regional development is the extension of the Pan-American Highway into the market town of Yaviza, connecting the far eastern part of the country to Panama City but leaving the gap between Yaviza and Colombia intact. This extension was completed in 1984–85 during my fieldwork. The highway is promoted as a new area to be colonized by campesino farmers and cattle ranchers. As did Torrijos himself, the campesinos come from western Panama, where the forest has long ago been destroyed by pasture-making activities unsuitable to tropical forest ecology (Heckadon and McKay 1982). In addition, the political stability of western Panama is threatened by large landowners who have squeezed the campesinos off most of the remaining fertile land. The highway takes pressure off the west, bringing campesinos into Darién, where they become *colonos* (colonizers). This third major ethnic group settling in the region, along with truckers coming in from Panama City, has disrupted the balance of relations historically developed between the blacks and Indians. Up until this point, the latter two groups had been living side by side in relative isolation, in slavery and in freedom, since the seventeenth century, when the blacks were first brought from West Africa to replace the Indians who died or escaped from the Spanish mines of Chocó and Darién.

With one hand, Torrijos increased the competition for land in Darién by bringing in campesinos. With the other, he offered the Emberá and Waunan grade schools, health posts, and voting booths in their upriver forest settlements. His strategy echoed that of the first waves of Spanish conquistadores and missionaries, whose repeated attempts to induce the Indians into villages failed.[5] Torrijos offered these things with the understanding that the emerging Emberá political structure based on village formation would support his ruling military party, the Democratic Revolutionary Party (PRD), in regional and national elections. Most important, they could work successfully, he promised, toward the establishment of their own semiautonomous reserve, a *comarca*. The partial fulfillment of these promises began to shift the balance of power toward the Indians and away from the blacks, for it created routes of exchange and systems of patronage that bypassed those that the blacks had created and controlled. Indeed, Torrijos's development strategy, whether intentional or not, served to weaken the links that connect the past and peoples of Darién to each other and to the Colombian Chocó, creating greater dependence on Panama City, his center of power.

Other influences promoted village formation as well, some of which preceded Torrijos. These include the Kuna, a neighboring indigenous group who already have an established *comarca* and who send representatives to speak to the Emberá and Waunan at political congresses.[6] North American missionaries continue to encourage them as well. One non-Emberá who stands out as an inspiration in the very beginning of the village movement is Harold Becker, alias "Peru," an eccentric former military-missionary-astrologer "gone native." An Emberá village head who was a boy in the early 1960s, when Peru was active in the movement, told me about how Peru used to wear a loincloth and live in the forest like the Indians. The authorities wanted to get him out, but the Emberá kept lookouts along the river. When they heard the first whine of the Guard's motor, they would hide Peru in the stand of *cativo* trees behind the village of Salto. He eventually fled to Colombia. No one has heard tell of his whereabouts since about 1981.[7]

For the first time since the Conquest, then, village formation seemed a viable if not uncontested solution to the Emberá's and Waunan's contemporary predicament, namely, the end of upriver forest to which they can retreat. As Torrijos's vision strengthened their movement, it became even more necessary for them to accept the place assigned them by development and environmental experts. Downriver campesino settlers cut down forest for pastures along the highway; upriver, between their proposed *comarca* and the Colombian border, a wildlife park is being established.

A few villages existed in the 1950s, the movement began to gain collective acceptance in the sixties, and by the mideighties, when a geographer counts and maps them, there are about eleven thousand Emberá and Waunan living along the rivers of Darién, 75 percent of whom have moved their households into fifty-three villages, 25 percent of whom continue to live in dispersed dwellings (Herlihy 1985). During this time, they constructed a political organization appropriate to Panama's particular mix of militarism, democracy, and an economy that was in large part based on foreign capital brought in by international banks, the canal, development funds, and the illegal drug trade.[8] At the local level, wherever possible, the Emberá have tenaciously resisted ceding authority in the domain of extended family households, the unit of autonomy that has provided for Emberá survival since what they call Ancient Times.

From the perspective of Emberá newcomers just arriving in Darién from the Chocó in the 1980s, however, there are a number of adjustments to make. Newcomers find themselves resettling, not at a comfortable distance of a river bend apart, as before, but just a few feet apart, within sight of unfamiliar neighbors. This situation breaks common magical codes at the same time as it requires elaboration of uncommon political codes. Agricultural patterns have changed dramatically as well. Unlike dispersed settlers, who plant corn and rice in forest cleared behind their house and plantain groves along the sandy stretches bordering the river, village newcomers find themselves walking quite a distance into the forest, past the other claimed fields radiating outward from the village, to clear a section for their own rice or corn. They are hard-pressed to find free land good for plantains, the basic subsistence crop, unless a relative offers it as a gift or they are willing to pay cash. They also find their children going to school, learning to read and write Spanish (a fact that some find acceptable or good, and some do not). If they are in a well-appointed village, they may have access to limited health services and occasional electricity. They also meet with new demands on their labor. For example, residents who are used to working only in fully autonomous household groups may occasionally have to work cooperatively on village projects. Households are also expected to participate in villagewide decision making, including choice of who represents them to their own new *comarca* organization and as an ethnic group in the halls of state.[9]

Villagers are represented to the state by a political structure that bears the name of the people but is in many respects experienced only indirectly. Each of the three subregions of the proposed *comarca* is governed by a "traditional" cacique, or chief, who is traditional only insofar as he is an unpaid older man who does not read and write and who draws legitimacy from family settlement history and kin networks. There is no evidence of a "tradition" of stable chieftainships existing, except maybe the one that the conquistadores and missionaries called forth between the sixteenth and the eighteenth centuries to address representatives of indigenous groups with whom they were at war, whom they used as laborers, or whom they taxed (Castrillón 1982:129, 156). In Torrijos's time, the contemporary Emberá chieftainship tradition is a reinvention based on the Kuna model. The new traditional Emberá caciques represent the political authority of a people who never before needed this kind of representation. The caciques are rendered effective articulators of the people and state through the collaboration of nontraditional, younger men (and in 1984–85 one college-educated woman) who represent the Emberá and Waunan by virtue of the fact that they are born to Emberá or Waunan parents. These younger leaders have grown up in towns and cities, and their qualifying experience is literacy in Spanish and experience with urban, non-Indian ways. Despite their limited knowledge of everyday life in the rainforest, it is the younger leaders who are voted into national office and onto committees that develop programs and policies for the Emberá. It is they who carry out most of the negotiations for the proposed *comarca* and organize the acquisition and distribution of village development funds. To bring the business of the nation-state to the people, the leadership stages riverwide, subregional, and *comarca*-level congresses on a regular basis. This type of organized political event is a completely new phenomenon in Emberá culture.

The liaison between traditional caciques and the young educated leaders produces communications that are regarded skeptically by villagers, most of whom do not attend political congresses themselves and hear reports only through their representative village heads. This skepticism derives from strongly held beliefs in household autonomy as a survival strategy and distrust of anyone who claims leadership, even when survival is now also framed in terms of struggling politically as an indigenous people for a land reserve through elected leaders. Informing this skepticism is the ecological knowledge that household dispersion is a more sustainable settlement pattern in the rainforest environment than is the concentration of households and food production areas in and around villages.

Fieldwork and Text

Entry/Exit

Although outsiders of European and North American descent have been arriving uninvited for centuries, the mechanism for seeking permission from the Emberá as an official entity, "a people," had not yet been explicitly worked out in 1983 and 1984 when I sought permission to study the social changes accompanying village formation. While it is conventional to speak in general terms, "the Emberá" exist only insofar as individuals are willing to assume authority to act as representatives in specific instances. In my case, no one was willing to decide the matter publicly. Their traditionally dispersed social organization generally discourages individuals from assuming decision-making power over others not in their household or kin group. At this historical moment, the village-*comarca*-state political organization was relatively new and constantly challenged by the strong commitment to household autonomy.

With letters in hand from Panama's National Institute of Culture, the Organization of American States (my funder), and the University of Texas,

Figure 4. Panama City bus: "Secret of Knowledge." Photo by J. Benson.

I met first with Emberá representatives elected into the national legislature
in Panama City (the young leadership). They sent me to a village in Darién
to find the traditional leader, the first cacique. He was en route to a political
congress in another river. I caught up and joined his group. Arriving at the
congress without proper permission, my presence provoked argument. I
was sent back to Panama City just in time to follow the young leadership
(and the women in the Emberá dance troupe) into the Indigenous World
Congress of 1984. It was bad timing. There were a few North American
missionaries. Otherwise, I was the only gringo around. My act of seeking
permission provided two or three of the Emberá representatives a perfect
opportunity to practice the anti-imperialist rhetoric that impassioned the
congress. Given my structural position, the fact that I consider my working
stance to be anti-imperialist began to seem like a delusion. The irony of
my situation was evident only to me and did nothing to soothe my frustration. Not to be dissuaded, I marshaled all the institutional pressure I
could.[10] Negotiations ended with both sides promising to lay out more
explicit procedures for obtaining permission to do fieldwork among the
Emberá in the future. The first cacique, who had been quietly supportive

of my endeavor all along, suggested that I work in one of the most traditional villages — that is, one of the smallest, most recently formed, distant, and isolated in his jurisdiction of Emberá-Drua, the proposed *comarca*. I accepted. This time — several weeks later — I departed for Darién with a letter of introduction from the head of the Emberá Teacher's Association to the head of Tamarinbó,[11] a village in the upriver section of the Tupisa River. As individuals educated in national schools engaged in bilingual education of village children, the Emberá teachers carry out a vital function that is well respected by both leadership and villagers. The letter from the head of the association served me well. Later that year, when I had become more accepted, I got permission to work in a second village on the Chico River. Working in two villages allowed me to assess the extent and kind of changes taking place over time. I compared the five-year-old, fourteen-household village of Tamarinbó with the fifteen-year-old, forty-household village of Palo Blanco, principally with respect to the politics and economics of land use and ownership practices.[12]

Initially, however, there was yet another barrier to my free movement in and out of Darién. I had to go through the market town of Yaviza to connect with people canoeing up the Tupisa River. In so doing, I passed the headquarters of Noriega's army, the Forces of Defense, better known by their previous name, the (National) Guard. Despite a letter of introduction from the head of their own Office of Indigenous Affairs (located in the central barracks that later got blown up in the U.S. invasion of Panama City), the Guard was slow to accept the explanation that I was in the region to study Emberá culture. The first few times I came through Yaviza or the regional capital of La Palma or attended some regional political event upriver, I was brought before military authorities for questioning. One time, the Guard sent an Emberá soldier to befriend me, get me drunk, and find out what I was *really* doing there. Coming from within the United States, I was unused to my presence eliciting official concern. And at that point in time, I was uncritical of the classic anthropological project of studying Indians. I thought that seeking such knowledge was a worthy endeavor in and of itself and did not yet perceive my activities as linked to the workings of empire. Eventually the soldiers let me pass with only glances of intimidation.

As for the people in the little village of fourteen houses, two days' poling upriver from Yaviza, the village head read them the letter from the Emberá Teachers Association. Like the Guard, the village residents also did not really understand what it was I wanted to do there. But some of them nevertheless took it as their responsibility to make sure I didn't get killed, a service that, in my naïveté, I did not fully appreciate at the time. For most of them, I was the first white woman to whom they had ever spoken; for me, they were the first Indians whom I had ever gotten to know. They got used to me walking around, writing everything down, recording stories, taking photos, helping them work, asking questions, mapping, going on journeys — and engaging in odd personal habits like bathing in my clothes and making a toilet of the ground instead of the river.

I remember the day months later that I left for the last time. My companions and teachers stood up on the bank and watched the canoe edge away, and I felt that they were again wondering what it was that I'd *really* been doing there. I told them I'd try to be back in about three years. After three years had passed, I had received grants from Fulbright and the Social Science Research Council to study Emberá culture again. This time, I planned a methodological experiment in positionality. Instead of establishing analytic perspective within the center of Emberá culture, in the more homogeneous and traditional villages, I planned to work more in town, analyzing Emberá culture at its interfaces with black culture. I wanted to see what that would do to ethnographic process and product. But it was 1988, the United States had changed its mind about General Noriega's involvements with the cocaine trade, and economic sanctions were imposed. I was concerned that it might not be safe for me in Darién, afraid disaffected guards might dump me in a river. I declined the Social Science Research Council grant. Fulbright let me wait it out for a year. When the year rolled around to November, I was glued to National Public Radio as the coup failed and the country was invaded by U.S. forces sheltered in its very midst within the Canal Zone. Large business and residential areas of Panama City were demolished, and hundreds — perhaps thousands — of civilians were killed (Weeks and Gunson 1991; Independent Commission of Inquiry on the U.S. Invasion of Panama 1991). I was allowed to use the funding for another project in Central America. Except for a brief report about the U.S. Special Forces roaming around the Darién jungle checking identity badges, I've heard nothing in the media about effects on regions outside the urban center of war and power. I wonder how the people are doing who took me in, watched out for me, and shared their experience and knowledge with me. I wanted to spend more time with them before I wrote this book, but as I began to search through my memories and documents, General Noriega sat in a Miami jail, and I realized that this was as good a time as any to write. For despite the classic tendency to produce impressions of a perpetual ethnographic present, anthropologists carry out research in a specific historical moment. The era that began with General Torrijos's seizure of power has come to an end. The Emberá are already living another turn in the cycle of disruptions and retrenchments that have reshaped the landscape since the Conquest.

Logistics and Epistemology

Classic ethnography is founded on a displacement — from home to "the field" — designed to precipitate constructive confrontation between the known and unknown. Conditioned by the precedents and procedures of academic discipline, this displacement provides a ready-made structure for fieldwork and its product — ethnographic discourse. Fieldwork process, learning to interpret a world from those who are most familiar with it ("the natives"), follows "naturally" in this structure.

Once in Panama, between August 1984 and July 1985, I went in and out between the city and "the field" seven times. Between four- to six-week stays in the villages, I'd use breaks in Panama City to type up field notes, go to movies, talk English, eat pizza, plan, and think. At first, I thought of these trips as logistic and emotional necessities. In time, however, I realized that the two to five days of traveling back and forth between village and capital represented more than a journey across space. It was a journey through a transnational structure of political and symbolic economies. The journey would begin with a two-day trip poling downstream in a dugout canoe with the Emberá from the little fourteen-house village of Tamarinbó to the market town of Yaviza. It usually took a day or two until I could get transport from Yaviza to Panama City (divining whether if I took the road, still under construction, it would be impassable in a rain; whether I was ready to sit through the night collecting folklore over the whine of a cargo boat's motor; or look past the demolished planes on the side of the Yaviza runway as I boarded a fast but unpredictable flight). Arriving in the city, I was greeted by the sight of big banks, hotels, casinos and gringo army bases (where I sometimes stayed).

The journey involves a shift in consciousness as well — and always a blindness to some things. For example, who would have thought that the Marriott Hotel, in whose pool I sometimes went for a swim, was (as I later found out) also the favored hangout of the U.S. Drug Enforcement Agency? While most Emberá in the upriver villages have never been to the

Figure 5. Pan-American Highway, Darién. Photo by L. Stoller.

city and probably have never seen a cement swimming pool, I, who may have actually swum with DEA agents, had no more idea of what was going on than the Emberá did. Copresence does not guarantee knowledge. The shifting political and economic forces that impinge on our lives are perhaps strangely felt but nevertheless remain largely unknown — unless catastrophe reveals them, that is. The display of forces in the U.S. invasion and postinvasion revelations fills in the public after the fact.[13] Up until the point where things blow up, gaps in perception, where sensed by the state and its citizenry, are traversed with imaginative insight (e.g., the Emberá's phantom gringo boat), repressed through information control (e.g., the CIA), bred to produce terror (e.g., Noriega's dictatorship), and resisted through uncensored channels (e.g., Panama's opposition). Where threats of violence shape symbolic process, as in this case, the partiality of knowledge can be a nerve-racking problem.

Although I was always a foreigner in the upriver villages in which I lived, fieldwork entailed a change in the way I thought about things. I didn't identify with the people I once lived among and now write about, but I did learn to see and speak about a world (mostly new to me) from

Figure 6. Noriega's Guard in Yaviza. Photo by J. Benson.

their point of view. I did not feel like an Emberá woman, but I did slip into the serenity of life in the upper reaches of the rivers, where the forest is beautiful and the ways of the people remarkably consistent. In this, I learned to see the blacks of Darién, of whom I knew little, from the Emberá perspective as allied but different. And coming down to Yaviza Town, I was often overcome by the kind of cognitive dissonance typical of border towns. I came to feel uncomfortable, somewhat in the way Emberá do, but not exactly, because of course people did not treat me as an Indian but as a gringa. In contrast, by the time I reached Panama City, I was "out of the field," out of range of most Emberá that I knew from the village, hence I constructed my own set of ideas in relation to the city, and it was not problematic in the same way Yaviza was. (There are many Emberá living in Panama City who rarely visit the Darién. I have met only a few.)

In this manner, ethnographers learn to replicate the anxieties and exploit the possibilities of intercultural and interracial contact that characterize the region in which they work. In this transformative process, the unconscious may bend the intellect's chosen stance of objectivity. It is this slippage of, not quite identity, but modes of perception and thought that lends authenticity to the ethnographer's voice.

Ethnographic Intentions

Between the time I was trained to do fieldwork and the time I wrote the dissertation that led to my doctorate, classic ethnography became a suspect endeavor, one that was all too adept at making "subjects" out of colonized peoples. Quaint. Ethnographers are now more conscious of the political implications of our changing roles. And we are somewhat baffled by the limits of participant observation in a world crisscrossed by satellite communication. To cope, we search (like shamans) for new strategies of representation that elude dominant regimes, that are open and quick to convey the instability and proliferation of meaning along the contours of social space. With doubts in tow, we push the forms of classic ethnography — our inheritance — into new shapes, watching to see if it will survive the changes and fulfill the promise heralded by feminist, "Third World"/minority anthropologist, and interdisciplinary critiques. As before, we mark off areas appropriate for description and frame moments of experience for telling. But these are no longer joined in a classically ordered sequence suggesting mastery through knowledge (Foucault 1980; Fabian 1983; Irigaray 1985; Clifford 1986; Haraway 1988; hooks 1990). Instead, systematic data are juxtaposed with interpretation in order to find a more resilient kind of truth.

In a reversal of classic ethnographic style, I do not describe the everyday in order to provide a foundation for intellectual abstraction. Abstractions, with which readers are by now probably familiar (e.g., the Indian, the state, magic, ideology, the Emberá, the Darién), are used as entry points. Like stage props, their usefulness lessens with the accumulation of the reader's local knowledge. The reader's experience thus mimics that of fieldworker and writer, who learns to appreciate the significance, complexity, and unruliness of the mundane. The goal is no more or no less than that. With a dash of intuition and wonder, the writer happily sacrifices her measure of ethnographic authority.

Figure 7. River bend prone to whirlpools, home of the mythical cosmo-snake Hëï, Chico River.

Local Magic and the Politics of International Development

A leap of imagination is required to grasp the local and global effects of power that are refashioning our planet and our selves, a process involving infinite sets of quandaries regarding agency and scale. That leap of imagination can be formulated in diverse modes of human thought and perception, but here I focus on one named "magic." Magical discourse begins where empirical observation (science) finds its limits. Among the Emberá, magical discourse, founded on the ancient and global practice of shamanism, is the language of argument and interpretation used to cross the gap between known and unknown.[14] In large part, Emberá magical discourse rides over the same semantic domain as that which Euramericans call politics and healing, with the important exception that it omits much of the patriarchal presumption common to these domains in other cultures.[15] In Emberá magical discourse the power to heal and/or kill is not specifically linked to gender.

Although deriving from a different intellectual history and serving different social functions, ethnography is like shamanism in its attempt to cross the gap between known and unknown. According to the empiricist presumptions of classic ethnography, however, the ethnographer and ethnographic analysis are rooted firmly in the known and knowable. The non-empirically verifiable unknown is broached only indirectly via the beliefs of other cultures. Euramericans mediate their fascination with magic by using other cultures as alibis. The distance they impose between their idea of themselves and the idea of magic is demonstrated in texts that clearly mark off the magical discourse of natives from the explanatory discourse of scientists or humanists. In contrast, this book does not dramatize the boundary between magic and empirical reality by contrasting voices of native and ethnographer. Out of respect for Emberá magical discourse, and as a strategy for conveying to the reader the structures of feeling associated with it,[16] I let its language and principles impinge on the ethnographic text in a less tractable way. Following memories' sensation, I try to write the magical real into the politics of the everyday.

two

Authentic Discontinuities

WhuuuuuUUSSHH! Inez flings her arms up into the air:

> The water burst forth from the wild cashew tree, creating rivers and lakes. In Ancient Times, Woodpecker and Horned Lizard were stealing water from the tree. Ankore [God] knew it: "Where'd you get that water?" he asked. They remained silent. Ankore got ANGRY and BURST the tree open. Each branch became a river. (−T/S)

I put this together with what I'd heard before: *In Ancient Times animals were people. Then the world changed. Woodpecker and Horned Lizard were skilled axmen. When the world changed, they were swinging their axes. And there the axes stayed, right on top of their heads.* Such words from the past remind us of the wonder and precariousness of human being: if the world changed once, it could change again. When it does, humans may find their positions reversed in the planetary hierarchy. And like the armies of deposed dictators, they may be subject to just retribution. But it would be far worse than even this, because as for the animals, the loss of power will be accompanied by a loss of speech and consciousness.

The Ancient Time story fragments intervene in the hot, bright scene in which we stand. Up on the spindly tips of second-growth *Cecropia* trees,

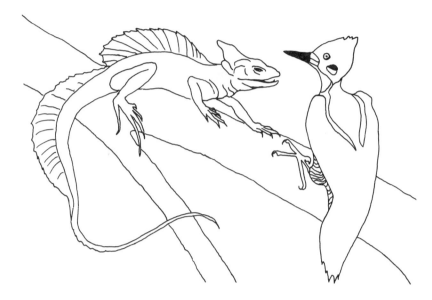

Figure 8. Woodpecker and Horned Lizard, the axmen.

mother iguanas warm their bellies full of eggs and watch the river. We wait
below on the stone beach for a rifle, a small group in two canoes traveling
downriver for a political congress. The first iguana is sighted not long after
we left the village. Inez's husband, Dalas, wades over to the grassy tangle
on the river edge and chops down the iguana tree so that it falls into the
water. Inez wades in too, staying waist deep till the tree falls, then
bounding through the water. Coming up triumphant after a sudden dive,
she bashes the iguana's head on the edge of the canoe. There's another
iguana a few feet away, but the tree it's on is leaning toward the forest. Inez
and her father's wife go to investigate. They try to change the tree's natural
inclination, but it falls inward, and the iguana takes off into the bush. Lost
it. "You see," Inez explains, "in the water the iguana only has its tail to
whip back and forth, but on land it can scuttle away on its four little legs."
Her father, Dzoshua, complains how the iguana always deceives people
(and I know him well enough by now to know that that's what he says
about all elusive prey).

We continue on downriver, scanning the treetops as we go. Somebody
spots another, then another and another. Dzoshua can't stand to lose these

opportunities and sends his wife back upriver to the village for his rifle. "After all," he said, "what would we do for food when we get to the congress?" When she got back, everybody disappeared into the bush. It seemed they were gone a long time. Finally, Dalas hazards a shot from the ground. No luck. Another long time passes before I see Dalas up in the tree pointing his rifle toward the end of the branch. (Iguanas' cryptic coloration make them practically invisible to me.) Poom. Nothing. Poom. A bullet grazes another. The bullets are few, and the iguanas won't die. If they're not hit in heart or brain, they can take several bullets without losing grip. The hunters consider sending a young boy up the tree, but he won't go. Poom. The iguana falls, gets stuck on a branch, is speared and handed to the boy, who knocks its head on a log as it claws the weeds. Poom. Dalas tries to get a third. It falls free, into the bush. Everybody starts running, calling, "Daidu! Daidu!" trying to steer it into the river, searching the river. Another one lost. "Deceived again," Dzoshua shakes his head.

We continue poling downstream, catching five iguanas in all. Luckily we stop seeing them after a while. It is nearly dark by the time we reach our destination. We set up camp on a sandy beach across from the village where the meeting is being held and make soup for dinner. I find the little floating arms and legs with claws slightly weird, but otherwise the soup is quite delicious.

An Aside

Since Ancient Times of the Emberá, being human is conceived in relation to that which human being is not. Through story, conception is lent reality. A primary distinction occurs between human and animal. *There's a story about a girl who falls in love with a shad. She feeds him with garbage. When her father discovers the relationship, he catches the fish and gives it to her to gut and boil. Realizing it is her lover, she cries as she watches her family eat soup.*

All humans define themselves by reference to that which they are not — in the unconscious (Freud 1913), in language (Saussure 1960), and in myth (Lévi-Strauss 1975). The Emberá girl who cries for her fish lover is caught in this paradox. The myth dramatizes a separation between human and animal, a basic process of differentiation that occurs on multiple levels simultaneously. Humans also distinguish themselves from each other by this same process. Time, race, culture, class, and forms of deviance are

Figure 9. Iguana with eggs and plantains.

common parameters of difference that bind human identities. Humans cultivate social relationships along these parameters, devoting themselves to those that they hope will fulfill expectations, sometimes reaching for the norm, sometimes for the unknown, evanescent, or unpredictable. Selves, cultures, and nations manifest themselves through this never-ending and often conflictive process of identification and separation. A great heterogeneity results. In this, each new historical intervention shifts the particular combination of distinctions used to create human order.

Because it is a discipline that tracks the shifting aspects of identity and difference, ethnography is deeply rooted in this paradoxical process. By stepping out of their own culture, ethnographers use disorientation to simulate independence from the particular set of distinctions embedded in their psyches. While this method is a useful way to understand and act on the world, it has also proved to be a way for Euramericans to create themselves as the West, the First World (cf. Fabian 1983; Clifford and Marcus 1986; Marcus and Fischer 1986; Trinh 1989). The diverse array of people who have been categorized as native others are no longer fixed safely in remote peripheries, however. Nor do they remain silent and unread. It is their challenge that currently enlivens debates.

The Congress

Hunting iguana, we missed the first afternoon of the congress. By the next morning, the olive green brass of Noriega's military, the Guard, have come upriver by motor. They inform the Emberá and Waunan in the audience that too many Colombians are entering Panama and getting identity cards. This is too easy. The government is changing the waiting period from one to five years. This includes Indians. (These restrictions are usually aimed at black migrants, who are not accorded the right of Indians to continue crossing the twentieth-century border without documents. These new rules are probably not independent of the Noriega-U.S. drug-trade controls.) Caught in Yaviza Town without an identity card, a person may be fined or jailed. This doesn't seem to worry Emberá I talk to (perhaps they are pleased by their own status in the national system, or secure in the system's inefficiencies). But to me it signals the intensifying surveillance that accompanies recent development — the construction of the first highway bringing trade, settlers, and cattle into the region; zoning plans with a reserve of nucleated settlements for the Emberá and Waunan, another for wildlife. Moving at will through the forest that extends across the low mountains between the Darién of Panama and into the Chocó of Colombia reaching as far as Ecuador may soon be spoken of as a freedom pertaining only to Ancient Times.

Dzoshua is the only man in his village who always wears a loincloth (E. *me,* S. *wayuko*), the traditional male dress. He is an elder who was never educated in parliamentary procedures. As he'd told me earlier, he came from Colombia as a young boy; "like a dog put out," he left the corpse that was his father, which he had lain next to for days when they both got sick and no one was there to care for them. It's painful to watch this man whose enduring wit and wisdom enlivens our evening as he shakes his head sadly, confessing that he doesn't really understand what goes on at these meetings, that he looks on like a toad. Earlier that day, waiting for the rifle on the beach, Dzoshua looks up at the sky and points to the vulture searching out Death. "It brings luck to the hunter," Inez points out. Dzoshua tells:

> You know how Vulture got to look like that? Vulture found a cow one day. Walking around it, around it, looking into its eyes: is it dead? The eyes are closed, yes. So Vulture sticks its head in Cow's anus. It works its way up inside. As its beak reaches her mouth, Cow tightens her anus. Pulling out, that's how Vulture lost its feathers. (−T/S)

Desire and deceit motivate culture's dynamic of difference in this Emberá tale, part of a vast genre of animal tales told by indigenous groups throughout North and South America. Tethered loosely to empirical observation, an allegorical array of personifications become points of reference for interpreting the profound complexity of life, which, like the ax on Woodpecker's and Horned Lizard's heads, got stuck in some confounded place. The Emberá stories from Ancient Times reassert themselves with joy and urgency, contributing a lively moral code to the pandemonium of the political unconscious in the lowland forest.

But are the Emberá being lured into development like Vulture into Cow, getting trapped as they try to make their way from anus to mouth? Are the people tired of eating predigested offerings from the huge, dull, stingy beast of a gringo system (would it were as peaceful as a cow)? A remnant from the Conquest sits in the plaza of the village in which the political meeting is held: a wooden stockade with chains wrapped around two slabs of wood with four holes for the feet of any two who try to avoid sitting on a log for two days of important but (for those uneducated in national schools or mostly monolingual in Emberá or Waunan) impenetrable discussions of property laws for the new reserve, maps, leadership, ecology, and education. Defeated but circulating still in the historic atmosphere of the Panama Canal is the unnamed Indian cacique who, having captured two Spanish marauders, fastened them to the ground, propped open their jaws, and poured molten gold down their throats while saying: "Here's gold, Spaniards! Here's gold. Take a plenty; drink it down! Here's more gold" (Abbot 1913:50).

I catch a ride downriver with a missionary/anthropologist from Winnipeg who'd built a well in the village where the meeting took place. He had a large canoe with a motor and motorist. Also hitching a ride was Benjamin Salazar, an Emberá man who has enjoyed a leadership role in the past, who now owns a store in Yaviza Town, and who wears an elegantly pressed shirt and slacks with black leather polished shoes. Benjamin tells me what I then considered exotica from the PR package of Emberá culture (about Aríbada, the cow with hooves as big as fifteen-liter pots, who claims dominion over all Darién when she calls from the Pirré Mountains; about floods that cause starvation; about evil in the form of a snake on the road causing death by vomiting; about Antumiá, the underwater black/human/animal that causes death by drowning; about the young woman who goes crazy and dies after meeting the devil in the forest). This talk of sad, bad, unchristian things took on the tone of comedy as the missionary's motorist, who didn't seem to have much experience navigating low and winding rivers, kept sliding the canoe ever so gently into the muddy banks.

Landscaped Figures of Imagination and Conquest

In the rush of the Conquest and the many arduous incursions into the dense and lonely bush of Darién that have occurred since, foreigners have brought with them an array of mismatched images that hang rather sloppily onto the figure of "Indian" (the name that is itself the result of a famous cartographic error). Because foreigners arrived with and sustained a disproportionate level of power, indigenous people have had to find ways to adjust to their strange vision. Because the array of images is inconsistent and changeable, adjustment has been a never-ending part of everyday life. Regional history cannot be understood without analysis of foreign imaginaries, because they mediate all indigenous understanding of foreigners and indigenous understanding of themselves as mirrored in the speech and action of foreigners. (The ethnographer is the experimental template upon which this dynamic is registered.) Indigenous people have negotiated these images, partially internalizing them or, better said, accepting the reality of the foreign imaginaries that are in their best interest to meet partway and doing their best to subvert or ignore the rest. In this process, they have developed a complex notion of who they are, as humans of a kind, compared to those others from a once-outside world. These negotiations, the contexts in which they have taken place, and their impact on indigenous culture are encoded and interpreted in stories from Ancient Times.[1]

Today's questions more often than not exceed the trick and wit found in animal tales, the recurrent logic of which depends on a measure of balance between contenders. To take on matters of extreme inhumanity, stories use human characters. For example, an Emberá man told me this piece of Conquest history:

> The Spanish came and captured many men, women, and children. They kept them in a round house closed in by high walls to await slaughter. The people inside wondered if they might escape out of a small opening at the top. They thought of using the wrapped bark of women's skirts. These were tied together for a rope, leaving the women nude. They began climbing out one by one. Among those inside was a shaman, a *häïmbaná*. Furious with the Spaniards, he caused a great storm to come. Heavy rains, thun-

Figure 10. Near the mooring site of the phantom gringo boat, Abebaiba poses for ethnographer.

der, and lightning filled the night. But when about half the people had climbed out, a tremendous bolt of lightning lit the sky, revealing the escape to the guards. The half remaining inside were killed, including the *häïm-baná*. Those who got free went far upriver and became *cimarones* with long hair down to their calves and white skin. For fear, the *cimarones* never came downriver again, not even for salt. (−T/S)

The women are returned to wildness (nudity). The shaman's power to wield lightning turns unpredictably against the people, thwarting escape. The Spaniards forced Emberá who wouldn't die or compromise to revert to animal-like creatures. Shunning all contact, evidence of the *cimarones'* mythical powers of fleet-footedness can still be witnessed in the upper reaches of the rivers, they say.[2]

The figure of the Indian is an essentializing concept historically bound

Figure 11. Baptismal procession led by Spanish priest in Palo Blanco.

to the feature of race — that is, it is a concept that lends a natural, homogeneous basis for identity to those who would call themselves or be called by its name. The figure erases differences among indigenous peoples and draws boundaries between them and other races. Such boundaries structure the distribution of resources and political power. In Darién at the end of the fifteenth century, boundaries between Indian and Spanish-white were drawn in blood and never forgotten. Three centuries later, the Spanish brought in Africans to replace the dying and intransigent Indians (Castrillón 1982). A new symbolic and economic space of mediation was created and filled by blacks. A tripartite social field was created: Indian, black, and Spanish-white. Enslaved, the blacks took certain heavy labors off the backs of Indians, mostly working the gold mines. After slavery, the blacks developed this space of mediation to their own advantage. In the contemporary context, the mediatory space once filled with unpaid, back-breaking black labor had been transformed into a biracial political economic structure centered in river port towns with cargo boats moving in and out laden with outgoing (mostly Indian) agricultural produce and incoming imported goods. As entrepreneurs and politicians, the blacks have linked the

Emberá to the world of outsiders, which had coalesced in the urban center of transnational linkage, Panama City, when Conquest ramified into colonialism, and as people of Spanish descent were joined by more whites from Europe and North America.

The Indians and blacks discovered different ways to adjust to post-Conquest life. From the Indian point of view, the blacks in Darién have had greater access to and affinity for the interlocking systems of white capitalism and Christianity. According to the Emberá system of social classification, the blacks share the category of *kampuniá* (non-Indian) with whites. The term can be linked to race (i.e., there are black-*kampuniá* and white-*kampuniá*), or race can remain ambiguous, as in this story Dzoshua told me:

> God was drinking *guarapo* [cane alcohol]. So we come up into the house, and there he was in the hammock, drunk. And the women come to relieve him, and then his eggs — "keck, keck, keck" — they were there outside. The women didn't take care of his eggs. He was naked, and the women were laughing.
>
> Then along comes this *kampuniá* and he says, "Hey man, why aren't you taking care? Why don't you cover that God? Poor God, I'll cover him." Well, if that were us, we would stay rich, like you all. But when God woke up, he said, "So you don't take care of my eggs, nor anything. You leave me naked? Then you will stay poor, like you are. You are going to stay poor, but the *kampuniá*, he is going to stay rich."
>
> It happened all at once, "You will stay poor, you will suffer to eat, to get money." For this, we are suffering, not like you. For this, they make money, I don't know where they coin it. But if it were we that took care, then they would deliver this money to us. But we didn't, so they bring it to you. This is. For this, it was.
>
> Ai. This is a story. A story from Ancient Times. (T/S)

With cynical humor, the story turns the spiritual ruler of all into just another home boy serviced by women and left to sleep in public with his balls hanging out. A farce, it doesn't pretend to explain the absurd position of the Indian in a by-now postcolonial hierarchy whose alignments have shifted here and there but have been through no revolution. Class consciousness cannot be separated from race in Darién, although cross-race identifications have been mobilized at certain historical moments.

The Emberá survived Conquest and colonization with a combination of retreat and controlled engagement. In the process, they were protected and exploited by the blacks, whose links to urban markets enhanced the quality of Emberá life in the upriver forests. Although not without its tensions and disputes, the Indians and blacks have achieved a peaceful and distinctive coexistence that is admirable. But the balance they have achieved may be contingent on the relative remoteness of the region they inhabit—and in today's crowded world, remoteness is another concept that seems to stir the imagination and invite sporadic manipulation by outsiders. In terms of market logic, remoteness inhibits efficient distribution of goods and services and is therefore seen as a negative quality, something to be overcome with development. A place that is remote (as defined by outsiders) has a certain allure as well—the next place to open up, full of hidden treasure, where adventure awaits, where the layers of domination are stark and thin and allow a different kind of freedom.

The Indian in a remote jungle is a landscaped figure of the imagination that attracts the manipulations of those from afar, manipulations that can thoughtlessly alter relations of power and cooperation that have been established over two centuries of coexistence. Focused frantically, romantically on the Indian, foreigners do not necessarily appreciate the peaceful relations between the races that exist. Some are just plain blind to the negative effects of interference (an overidentification with God, capitalism, or environmentalism perhaps).

The body of the bare-breasted Indian in a tropical paradise/jungle hell is an ideological site. The Indian is a fiction onto which the savagery of Conquest can be projected and through which the powers of terror and healing can be forged (Taussig 1987). The Indian is a fiction through which the optimism of capitalist development and pessimism of military dictatorship can be managed. The Indian is a fiction that focuses the sight lines of salvation sellers, wildlife protectors, and ethnographic knowledge-producers. Into this field of contrasting figurations walk the Emberá. Assuming the ascription of Indian, they represent that which is required to elicit whatever is obtainable in each arrangement, knowing each figural variant presupposes a particular set of imaginary associations that fill the space between selves and others so necessary to human being. But they never forget, through all the ins and outs, booms and busts of these part-rational, part-fantastic models of regional structure and function that figure in and through the Indian, that these outsiders, especially the white ones, tend to have a quite erratic interest in local matters. Since Ancient Times, the terms and rules in the game of desire and deceit have been elaborated and confused. In the context of contemporary development, the game must be played adroitly. At the same time that the Emberá may reap benefits from a new market economy, they must sustain ecological survival at the level of the autonomous household.

Flood Memories

Most perplexing to the person who explores far and wide in search of different forms of apprehension is the encounter with images that come from home, images that were given away, spread around, stolen, and transformed. Governed by a peculiar distortion, images may retain a name and a trope, but the familiar exists in a changed media, its elements conjoin with new ones according to a different code. The new combination of elements conveys structures of feeling from opposing sources, sends conflicting qualities to the brain, and stimulates awareness of the cultural production of difference.

The homogeneous merging of cultures that hypothetically takes place after prolonged contact and has been called acculturation seems to occur only superficially. The presence of borrowed terms may seem to support the notion of an unproblematic and inevitable assimilation of indigenous cultures only if the deep suspiciousness installed with Conquest's treacheries are erased. Indeed, the traces of borrowed traits is just as often a deceit that defeats the desire of a conquering order. The use of the word *devil* in shamanic discourse is an example. It threw me off at first, when I was doing preliminary fieldwork in 1983 in a village along the highway. I hadn't developed the more receptive approach to learning about magic yet and was asking what and why questions about what a shaman was doing. (What he was physically doing was bathing and chanting over a woman sitting before him up in a house.) He looked down at me standing on the ground below and said he was "getting the devil out." I assumed he was talking about devil with a capital *D* and was dismayed at what seemed to be a Waunan adaptation of an invasive Christian theology. Then I learned that for the Waunan and Emberá there are lots of devils—in fact, the shaman's song was as much about calling ones to aid in curing as about getting rid of others. These little devils—*diablitos* or *animalitos* in Spanish, or *hai* in Emberá—aren't particularly good or bad. They are governed by intent, by the heart of the shaman that employs them. Little by little I began to unpack the concept of devil and eventually have come to understand the use of the term as a particular, limited kind of acceptance of Christian dogma that avoids conflict with missionaries. Acceptance is limited because the term *devil* is put in a different context and is invested with Emberá meanings and functions that are consistent with shamanic practice. The term is a guise that does not change shamanic practice in any fundamental way.

Most linguistic markers of cultural contact do not need to be guarded as effectively as the term *devil*. Some have a more neutral capacity for simultaneously conveying universality and cultural difference. Words, images, and tropes have universal appeal because they have potential to be transformed in ways that make their meanings pertinent to the history of their narrators. The flood myth is an example of this. One of the first myths presented to foreigners, in the Emberá corpus Noah becomes Nué, his boat a giant dugout canoe (E. *hampá,* S. *piragua*). The animals that are taken on board two by two include a female devil and her husband and a male devil and his wife. Here follows a version most clearly related to biblical tradition told to me by Celestina of Tamarinbó on July 15, 1985.

Nué

In Ancient Times the rains came.
Nué built a boat, built a dugout canoe.
"Rains are coming.
Achira,[3] rains are coming.
They're going to come today.
Within three days, the floods will come."
Nué.

Nué dug out a canoe.
He is going out into the heavy rains in the canoe he built.
In the heavy rains, Nué is going out in the canoe he built.
He'd go when they came. He'd go when they came, in the canoe he built.
I'm making a canoe, he'd say.
Big, was the canoe Nué made. He built it all, finished, he completed it.

The big river came.
That flood that destroys everything came.
The whole earth was filled.
That, in that time it was done.
He was building his canoe every day, building the canoe, night fell.
Building the canoe. Then Nué finished the canoe.
Biiiiig, it came.
"I'm not going to make you embark," Nué told them.
"You all," he told them, it is said.

"The flood comes, you don't believe, and you stay thus."

"It comes," he told them.

A raft, Nué made.

He was cutting balsa logs and sticking them together, he was making it.

In this already one year past.

Then the flood came.

Nué made a canoe, the flood came.

The whooooole world was filled.

Full it was, thus Nué told them.

Full it was, thus Nué told them.

His wife he took.

An old woman devil that was with her husband he took.

The devil with his wife he took. He put them inside.

Then, he let them embark.

With the spouses that were, he took all.

Wildcat was there with his spouse, he took.

Little ant that was there with her husband he took.

All the animals that were there,

The snake that was there with her spouse, he took.

The snake, the deer that was there with her husband, he took.

He made them embark in the boat.

That [gesturing all around] filled up and stayed that way, it is said.

Everyone came, it is said, this [gesturing all around] thus was filled.

They sent forth the dove, it is said.

The little dove, thus, said "um-umm," it didn't see the branch.

Thus it was full where it was going to get it, it is said.

Nué remained.

There he was, then, they were shouting, the others went below, it took them.

They took the Emberá multitudes to the waters below.

Then, thus said, the canoe that he made, it is said.

Now yes, he would not have made me embark in the canoe. (T/E)

The missionaries may have translated the flood myth into the languages of Emberá and Waunan as their way of teaching God and Spanish to the Indians, but the Indians transcode it according to a cosmology of rainforest survival. The teller personalizes it, ending pensively with the thought that she would not have been one of the ones to be saved. The gentle tropical breezes of the Emberá environment belie an ecology of disaster. Floods of devastating proportions take place periodically and unpredictably. In Nué's story, real and mythical floods are conflated, empowering a generalized morality tale with an air of historicity. For example, another woman in Tupisa told me a version that locates the event in the landscape of the Chocó: *The water was already deep on the hill in Chitre, where they waited and withstood, till the flood of forty days began to subside.* Others have used their versions to support Emberá claims to pre-Conquest settlement in Darién. Through the work of Indians and missionaries the biblical myth has become a vehicle through which the site of human survival is transposed from desert to jungle, an ongoing part of their cataclysmic oral history.

There were two major floods in Darién's recent past, in the early 1950s and early 1960s. When rainforest rivers flood, they take everything with them. Desperation is grafted vividly to memory; floods become turning points in family histories, devices for the organization of experience.

A man from the Chico River tells of the flood he experienced in the early 1950s, when he was a young boy living upriver from where the most upstream village (an Evangelical mission site) is now:

> When the flood came, the family crossed downriver to the other side, but not everyone fit in the canoe. We couldn't get back to pick up the second load of four people. The river was raging. It carried away the house we were waiting in and the house upriver where the four others were. I held onto a tree and eventually went with the water downriver. One woman who'd been left up at the other place somehow got hooked onto a tree with a vine and survived, although she lost her *paruma* [S. wrap-around skirt, E. *wa*]. A small girl got carried away and drowned. It all happened in the dark of night. The flood finally subsided about dawn. All the plantain orchards were destroyed, all the houses gone.
>
> All we had was a little bedding we'd grabbed before leaving. We came downriver to where our uncle lived, but there was nothing to eat, only some plantains that had gotten carried away by the current and wedged into a crevice here and there. So we left and went to the Congo River. [The Congo River is quite far from the Chico, on the other side of the Gulf of San Miguel. It was also the site of the buried gold that the grandfather-shaman and his two grandsons were seeking on the Easter that they encoun-

tered the phantom gringo boat; see Chap. 8.] We had family there. The flood had not affected that area. In that time there were two lumber companies in operation getting *kaóa* [a hardwood]. We worked for this company one year till we saved enough money to buy bedding, pots, and other things we needed and then came up back here. We moved down to the village of Palo Blanco later when the school was founded. (−T/S)

After the flood, people's lives, like the paths of the rivers, are diverted in unforeseen ways. In such times, Emberá resources may be insufficient to survive. They depend on kin where they can and take advantage of whatever wage-labor opportunities are available. In times of ecological crisis, the system of foreign-owned capitalist enterprise that has been established in the region provides an important back-up mode of survival. Those with more established kin may not need to appeal to the wage-labor system so directly, or at least they may not have to go so far away from home to do so. For example, Larú tells me his story of the 1961 flood in the Tupisa River. It's Easter Thursday in Tamarinbó. As people are lying around in the midday heat, talking vaguely if at all, sleeping off the holiday meal, he tells how the flood was the first event in a sequence of family disasters:

I was working contract labor clearing bush for Onofre's father. That downpour came, then the flood. It came when I was working downriver on the other bank. I couldn't make it back to my house where I had left two little girls (one of them later died from snakebite). There on the path that now goes past Roberto's house I mounted a *ranchito* [temporary shelter built at work sites] with my daughter. We thought we were going to die. The flood took the *ranchito,* and we grabbed on to a tree, then that broke too. My daughter fell in the river, and I grabbed her by the hair. When the tree broke, we just rode the river till it subsided. Then we returned to the house. The little girls were crying.

Later my wife got sick, something with her foot. I took her to her brother in the Tuquesa River who was a shaman, now dead. [The Tuquesa is the next river over, about six hours' walk away.] "Work here, here is forest [*monte*]," they said to me. (Before I left, most of my orchard was destroyed by the flood, and I'd sold four trees, though I still have a pejibaye palm, mango, and calabash.) I called my son from Sambu to come with me (he had a different wife then). My other son got murdered with poison. So we stayed there with just the one son that had come from Sambu. One day this son took a sister to hunt in Charco Peje. They were cutting sticks to make a hearth fan. It was on a steep bank, and as she was grabbing the last piece, a snake bit her in the chest. It happened in the morning, and she died by that afternoon. Eventually, we came back here. (−T/S)

The myths of Ancient Times echo through the atmosphere of the living. In the language of rivers, each flood, each small war, each deceit contains within it the potential for complete reversion, an unconscious devastation of that which is known in all its diversity as human being. As the Emberá struggle to survive in their way, they know that complete restoration after every cataclysm cannot be expected. People move on, others preserve and restore what is left. When movements and labor investments overlap, conflict may result.

In the time frame of the living—about three or four generations—things get sorted out one way or another. Everyone over twenty-five has experienced at least one flood, the meaning of which gets interpreted in the frame of Ancient Times. Mythical meaning confronts historical conditions that have changed in many ways since Noah/Nué built his boat/canoe.[4] The regional presence of a cash economy is more than just an alternative to traditional subsistence practices (the man said his son was killed by poison because people envied his means of production, i.e., his motor). As the cash economy ramifies and gets institutionalized in the region, it intrudes into the most isolated human sanctuaries of the upriver forest. Money brings its own terms and its own codes, which, spoken through the imaginary figure of the (male) Indian, begins to weigh on people's minds. The outside world is now inside the borders of even a small family garden.

Social History of a Garden

A week before I went downriver to the congress with Inez and Dzoshua, it was an ordinary day in the village, early February, just about the end of the rains. Machete in hand, I head upriver past Zelda's house, looking for something to get involved in. As usual, she asks me what I'm doing, then says, "Tiger's going to get you! Tiger's going to get you! Haaa, ha, ha ha!" Her peals of warm, gently mocking laughter follow me down the path. Just outside the village, I find Inez clearing a fruit orchard. The prodigious growth of weeds will slow down with the rains, so it's a good time for cleaning up, leaving some overgrowth to protect the trees from the strong summer sun to come. Inez accepts my offer of help. She sets me working by the papaya, and we talk with the swings and chops of machetes. She's both annoyed and proud of the fact that out of all her siblings, only she, the eldest daughter, takes care of this place, even though everyone benefits from its produce. That suggests to me that there's more to the orchard than chopping and eating, and I begin asking her how this orchard with its abandoned house sites has come to be. She tells me its history, a series of selected statements about who owned what, where houses were located, and how the family moved around with changes in circumstance. She composes her discourse using the objects around her: the different kinds of trees whose size and position recall their conditions of planting, the fallen remains of the last house her family lived in together, a post that marks the orchard boundary as well as her brother's separation upon marriage. The river to the front and forest to the back orient her memory. What I don't realize until later, when I learn of contesting interpretations of the orchard's history, is that her telling is more than an evocation of people/object/place configurations from the past; her telling is also an invocation of support for present family claims that must bear the burden of proof. Shaping her statements about the past are present, conflicting interfamily claims. As I was to find out a month later on Easter Thursday in a parenthetical remark within Larú's flood story (in the previous section), he and his wife, Beatriz, lived on the orchard site before the 1961 flood. The pejibaye palm, mango, and calabash trees that Larú claimed he owned in his family history are the very same ones Inez was caring for this day. At this point in time, however, I do not understand the influences that compel her to select and order her memories in a particular way.

Inez calls her telling into mind bit by bit, referring to whatever objects happen to be closest to our working space. While she talks, she works and keeps an eye on my work to make sure in my ignorance I don't cut the inconspicuous new growth of squash vines. When we rest, I note down her words with the aid of a map, later reordering them to go forward from past to present. Later, when I finish abstracting the chronological sequence from the topographical one, I go to her house to retell her story, and she confirms its correctness.

> When the family first came from Sambu, we settled on the opposite bank, where Dzoshua's plantains and bananas are now. We had pigs, chickens, and an orchard when the big flood came in 1961 and took nearly everything out to sea. After the flood, we moved to higher ground, the orchard in which we now stand. We built the first house in the center of the or-

chard near the chocolate tree. My mother's brother, Andreas, came soon after and built a house closer to the river.

My deceased mother, Dzoshua's first wife, planted many of the trees in the orchard. These have been cared for all these years. It is these trees that belong to us. My mother planted much, and much of what she planted has died. She herself died about fifteen years ago. [She tells about how Dzoshua brought her mother to the hospital in Panama, how it was a holiday and they got turned away, and how she died on the way back.] After my mother died, I, the eldest, took care of all the others. Ritali and Oliver, the two youngest siblings, were still little then.

Some time later my mother's brother Andreas was about to build a new house. He had three poles up when his wife got sick. He took her to Tuquesa [the next river over, about six hours' walk away], then sent her to Panama for treatment. She died there. After the deaths of first his sister and then his wife, Andreas didn't want to live here anymore. He said he was going to Uncle Beté and went *con cabanga* [in an extremely disturbed state]. And he said to Dzoshua, "Brother-in-law, make a house for yourself," and this Dzoshua did.

Andreas sold the *finca* [S. farm] to the family. Well, actually, he only sold the coconuts, for five dollars apiece. They were young at the time, only about four or five feet tall including the young shoots. There are five of them, owned by myself, my sister, brother, father, and husband. All the rest of the trees were still small then too. Other family members have planted trees here through the years, and they are still here. Now we will plant more. When my mother was alive, we always stayed together, but after her death, we began to build separate houses.

In the meantime, newcomers arrived. Omar, his unmarried sister Zelda, and daughter Norma. Omar built the house at the edge of the village, where they still live. Dzoshua moved in with them. The rest of us moved into another house, the remains of which still hang together in the back of the orchard. When Dzoshua married Omar's daughter, Norma, the new in-laws, Omar and Dzoshua, built another house for all of them to live in together. When Norma gave birth to her first son with Dzoshua, they built their own house. Later my brother Edi married Melani of Promesa, and they built their own house. Just about then, Onofre's family (with others) decided to found the village in its present location, and one by one my family moved into it. Edi and Melani were the last to move, building their present house site in the village about a year ago [early 1984]. (−T/S)

Inez's garden exists in two systems of meaning and economy simultaneously. In the indigenous system that derives from an isolated, land-rich geography, the garden is a subsistence base in which the meaning of fruit trees resides in the actions of planting and care. In the indigenous system that is partially integrated within a developing nation-state, however, the garden is also becoming a piece of property in which fruit trees are exchangeable for money and may be alienated from the actions of planting and care. The incorporation of capitalist measures of value has been accelerated by increased competition for land resulting from household concentration in villages. Land claims, of which Inez's family history is a version, have thus become a discursive form that strongly reflects the juxtaposition of codes derived from different systems of value. Multiple code use is an index of Emberá articulation into national society and international markets.

In her garden's history, Inez states that the orchard belongs to her family and that others should not touch it. She accounts for her family's ownership with the following arguments that make use of both subsistence and market codes: (1) her mother planted the trees; (2) all trees planted by her mother belong to the family as a whole; (3) any tree planted by a family member is owned by that family member, yet the work involved and fruit produced is shared by the family as a whole; (4) her mother's brother sold her family the young coconut trees, hence the orchard; (5) her family has been taking care of the orchard for some years.

The set of contradictions that arise from the articulation of subsistence and international market economies constitute one layer of meaning in Inez's discourse, but her predicament is multilayered. And indeed, she uses the different codes as resources to strengthen her position vis-à-vis her local community. For while she is concerned about the shifting ways of determining value, she is also grappling with contradictions arising from principles of social organization that are applied to families and communities with changing memberships. In Emberá communities, membership fluctuates fairly frequently and often suddenly because of death and migration. Garden histories trace the contours of care and conflict that result, encoding changing alliances and tensions. When extended families are dispersed in a spacious and fertile landscape, the complications of property claims that may result from families who occupied the same land at different points of time are less problematic. Tensions between families are exacerbated in the village context.

In her talk that day in the orchard, only a hint of the conflict with Larú's family appears. Coming across the big mango tree, Inez says: "Beatriz [Larú's wife] is scheming. She says the big mango is hers." Inez doesn't think so. "Of course, Beatriz's family did live in the orchard site before the flood when we came across from the other side [of the river]. But when they left for Tuquesa, that mango was just a bitty sapling. It is only our care all these years that has made it a big fruit producer. Why, only a week ago Beatriz's daughter-in-law said the mango was here before us! I kept my mouth shut. I answered nothing," pronounces Inez indignantly.

In asking around, I discovered a loose knot of conflicting opinion. These are the details: One young man, who himself had bought *rastrojo* (cleared crop land) from Inez's uncle Andreas for $400 (a price set as much by labor invested in clearing as for the land per se), said that Inez's family never bought the coco trees, that the coco trees were a gift from Andreas because they had no money. Omar, the father of Dzoshua's wife, said they bought the coco trees but never actually paid money for them. (This suggests that among kin, the agreement that money is to be transferred may provide sufficient precedent for ownership.) Moreover, Omar said that the trees were not five feet tall when they bought them, as Inez said, but twenty-five feet (thereby diminishing the labor investment of Inez's family). He was quite upset about the whole thing because Beatriz told him she wanted *her* land back — her land is the site on which his and his sister Zelda's house now stands, which he said he bought from her when Beatriz and Larú went to Tuquesa. Omar told Beatriz it would be impossible for him to move, but pointing to the other side of the boundary marking Inez's orchard, he told her he'd be glad to let her live on his upriver side. When he told me that, I said, "But that belongs to Dzoshua's family!" And he replied that Inez told him she doesn't care; if Andreas wants to come back and sell it, they've already gotten their use out of it. (Note how Inez delegates the decision to a family member who is no longer living in the community, displacing it in space and time.) Eva, the granddaughter of Dzoshua's uncle, the first settler, and Beatriz's niece, said that Omar didn't buy the land from Beatriz when she left, but rather some orange trees. Eva's brother Agouti confirmed what Eva said, saying that Omar bought oranges and pejibaye palms. But then Agouti put it all in perspective for me. He explained that of all the people here, almost no one had to buy land. Buying and selling land only began in 1981, about a decade after village formation.

The emergence of discourse presenting competing land claims indicates that this is a pivotal moment in the history of land transaction in the upper Tupisa River. Again, Inez is not unaware of this fact, but there is as yet another layer of intention represented in her garden's history. On the most personal level, Inez is grappling with the very definition of the term *family.* Her predicament, while tied to tensions between her family and others, is also related to tensions within her own extended family. Through the last marriage of her father, Dzoshua, her family was joined with a previously independent family. In her history of the garden, she guards against the potential consequences that could arise from her father's second marriage. Indeed, she subjects the term *family* to strategic definition that changes with context. Inez tells how she assumed the role of female household head upon the death of her mother. She had to take care of her siblings and do her share of a wife's work as well. Now that her siblings are grown and Dzoshua remarried, her responsibility has been eased, but her life is not less complicated. Dzoshua has widened his responsibilities; Inez feels it is her responsibility to protect herself and her siblings, that is, her mother's family's interests as distinct from those of the family of her father's second wife. When Inez talks about "us" in the orchard, she means her siblings and her father, but not his father's wife and their children. This orchard "us" is connected to the maternal ties that her claims recall, namely, her deceased mother and her deceased mother's absent brother, rather than her ties to her living father. Her discourse, then, not only supports her claims to owning the orchard but defines family specifically for this context. In most other contexts, however, this distinction is not appropriate, for Dzoshua's first and second families both live nearby, sharing food and work (e.g., see Chap. 5 on canoe construction). As female head of household, daughter, sister, and wife, Inez participates in a range of activities where "us" means everyone. As chief strategist in the interfamily arena, Inez balances the respect she has for her father as male elder with her need to protect her (mother's) family.

Inez's multilayered predicament can be read in the history of her garden. Her position, her subjectivity, and her politics can be deciphered by means of her memory's text and the little knot of conflict in which it is embedded. In the entanglements and antagonisms that are stored in the interstices of everyday life, the meaning of things is changing. Fruit trees, for one, are acquiring a meaning they never had before. Through their indexical relation to the land in which they are planted, they are becoming equivalent to land in the context of money transfers. But as a term of exchange, fruit trees are complicated by the need to evaluate the extent of care provided by a sequence of owners/tenders, which, I believe, is precisely how Inez wants social life to be complicated. It seems that for her part, although she is willing to prop up her argument with cash value (point 4 in her series of arguments above), using a range of available discursive forms for the purpose of argument, it is the right relation between people, not the dollars that people hand one to another, that is paramount, that seems most reliable in the long run. In her equation for determining ownership, she gives the most weight to kinship and extent of care. In practice, these aspects are inseparable. Being in someone's family means that you take responsibility for caring for them. Owning an orchard is just part of that. Holding tightly to traditional values, Inez wants her family to own the orchard because it produces fruit, not capital, for people to eat, not sell. She struggles here not only for an orchard but, in the context of adjustment to changing historical codes and conditions, to keep Emberá values of kinship and care, to keep some orientation to the qualities of social life that have nurtured her sense of herself, now shifting too with the contending discourses on the landscape. The availability of alternative codes creates contradictions and ambiguities that are loci of struggle and creativity. Thus with intelligence and caution, capitalism can be put at the service of indigenous values. This creative struggle can be traced not only within the discourse of differentially aligned groups but within the discourse of a single person like Inez.[5]

When we finish our work that day, Inez hands me a big round calabash (E. *säö*) to cut in half and scrape smooth as a bowl, some superhot peppers, and a few little odd-shaped gourds that she says kill cockroaches, all in exchange for my labor.

Nomads?

In Inez's garden history, village formation is the last in a series of events (following flood, illness and death, newcomers, marriage and birth) that have triggered household movement. Indeed, micromovement of settlement sites within an established area and macromovement across regions have been part of Emberá life since Ancient Times. In the twenty-odd years before fieldwork, the mass movement of Emberá households from dispersed sites into villages was enabled by practices that continually reproduce the potential for mobility (e.g., canoe construction, transfer of plantain stocks, use of forest materials for house construction). The micromovement that constitutes village formation is a variant of Emberá survival strategies keyed to the particular constellation of forces that have come together at this point in time—local impact of world population growth, deforestation, militarization, and world system integration. While these forces may be irreversible, that does not necessarily imply that nucleated villages will always be the best survival strategy for the Emberá.[6] The development model, based on Euramerican urban history, in which a dispersed settlement to village transition heralds the establishment of towns, cities, suburbias and tourist sites, is sure to meet ecological and cultural resistance when put into practice. Adequate models of human habitation in the late twentieth-century tropical forest, yet unformulated, will (I hope) arise from the intersection of indigenous and postindustrial cultures and technologies.

If a foreigner goes by this orchard of Inez's, he or she might think it was abandoned. It might seem as if the people who built the houses now in remnants have moved on, confirming popular characterizations of the Emberá as nomads. The trees, he or she might think, once planted, grow naturally. But in fact, there are people who belong to this place, and they live not far away. Most of the trees, and certainly the squash, peppers, herbs, and sugarcane, would sicken and die if nobody cared for them. The people come every now and then; they sustain the orchard, and it sustains them. Orchards like these look like nothing much, but they feed people who have little money and no stores, who know little (or more than enough) of urban strife.

The Emberá do not dominate the landscape of which they are a part. Although their stilt houses open to the breeze and built on the tops of levees are distinctive, they last only about ten or fifteen years before they are allowed to come apart, become enveloped in new growth, and fall back into the earth. If all is well, another house is built nearby. They are a people who until recently had no interest in building towns or forming governments. They don't even boast the ruins of "high civilization." Many still know how to survive without all the things many city folk take for granted — electricity, cars, ozone, fast food, bridges, plumbing, and nuclear weapons. If by some unlikely miracle the "outside world" (e.g., loggers, miners, pesticide experts) can learn to forget this piece of forest, leaving a small gap in the destruction, the Emberá of Darién may survive a good deal longer than the rest of humankind. But this is probably an overly romantic evocation on my part. For now, the Emberá, just like the *kampuniá*, must struggle with the contradictions of capitalism, which, following Chantal Mouffe (1988), is best understood in its most pervasive sense as the commodification of social life. At the same time, they must sustain the piece of forest that gives them food and shelter and must adjust their sense of human being to the currents and currencies of global import.

Of all the aspects of life in the upriver forest that is the most authentic, it is the discontinuities that present themselves. This is, in part, a function

Figure 12. First cacique's Emberá-style *(right)* and *kampuniá*-style *(left)* houses in Union Chocó.

of the intercultural epistemological and logistic grounds of this ethnography, which I have been careful not to erase from my writing. But this ethnography is just a symptom of the much broader process of world system intrusion into all indigenous enclaves, an economic and symbolic process that creates discontinuities, inexorably forcing distinctive cultures to come to terms with the hierarchies and homogeneities that result from market-driven abstractions of human value.

As bald-headed Vulture looks again at Cow and considers its chances, we need not worry that desire may be tricked by deceit once again. For the wisdom of Ancient Times has prepared us with the knowledge that it is deceit, after all, and in the beginning, that motivates creation. As the Emberá engage in the kind of things they have always done—hunt iguana, tend gardens—they engage as well with a soon-to-be-overthrown U.S.-backed military junta professing revolutionary democracy, with the fear of flood, with the changing significance of trees, and with the multifaceted figure of the Indian.

three

Transformation and Taboo (Burning Forests)

In chaos, the cosmos seizes two lovers engaged in anal sex. Simone reminds her listeners of her version of Noah/Nué:

> The old woman told son not to do it from behind, but he didn't listen. They didn't even have time to take the lamp with them when the floods came. When the waters subsided, she told them again: "It's a dangerous time, don't do it from behind." But son didn't listen, and they got stuck. They stayed stuck; like cement they stayed. Turned to stone. There is nothing to be done about it now. (T/E)

A form of human interpenetration that is nonreproductive may be thought of as excessive; its intimate excess attracts co-occurring cosmic transformations. Cosmic and human excess resonate. "In this day it was sticky," tells Simone in her tale. "Because it was the time of creation, the world was still in the works," my translator explains. In this mythical case, excess is a kind of similarity that sets up a sympathetic vibration between cosmos and human couple. In other words, similarity activates the indexical relationship between couple and cosmos. But the power of the cosmos is too much: it leaves the couple petrified. This combination of similarity and indexicality, or contact, may be related to the two principles of sympathetic magic that

Frazer identifies in *The Golden Bough* (1911:52) as underlying the magical efficacy of fetishes—namely, the Law of Similarity, in which a likeness can affect or draw power from the original, and the Law of Contact or Contagion, in which things that have been in contact can continue to act upon one another even after contact has been severed. As Taussig (1993:55) points out in his study of mimesis, Frazer's principles are usually combined in magical practice. The Emberá mythical conception of how human action connects to the cosmos points to the utter naturalness of the combination of these laws in practice, as everything in the cosmos may be perceived as always already in potential contact. According to this mythical conception, magical transformation is not necessarily a matter of fetishes but a matter of timing.

Woodpecker and Horned Lizard, engaged in the transformative activity of ax work in the very moment that the world changed lost the power of speech and had their axes stuck up on the top of their heads (see Chap. 2). Similarly, humans can be stopped in the very midst of movement, say the stories from Ancient Times. The moral, spoken in the voice of an old woman, passed down through time and many tellers, is that it is safer to avoid excessive conduct altogether, for moments of chaotic creation are so unpredictable.

This mythical knowledge teaches people to avoid setting up situations in which excess activates untoward cosmic contact. Taboos are set in place to guard human behavior, especially behavior that is transformative in nature. Because it is the epitome of human transformation, sex is particularly subject to such taboo. Incorporative, like eating, and also reciprocal, like talking, sex engulfs other concepts of exchange. Sex is the purest embodiment of myth, a model of potential. Its images of abuse and resurrection cue unpredictable effects; its images of intimacy offer grounds for social control. The discourse of sexuality circulates, substituting for other modes of signification.

Enforcement of taboos becomes intensified during recognized cycles of celestial disruption such as Easter week (S. *Semana Santa*). You are not supposed to have sexual intercourse on Easter week (especially on Good Friday), which celebrates Jesus' rising from the dead.

There's the story about the blacks [*libres*] from Antiochia in Colombia who didn't pay attention to the sexual prohibitions on Easter. They had intercourse on the holiest of holies and got stuck. Their friends charged thirty pesos to whomever wanted to watch. Felipe knows someone who actually

went and saw. And there's that Emberá couple who went out to cut plantains on Good Friday [trees are known to speak or bleed when cut on this
day of rampant animation] and they wanted sex and so they did it, and the
man's penis grew abnormally large and they stuck. Ai, there are lots of
stories. (−T/S)

A chain of taboos concerning the body are observed more strictly as
Easter Thursday and Friday approach. In addition to prohibitions against
sex, there are prohibitions against sleep, (long) baths in the river, going to
the forest or orchard (all food and firewood is gathered, hunted, fished,
and processed before the holiday), cutting or cooking food too briskly,
handling money, and letting dogs sleep in the house at night. Because exchange sets up the possibility for transformation, sites and actions that en-
tail exchange are to be avoided. After the hectic period of preparation when
everything is readied, there is a slowing down of everyday life, a suspension, a unification of the people. If these taboos are broken, some fear the
world will end. In the same breath, however, people may note that of
course everybody disrespects Easter these days.

Burning Forests

Where the cosmos has order, take advantage and prepare. Where its
tempos can be discerned and qualities balanced, attend and act. When the
heavens are about to change from dry season to rain, prepare for destruction and rebirth: make black smoke billow from crackling hot fire. With a
blaze of synchronicity, bring on the hard rains and tender green shoots.
Out of the fire, the people bring bright life. Every year at Easter time,
public life turns toward creation.

The timing for setting the cut forest afire is critical to agricultural success. Optimally, things get so dried out by the summer sun that they catch
well, leaving large areas covered with rich ash in which seeds can be planted
after the burn. Once planted, the rains must come hard and sure if seedlings are to grow. If you wait too long and rains come before the big burning, the cut forest may be damp and burn poorly, leaving big tree trunks
that obstruct the planting area. If the rains are weak and sporadic after
the burning and planting, weeds will compete with edible plants, stealing
nutrients and requiring extra labor for clearing. According to Emberá tradition, the ideal time for burning the fields is Saturday of Glory, the day

after Good Friday. When I asked Dzoshua about it, he said that before, everybody burned on Saturday of Glory, then PO! the rains came all at once and everybody planted. Looking out across the landscape then, one could see the fires rising out of all the dispersed sites. Today, however, this one here, that one there burns. This one calls the rain too soon and spoils it for that one who has waited.

The problem is that it's impossible to predict the exact moment when any particular dry season will end and rainy season begin. In fact, there is no precise change of seasons as the ideal would suggest: dry one day, rainy season the next. As it happened this year, almost everybody burned on a so-so day before the proper time (April 1). Then there was a week of blazing sun, hotter than all year, and the *monte* (S. forest) kept igniting and burning areas that were not meant to be burned. Then Saturday of Glory came, and those few who had waited for it burned. It was hot hot hot till late afternoon, when there was a light rain that messed things up. People were still burning up and down the river when I traveled down on the ninth, and the highway was alight in many places on the fourteenth when I took a night bus trip from Yaviza to Panama. It looked like hell.[1]

After seeing the inferno searing down the center of the Darién isthmus in 1985 and the Amazon burning in 1980, and having learned the planetary implications of this process, whenever I saw forest burning, I saw only destruction. And so I was shocked into attention when my Emberá companion remarked on the prettiness of a charred space. I hadn't seen past the destruction because, having grown up in New York City, it was not within my experience. Being with the Emberá taught me how to see the beauty of bright dark green shoots of corn and rice shining against charcoal and ash. I learned how to feel satisfaction at a well-burned field.

A not uncommon mistake that results from overdoing things and suddenly waking up to the damage, as has happened with U.S. citizens and their environment, is to misperceive all related actions as being equally damaging. Indigenous people have engaged in slash-and-burn agriculture for centuries without the kind of devastation now being brought on by vast clearings created for lumber, cattle, and agricultural industries. According to the Emberá way, in previllage days forest was cleared for dooryard gardens (with herbs, fruit trees, and roots), fields of rice and corn (S. *monte*), plantain and banana orchards (S. *tallos*), spreading outward in a circle, scattering around a river-edge clearing with one or two stilt houses. For environmentalists, this is a model of sustainable tropical forest agriculture. But it is not environmentalists, mostly living comfortably in dwellings with heat, plumbing, and electricity and in proximity to schools and hospitals, who sustain the hardships that living in isolation entails. And it is not environmentalists, but economists, who offer models for improving the standard of living of the Emberá. Now houses stand fifteen to a hundred in a clearing, people work their lands side by side, every season cutting deeper into the *monte virgen*. After vines and small trees are macheteyed, the men ax the big trees. The bigger the areas, the further the wild seeds have to travel to replant themselves, which is initially good for agriculture. But when the land is left fallow, the bigger areas take longer to become forested again, and they will be left fallow less and less if village populations are to be sustained. The dispersed settlement pattern is better ecologically, but it is not safer (remember Dzoshua, who lay sick by his father's dead body for days before anyone found him), nor, from the official national government perspective, is it efficient, in terms of the distribution of goods and services.

The world is changing, the elders say.

Celebration

Easter is a time for affirmation and sharing. It is a time for people from villages and dispersed sites up and down the drying river to haul their canoes toward the mountain headwaters, where animals in relative abundance can be tracked as they seek dry-season streams. They can then be killed and smoked for the coming holidays. It's a time when sites along the paths leading to the Colombian border jar memories of events: the rock face called *ürähó* (E. honey), where Roberto's wife built a ladder to get the honeybees' hive, there by the path the fox (S. *zorro*) takes to reach the palm fruit *(trupa, uruta)* within the forest; and *do imamá de,* the cave at the river's edge where the jaguar once sat to sun, and *chorromai kampuniá peútumá,* the waterfall where two *kampuniá* were murdered (see Chap. 6). It's a time when the spinning architecture of winged *cuipo* seeds falls on the stone beach, a sign that parakeets are maturing and the heavy rains will come soon; a time to camp out and hunt and smoke provisions and gather the sweetest, slightly boozy, and tenderest wild tamarinds *(tamarinbó)* on the planet and those strange *algorobo* fruits with Masonite exteriors you crack open with a stone to find fruit like animal fur.

Easter is a time to bring wild and cultivated sources of nourishment

Figure 13. Awaiting Easter Thursday meal in Tamarinbó.

into the home by the Wednesday before Good Friday. Then you must enhance the kindred's ring of mutual transformation through synchronous eating: armored catfish (S. *humpé*) in soup with cilantro and rice, smoked guan (E. *samó*), deer (E. *begí*), tinamou, or the Emberá chicken (E. *so-korro*), peccary (E. *bidó*), paca (E. *përöwära*), toucan (S. *pico*), corn, drink of the pejibaye palm fruit (E. *hëä chicha*), and the honey and fermented *guarapo* drink prepared from women's cane.

[High-noon meals, Easter Thursday and Friday, field notes, April 4, 1985, Easter Thursday, Tamarinbó] About 9:45 A.M. Rubén, the village head, came with his family's share of catfish in a basin to Inez's house (Inez has the biggest house) and asked, "Well, are we going to do it? If so, I'll go around and collect catfish from all the houses." So Inez threw in her share, and in a while Rubén returned with a full basin. [It never seemed sure that the communal meal would happen until it did. Rubén and Eva's family and I had gone *monteando* (S. forest activities that include hunting, fishing, gathering) upriver the week before, coming back with a fairly large supply of smoked catfish and tamarinds, most of which was already gone. Dzoshua's gang had gone upriver to fish with poison (E. *dokán*) a few days ago. Just last Sunday Eva and Dzoshua started to think about organizing the meals. She said it would depend on whether or not Dzoshua's folks would catch fish. If everybody would contribute five catfish to make a soup, she would do it, she said.] I contributed two pounds of rice (all I had left; I was going to the city after the holidays and was nearing the end of my supplies) and so did Dzoshua's wife, Norma, Inez, and I guess some other people as well because they wound up with a giant pot full. Inez was in charge of making and distributing the rice; Eva was in charge of making and distributing the catfish soup. [The actions and spatial organization of their culinary roles reflect the structure of village kinship. The women are the active female household heads of the two major families: Eva is the granddaughter of the first settler of this area of the river; Inez is the daughter of Dzoshua, the nephew of the first settler and initiator of a collateral line of descendants.]

When Simón arrived at Inez's for the meal, she started crying about her brother, Eva's father, Onofre, who had been killed some months before [see Chap. 4]. Then she, Eva, and Eva's mother wailed in grief.[2] Everyone in the village came (some had gone to visit relatives in other parts of the river, others had relatives visiting here), except for Margarita and Felipe's family, who said they were ashamed because they had nothing to bring. Everybody who wasn't cooking was concerned that things be done exactly at high noon (E. *umatipa*). We ate by 1:00 P.M. Dzoshua's wife, Norma, laid out the broad green leaves (S. *hoja vijado*) in the central floor space. And the plates of food were put down there along with side dishes of avocados, plates of honey for dipping, fried plantains, a calabash full of nuts and raisins I brought (protectively distributed by the spoonful by Inez, who said people would take too much otherwise). Carolina, whose husband didn't come, went around dishing out spaghetti with tomato sauce, and Simón spooned out some of her *cocada* on each plate (grated coconut cooked down with honey), commenting about how this *cocada* was for everyone to eat and not to sell. Male and female guests were served first, eating out of their own plates, which they or their wives or daughters had brought for them. Then the women and children ate, finishing up all the stuff in the big pots and eventually cleaning up. Then everybody rested. (This is when Larú told me his story of the 1961 flood; see Chap. 2.)

[April 5, 1985, Easter Friday] It went pretty much the same way, except I didn't eat. When I went over to Inez's about 10:30, I brought some canned food I had, but no rice because I didn't have any left. It was a mistake not to divide what I had in half yesterday, part for Thursday, part for Friday. Simón gave me some of her wonderful fried corn cakes and *cocada* to eat, and when Inez came in, she looked and said meanly, "Didn't you already eat over there with Eva?" [I lived alone, cooking and eating my own food, partially in an attempt to remain nonaligned in respect to any particular household. But going upriver with Eva's family on Easter reinforced the relationship I had developed with them. Inez's comment highlights the current village perspective on my status that now made me a member of Eva's household.] Later Incz, who was usually so friendly to me, was even meaner about my not bringing rice. When I went over at noon, I was angry and didn't bring my plate. I just sat down near Dzoshua when I saw Anton walk past the house with a plant over his shoulder. I climbed out and down and followed him. He was going to put medicine on his trees. Some of them were dropping their fruit before they were ripe. He treated these, and while he was at it, he treated the rest of them. With a branch of nettles (E. *huéchichi*), the lower section of which had been scraped free of thorns so it could be held, he whipped the tree trunks and then scraped them with a white-lipped peccary jawbone (E. *bidó kitatri*).[3] He scraped the sides (E. *orrekuabua*) so it carries (E. *saumarea*) fruit. He did this two or three times to each tree, not saying anything out loud.

Easter is a time to restore vibrancy to body, earth, and magic formulas. It is a good time to buy and learn *secretos,* verbal (often one-word) formulas for the treatment of specific ills, such as stopping the flow of blood from a machete wound, stopping the *casanga* bird from eating a corn crop, stopping the pain of snakebite, or curing warts. If your *secreto* has gotten stale, write it down on a piece of paper and bring it to the forest on noon on Good Friday, the same time Anton went to heal his plants, and put it in the crotch of a tree. When you pick it up at 1:00 P.M., say a prayer to Jesus or Ankore (E. God) to "please restore this *secreto.*" Rubén said there are lots of things people do on Easter. They say if you mark your bullets, each with a little cross on top, this assures that they will kill their mark. But, Rubén adds, I don't believe this bullet thing works. Easter is the best time to make a pact with the Devil and to discover buried pots or chests of Spanish gold (as thought the grandfather-shaman who encountered the phantom gringo boat; see Chaps. 1 and 8).

While talking with Dzoshua about Saturday of Glory burning practices, I mentioned that I recorded a *dogowiru* bird who was calling near my house the night before. When I played it for him, the recording set off a stream of Easter devil stories:

The *dogowiru* is the Devil's chicken. If you catch it on Easter, it brings luck and money. You catch it (it only sings at night), walk on the beach, pull out its tail feathers, and the Devil will come. In a gruff voice he will demand:

"Why have you killed my chicken? What do you want?" If your heart is strong enough, you say: "I want *plata* [S. silver, money]." And you will get it.

Like the fig tree over there (whose flowers fall during Easter): At night, if you go and gather the flowers and wait there under the tree, the Devil will come. In a gruff voice he will demand: "Why have you killed my chicken? What do you want?" If your heart is strong enough, you say: "I want *plata*." And you will get it.

We are so poor, sometimes a man gets fed up. During Easter, then, he starts walking, walking, walking — like to that hillside over there [points]. Walking, walking, and when he comes to the top of the hill, it is already midday, and he shouts: "Pedro, or Fulano, or Don Juan, I want money." Then he walks again until he reaches the next hill and again: "Pedro, or Fulano, or Don Juan, I want money." And from there, the Devil comes: "What do you want? Do you want *plata*, or gold, or in bills?" If your heart is strong, you answer: "I want gold." Then, the Devil leaves. The man stays waiting, waiting. And then he gets it — a big, heavy sack full of gold. For this, in ten years, or twenty years, the Devil will eat him. (−T/S)

"It hardly seems worth it," I say, "unless you're already very old." Dzoshua says, "Well, yes, but we can enjoy [the money]. In Ancient Times we were brutes, but now we know plants to put on us that protect us from the Devil. You apply the plant [washing motion with arms], and the body is like kindling [points to the forest on the outskirts of the village]. Like when we set this forest afire, you can't get close right? So is the body of a man when he is like kindling, the Devil can't come close." "Ah, so Saturday of Glory is a good day because the Devil can't come close — it's the big fire." He said yes. Then he went on to the theme about why *kampuniá* are rich; he told me the one about God's uncovered balls again (see Chap. 1). And another one about how:

Cholos [Indians from Chocó] grab the wild and edible *sokorro,* the Emberá chicken, by the tail feathers and of course lose it. And the same with deer — the *cholo* grabs it by the tail and it breaks off, and the cow and the horse. But no, not the *kampuniá.* The *kampuniá* grabs it by the foot, and it can't get away. He puts it aside to raise so he can keep it. Like money: the *cholo*? $30, $50, $100, it's eaten [gestures hand to mouth]. But not the *kampuniá.* He's got $100, and suddenly he has more! (−T/S)

Dzoshua is uncomfortable with the new politics that takes place in formal congresses (see Chap. 2). But in informal, interpersonal contexts, his politics shines through, providing a crucial indigenous perspective on the irrational and unfair bases of racial inequalities. His tales use these imported figures of good and evil, God and the Devil, with humor and irony. Basically, I think they reflect the social fact that many Emberá don't take these Christian images very seriously; they have a more expansive, fluid notion of spiritual embodiment and codification. Hence the comedy of the Indian playing fool, whose cash always seems to loose itself from his fingers and whose source always seem to be some Spanish or gringo devil. And the light way Dzoshua sloughs off the consequences of Devil pacts, which have been considered as a means of capitalist critique (Taussig 1980; Crain 1991) and overcoming alienation (Nash 1979) in the context of the proletarianization of indigenous peoples, suggests that perhaps not everyone takes the Devil's terms as seriously.[4]

These stories, and the Easter adventures they provoke, are anchored by the set of taboos that attempt to avoid mixing transformational behavior with chaos. And they are contextualized by the warm celebrations of kinship and community that have arisen in the villages of Darién. Easter is not celebrated this way among all Emberá. And although the Emberá are wont to say, "Gringos may know Christmas, but only the Emberá know how to celebrate Easter properly," many of the customs and concepts attendant on the celebration are shared in the neighboring black communities in the Darién and the Chocó. Emberá shrug off implication of their mutual influence. In the end, it doesn't seem to matter who belongs to which idea. The holiday attests to the fluidity of cultural motifs and suggests that cultural identity is not bound to content or place but, rather, to process and perspective.

The Emberá meanings of Easter are bound to the rhythms of forest, river, and sky, integrating symbolic and material dimensions of culture with rainforest ecology. Even as cosmological knowledge from Ancient Times is reinterpreted for each Easter season, its priority still engages those who continue to realize the pattern of its tales and organize its happenings. And for those who don't, well, *remember the father who did not respect the Santa and who let his son bathe for too long when the boy turned into a fish and swam downriver to the sea, and the libre in Colombia who didn't believe and went to the orchard to cut plantains and when he cut, a bee came and stung him in the eye and he went screaming back to his house and said "Wife, I got stung by a bee," and she said, "told you so," and he went and lay down on his bed and died, at once.*

four

The Absent Patriarch

We go clean the cemetery on Easter's Saturday of Glory. Eva carries a cup of coffee for Elia (Elijah). Filing out the village down the river path, we pass Carolina in the lemon tree. She's picking leaves with which to bathe her baby. We do not know it then, but the baby is soon to join the others in the circle of earth that is our destination.[1] We turn into the inner forest, through land of Eva's father, Onofre, to the bright green circle where he now lies. His is the only grave that has not yet fallen back into the earth. The first to be buried here was Onofre's cousin, a deaf boy, cared for by his mother alone (she had no husband). That was when the cemetery was on the river. When the boy got sick and died, his mother said, "Who will take my son away and leave him in Yaviza?" At that time the dead were supposed to be taken to Yaviza, two days' journey away. Onofre said to his sister, the boy's mother: "Let's put him under the house so that he won't have to stay alone." Onofre's sister stayed in the house above the grave, separate but close to the rest of the family. Three more of her daughters died. Only one son survived, Januario. He lives in the village now. She eventually married downriver to Ramondo (the first Emberá man to settle the Tupisa) but never had any more children. She may have been poisoned, for she died suddenly. There was another wife.

The story of the first burial is part of the family history according to Agouti, recorded earlier in the village.

Onofre's father and mother came up here sometime before the 1950 flood. Ramondo was already settled downriver. They came from the Jurubidá River on the Pacific coast of the Chocó [through Balsa] to the port town of Jaqué. They took a ride upriver and decided to stay. It was pretty here. Why go back to Colombia? Lots of peccaries. ["Actually," interrupts Anton, "they went back to Balsa for about a year, but the family was afraid Onofre's father's first cousin wanted to kill him, so they came back to Tupisa, never to leave again."] We all lived in one house in what is now the cemetery. Then the family split into three adjacent houses. After the big flood of 1950, when the river broke through to its present course, the family moved out to the new riverbank, where the pejibaye palm stands now. The house at the pejibaye was big, and everybody lived together again [Onofre and Grandmother, their eldest son and the daughter of Ramondo, whom he married; their second son Agouti and his wife, Celestina, from the Baudó River in the Chocó; their only daughter Eva and her husband, Rubén, from Sambu; and Onofre's brother Anton (who cured his trees on Good Friday)]. Some time before the others came (Dzoshua, Dalas, Omar, and Coco), before the village was formed, Onofre's father went down to Yaviza to get permission from the mayor to bury the dead upriver where they lived instead of having to take them on that long journey. And because he got permission to establish a cemetery here, he became the first *regidor* [alderman]. Everybody was happy about this because dead bodies smell awful by the time they get to Yaviza. In this way, Onofre's father became the first representative of state law. (−T/S)

(Not all would present village history quite the way Agouti does, invoking authority of a line of male descendants leading directly to him. For example, the family history presented by his sister Eva, which I do not present here because it's not all of a piece, also legitimates their family's precedence as first settlers. But her history focuses on ties between mothers, daughters, and sisters.)

The bright green circle where the dead live had not been cleared for some months. The shoots stand waist high against the forest's dark surround. The men form a line across the center and move slowly outward, slashing at the regrowth, faces pensive, deliberate (it seems to me). Eva is at the grave of her father Onofre, the other women by her side, crying softly. Dzoshua's young wife draws her little daughter close and makes the motions of checking her head for lice. The women start talking, remembering who was in which grave. Tennis shoes, toys, pots, cups, lamps, and clothes mark the graves. The women move among them, fixing them up a bit. The men continue to push the forest back.[2]

Grandmother sings mournfully at the foot of her husband's grave, marked with a cross and an inscription including year, day of the week, date, and name, Onofre Abenamaché. He was killed just a few months before. Her wail fills the circle's space, as it fills the space around her house every dawn and dusk. Eva cries and draws nearer her mother, walking around the grave, making clearing motions with her machete.

I had been here with Grandmother, Eva, and her sister-in-law Celestina back in December, gathering food and recollecting the dead. When we reached the cemetery the previous time, Grandmother had stopped at the edge of the forest opening, stretched out her machete-holding arm, and traced a wide arc across the circle. "That here. All are people. All are people." We cried as we cleared around the grave that day too. On the grave was the knife that Grandfather always carried, wrapped in the loin-cloth he had been wearing when they found him (they dressed him in the dry one for burial), wrapped again in an envelope of dry *Heliconia* leaf and tied with the string that held up his loincloth. The machete with a yellow handle he'd made from the melted plastic of a bucket was there. The bottle of rum that he'd been drinking when he died was there. A cup was there. Grandmother opened each one and softly explained the relation between Onofre and the objects. They seem to mark the edges of material existence. After holding each in her hands for a while, she replaced them in fresh-cut leaves. When the grave was cleared of weeds and fresh leaves replaced the dried ones on the grave and on the sunshade built to shield it, we followed the path out around the circle. Before entering the forest, Grandmother turned to face the dead. In a pressed voice of controlled anger I had come to identify with the shaman's spirit-talk, she reprimanded them.

On Saturday of Glory, Eva pours the coffee she brought into a yellow plastic container on her father's grave. Larú replaces an orange plastic cup that had strayed from its proper grave. Melani puts a candle on the grave of her two-month-old. I had my camera but was afraid that it would be disrespectful to take pictures. I eventually pulled it out as inconspicuously as possible to record some inanimate thing. One of the men sees me and says, "Hey, everybody, she's got a camera!" and proceeds to gather everyone together for a group portrait. We are positively gay as we circle out of the cemetery that day, Raúl naming the people in graves as we pass: "Ai, there's a lot of people here." On the forest path again, Anton tells me about how he was in Yaviza when Onofre got killed. How for three or four days he tried to find out who had died. First he thought it was Dzoshua, as he'd been sick, then someone said that they saw Dzoshua at the mouth of Maraganti. Finally, he heard. But it was too late to bring Onofre to Yaviza as he would have liked. They had already buried him. He said the Guard, a *cholo*, asked at the last congress downriver if they had learned anything about the death yet. Anton told him, "Not a thing." Actually, as I found out in time, some things had been learned. But these things could not yet be publicly shared. They waited not only until the killer was identified, but also until the killer slipped up and incriminated himself. Basically, the solution to the murder would be reported to the state once the indigenous system of justice discovered the truth.

Mudhole Fishing

When an important man like Onofre dies, a man around whom others organize their emotions and interests, he is not soon forgotten. If he is murdered, memories are warped by severe doubt. If neither reason nor killer is known, yearning and fear alter the rhythm of talk, folding questions and theories into whispers. The landscape of everyday life holds the breath of the absent patriarch.

Near the beginning of the dry season, late January, we search for food in the bottoms of diminishing streams. Eva, Celestina, Grandmother, two little boys, and I walk in line out of the village and turn down an inner path through the forest Onofre cut. From beach to uncut forest, the land is full of the fruit trees planted when the family lived on the cemetery site and then, when the river moved, on the pejibaye palm site. It's just down from the village. First we pass land that was planted with rice two years before. Mimicking the banana with its inedible broad leaves, the *Heliconia* now stand tight and tall. In an adjacent piece of land, planted with rice one year before, sugarcane now stands. This is the last field Grandmother worked with Onofre before he died. The three women come through here regularly, mourning and thinking as they search for food. Before turning into the forest, as always, they point out the rocky beach where Onofre's body was found.

59

The first December day they pointed out that place on the beach was the time Eva, Grandmother, Celestina, and I went to the cemetery to clean his grave, the same day Grandmother unwrapped his personal effects and explained them to me. On the way out that day, they showed me the one-inch piece of candle. On the last stretch of dark forest before coming out into the opening of the river, in the hollow of a large tree on the left edge of the path: Eva put it there. She found it on the day after her father died, there at the spot to which she pointed. Thrown into the bush it was. Onofre may have been killed in his own orchard at nightfall and dragged out onto the beach (to make it look like an outsider did it), the murderer using the candle to light his way. "We think this way, so. That is our thought. It was thrown here. She found it and left it there." "But couldn't some visitor to the cemetery leave a candle on the way?" I asked, then realized that it wouldn't make sense to leave a candle *there*. They agreed: "Here we do not leave [a candle] that way."

One inch of candle out of place. With habit secure, out-of-order events can be more readily deciphered.

On this day of mudhole fishing, several weeks later, life is as ordinary as it gets. Celestina explains the ownership and use history of the land we pass through. "Onofre turned this section of four *kabuyas* [about four hectares] from *monte* to *rastrojo*." (By implication, this also informs me of her rights to the land as his daughter-in-law.) Turning into uncut forest, Celestina shrugs and says: "There's still plenty of this left. The only reason the whole forest hasn't been turned into farmland is that the men don't work. They're afraid to fell the big trees." It was late morning by the time we left, and the children were already hungry. Winding through the trees, we climb down the wooded slope of a drying streambed. A shallow pool of muddy water sits where it loops abruptly, all that remains of winter's rushing waters. Celestina and Eva get in and walk around slowly, poking their machetes down to the pool bottom looking for buried turtles (E. *chibigi*). Only bubbles come up. Reaching as far she can go, face horizontal to surface, Celestina reaches underwater into holes in the bank and comes out with a crab (E. *chikwé*) about the size of her hand. We walk up the streambed, looking under rocks for snails (E. *korogó*) and iguana eggs (E. *opogá imi*). Nothing.

Already midday, we cut through the woods again. Celestina finds and cuts two saplings to use as canoe poles (E. *doté*). Eva's son Tomás fells a young pejibaye palm in order to get a bunch of the ripe red fruits, which taste like chestnuts when cooked. In the lead, Eva gets disoriented. We joke about her abilities as guide and descend again into a drying stream-bed. A foot-long catfish (E. *chícharro*) scuttles off to the edge: a sign of more. Celestina and Eva and the two boys begin to fish. The women use various methods. Turning their *chiles* sideways, holding the top rim above water, they transform their loose-weave *pikiwa* vine-work baskets into nets. They walk side by side slowly moving across the puddle (about twenty by twelve feet). Or they slowly come toward one another walking from different points along the circumference. The mud hides the fish from them and them from the fish (and who knows what other creatures). Some fish herd into a place that the women discover with systematic patience. Trapped on the edge, the fish jump out in front of or between the baskets, and the women grab them with their hands. A few pop right in. Not satisfied, the women look beneath rocks around the edge, then throw the rocks aside. Ineffective. Some fish jump to the surface, and Eva tries whacking them with her machete blade. That works once or twice. Bending sideways with her lips just above the water, Celestina reaches down into the mud walls of the puddle and gets another big crab.

The little boys are also fishing, but they are learning to fish with spears like men. Eleven-year-old Tomás spears a couple of four to seven inchers, and five-year-old Roke spears a couple of one-inchers. Grandmother and I sit on the side. I have nothing to fish with, and I am bored. We are there two hours. Counting only the larger ten to twelve inch fish, the women catch an average of one every twelve minutes. At least three times during the two hours we spend at the puddle, over twenty minutes pass when nothing is caught. When it seems certain there are no more fish in there, someone gets another, and the tedious mud walk continues.

The women coordinate their movements to corral fish that luck flips into one or the other basket. They nevertheless keep their catches separate. They toss the fish out of the pool as they catch them. Eva and her son Tomás throw all their fish to Grandmother, who begins gutting them. Celestina and her son Roke throw their fish off into a separate pile. As her daughter, Eva has a closer relationship to Grandmother than Celestina, who is her daughter-in-law. The organization of work materializes this difference in their relationship.

All three women are temporarily living in the same household. When Grandfather Onofre died, Celestina moved next door with her husband and children to provide further support. (When I arrived, I moved into Celestina's vacated house.) Grandmother's house now includes two nuclear families and herself. As female heads of nuclear households, both Eva and Celestina are responsible for caring for only their own husbands and children, but as daughter and daughter-in-law, both women are responsible for Grandmother. The precise distribution of that responsibility is determined by the difference in distance between lineal (Eva) and affinal (Celestina) relatives. Work responsibilities are thus organized into areas of independence (serving respective husband and children) and overlap (serving Grandmother). Most activities involve both cooperation (fishing and cooking together) and calculated difference (separating catches and cooking pots).

This organization is not equally compatible for all. As the in-marrying wife, Celestina has to leave some loved ones out of this circle of care. She came to Panama with a man from the Baudó River in the Chocó. She had one son before she left him. When she married Agouti, this son stayed with them until he was sixteen, then left, and has never returned. But his wife, her daughter-in-law, did, bringing along one of her little girls to stay with Celestina, her grandmother (a second little girl was left with the other grandmother downriver). After about a month, Agouti got tired of having another mouth to feed (they have six children between three months and sixteen years) and wrote Celestina's daughter-in-law a letter telling her she at least ought to come and take care of her child for a week every once in a while. The daughter-in-law arrived when Celestina and Agouti were away downriver and took the child back with her to Tuquesa. The child caught a fever on the way and died a day after reaching there. The news brought great sadness to Celestina, evoking the mourning song. Celestina struggles to keep the future secure for the six children born to her and Agouti, all the while accepting the limits on the distribution of food and land negotiated with her husband's family, painfully aware that they exclude others she loves. Because serial marriage is common, the limits drawn around successive "families" affect the welfare and inheritance possibilities of many children.

When the three women figure they've already gotten most of what the mudhole has to offer (all the time worrying aloud about their family's empty bellies), they quit and assess. They find that each has about the same size pile and decide to divide the catch into two *chiles,* transformed into baskets for carrying, according to whether or not they had been cleaned, instead of to whom they belong. Tired and hungry, but pleased with their success, we head back through the forest to the village with about six to eight pounds of catfish (*koromá, chícharro, baú,* and some I don't recognize), crabs, and shrimp. Not bad for a mudhole.

While mudhole fishing, the three women reinforce the bonds between them, enacting difference and shared responsibility, filling terms of address like *kau* (daughter, daughter-in-law) with meaning in an active mode. Brought by tragedy to a shared hearth, the women are in the process of negotiating another cycle of household coalescence and dispersal. Each acts from the perspective on and in the family that is unique to her birth and experience. Each inherits differently and has a different domain of care. But they both share an orientation of interests and emotions that turns toward an absent patriarch. The structure of family relations does not terminate with the patriarch gone, for its continuity draws back into time incorporeal. The matriarch still lives, but she ages quickly with grief.

Afterlife: Accounts and Visions

Onofre was asked: "Why didn't you come home?" He was singing (itself a shamanic act). In the song he said: "That night I was sick. That's why I didn't come. They murdered me. That's why I didn't come." His head wounds were already healed. Yes, they have healed well.

A family dream

Onofre was calling from the edge of the woods.

A family sighting using the hallucinogenic vine Datura *(S. pindé, E. iwá)*

In November, soon after we'd become friends, Eva told me about Onofre's terrible end. We'd been sitting together in her house. All the little ones took off (she had six children between one and a half and eighteen years old). She was quiet for a time and then spoke: "We're in a bad way. We can't stop thinking about my father's death. It happened so suddenly." "Oh, I thought he was very old and died of some sickness," I said. "No," she said, and on November 24, 1985, told me this account:

> Onofre left early that morning to go fishing upriver by the post. It was just three months ago. He was out all day and came back in the afternoon, about this time of day. What time is it now? [My watch showed 3:00 P.M.] He hadn't caught any fish. Not a bite. He came to the house and asked: "Daughter, what are you cooking there?" and I answered, "I'm cooking plantains," and he said, "Good." Then he took out his bullets; he had three or four that he reworked to use again. Then he said, "Daughter, I'm going

63

down(river) to the orchard to kill a toucan." And so he went off. I never saw him again.

Night closed in, and still he didn't come back. We wondered where he could be. "What could he be doing in this darkness?" said the old woman [Grandmother]. Well, it got later and later, and still he didn't come back. So we went to look for him. In the dark, we went down to the orchard. We shouted, "Tata, Tata!" "Uncle!" But nobody answered. We gave up and came home. We went to sleep but woke up early, early, barely 5:00 [A.M.], and went to search again. This time many people of the village went, down the path along the riverbank, to the orchard and past. We looked and looked but couldn't find him. But one young boy (that one that lives up front) went looking down the river, and there he was walking by the beach at the second bend, he heard the sound, "Wish, wish, . . . wish, wish, wish." He turned and saw Onofre lying there dead on the rocks. "Ai, my uncle, dead!" And he came running to the house to tell me. I went running, running to the place, and there was my father, dead. A big bloody blow on the back of his head. How could this have happened?

This is what the people keep thinking. He couldn't have just fallen from the canoe. Someone must have killed him. . . . But we all remain silent. We can't say anything, we just live thinking this. (−T/S)

In those days I would hear Grandmother's mourning song from the house next door at dawn, at dusk, and at times of arrival. She chants, "I am sad" in minor tones, a beautiful melody I did not have the heart to record. Eva calls it simply "crying."

Every time I went gathering fruit, medicines, or household items in the woods with Grandmother and her sister Beatriz (now acting as village shaman, doing her best to replace Onofre), they would mime the killer's motions. Holding her hand stiff like a knife toward the back of her head, one or the other of the sisters would perform the gesture of reconstructed animosity. Raising her arms, she'd then look at me in questioning challenge. Each time it was the same, without words, and like everyone else, I had no answer.

One day when I climbed up into Eva's house, there were several other people there. She was sitting on her wooden bench by the hearth, stirring the pot and talking in Emberá in a style that sounded like storytelling. It caught my attention because Eva is not one to tell stories as such and because it was daytime, not the usual time for storytelling. So later I asked her to repeat it so I could tape-record and translate it with her eldest son,

Gregorio. It wasn't a story from Ancient Times but a story of something that happened to her teenage nephew Ako. He was on his way to the village upriver, on a break from high school in Yaviza. When he was just a couple of miles from home, he experienced an encounter with his grandfather Onofre. This was some months after Onofre was dead and buried.

Thus Ako told it.

Then, Ako was coming up from town to here by Bodin's plantains.

From there he came out [of the forest to the river].

He came out by Chichu's *rancho.*

From there, he saw the figure of Dzoshua.

He looked upriver: the figure passed in front of him.

It was the figure of Dzoshua.

On a horse [Ako thought]: "I'll catch up to the old man."

And for that reason, he came running.

Running, running, the horse brought him.

Already truth running, running, he was brought.

He saw Chichu's *rancho* that was there.

And then he didn't see him anymore.

He came running, running, running to where the avocado tree is.

He arrived at the avocado tree.

Then his head felt large. [TN: As if a bad spirit were entering, he had fear in his head].

Then he was.

The horse could not endure, so fast did he, running, running, bring him.

Then he was.

He brought him running, running, running, running, running.

Yes, here to Vincente's avocado tree.

There by the boundary with Orlaf's plantain orchard he came.

Then the horse was almost exhausted, it was tired.

Then he came, came, came, came, came here.

It was below the chocolate tree.

There he kept whistling. [TN: He whistled to himself so he wouldn't be afraid.]

With fear, he came with fear, his head stayed large.

He got scared, the horse brought him thus.

His head stayed large.

Then there by the chocolate tree it was.

Robaldo's plantains that it was.

There he was, he kept whistling, he kept singing.

He sang as he walked.

He sang as he walked.

He was there a bit below the house.

He called him, [at] the house of Vincente, he called him.

Then, he remained silent.

There at Vincente's house, he called. [TN: To see if anyone was there].

Then it was, as if from the house, as if [somebody or something] jumped to the ground.

Thus: "kururu," it sounded.

Thus, when he sensed this, his body could not withstand his large head.

Already his body could not withstand.

He came.

Thus he held on to the belly of the horse.

Then it was the horse brought him running.

One brought him running, one, up to my brother Anton's house.

That little stream below, he jumped, he came.

And then it was as if sand were being thrown at him. [TN: He felt someone invisible throwing sand at him from behind.]

Sand.

That was thrown, it was fast, he cried.

He came crying on top of the horse, "Wëramë!" [urgent appeal].

He was up high, he almost fell to the ground.

He held on, grabbing the horse's neck.

Then crossed [the river]. Cha! He brought him.

Then it was as if from behind he came, as if from behind.

How he cried, he came.

Then it was, all of a sudden, came the word. [TN: Thinking it was the spirit of Onofre, the boy spoke:]

"Ai, brother," said.

"Why are you treating me this way? I who come to see you. Why are you treating me this way?"

He said to him, then it was, as if he left him alone, as if he sensed it thus.

> [TN: When Ako spoke, he felt the spirit-animal heard him and would
> quit his pursuit.]
  To there no more. Done. (T/E)

Sensing Grandfather's spirit, Ako defends himself from its dreadful pursuit. He refers to his visit back home as proof of continuing his obligation to kin. He has not contributed an improper lack of attention to kindred that might cause a rent in the boundary of the real, an opening between worlds through which a boy might be drawn away from life. He claims his right to move through familiar places without fear of unsolicited communications. The act of asserting his claim of being kin in good standing and his sense of Grandfather's acceptance releases him from fear.

Grandfather is dead, but his projected desires motivate the living. His absence is apparent only to those who do not sense his presence. For those who do, he is one of the more or less identifiable sentient beings living in the screen at the edge of the world. Ghosts, along with devils, animals, maybe even some *kampuniá* (E. non-Indians), edge along culture's seams where, through desire and deceit, action can be taken on the real. They are free to assume or enter or possess nature and humanity in unpredictable ways and times. Grandfather's ghost is a rift in the heart of kindred's domain, sketched in this narrative of family geography—Chichu's *rancho*, Vincente's avocado tree, Orlaf's plantain orchard—the same map that would be used to justify claims in historical accounts. The family tries to discover and mend the cause of the rift through empirical investigation matched with the visions of dream, song, and the *Datura* vine's hallucination.

I heard one more account of the sequence of events leading to the discovery of Grandfather's death. His ten-year-old grandson, Eva's son Miguel, told me the following story a couple of days after the village cleared the cemetery. The Easter fires were still burning around the village on April 7.

> That night he didn't come back. The people were searching everywhere.
> The moon was bright. I was already in bed, and I knew he had died. Early
> morning, Coco was in the river squatting down on a rock to take a shit. He
> pulled his pants down and heard a sound like the letting out of breath,
> blowing: it was the sign of my Grandfather's spirit. But Coco of course

wasn't thinking this. He looked around, didn't see anything, got back to business. Again he heard the sound. This time he looked behind him. There was the body lying in the rocks with an arm crooked upward. He got frightened and ran to the village. Never took his shit. First told Melani, then Eva: "Daughter, your father is dead." Meanwhile Luís and I had gone running up to the post to tell Ivan and Samson [the COPFA border official and his mariner] that Grandfather was missing. We came running back, and when we got here, I already knew. I said to Luís, "My grandfather is dead." Then we heard. We went running down to the beach. There was a crowd of people. When I saw Grandfather's upraised arm, I thought, "He is alive"—but no. He was still as energetic as a bee.

Many people came to our house that day. As he was discovered in the early morning, Ivan had gone down to Ansabidá right away to tell Bartolo [Onofre's eldest son]. He was here by 4:00 [P.M.]. People from all up and down the river—Promesa, Ansabidá, Bocadura—came here to the *vela* [wake].[3] We kept the body for three days. We didn't want to part with it. I would grab it every once in a while. (−T/S)

Miguel was worried. We talked together:

M: When Grandmother dies, I'll be all alone. Then what? I was raised by my grandparents, not my parents. I lived with them in the house near the cane, on the inside river path. Now it's all falling apart. It's already *monte*.

SK: Why don't you show me tomorrow?

M: I'm too scared to go there.

SK: Why?

M: It's too close to the cemetery.

SK: Why are you scared of the cemetery?

M: There are dead spirits around. The elders say that when people die, their spirits go to heaven, but not really they say—really they stick around.

SK: You mean the cemetery is full of spirits?

M: Yeah. They like to drink and eat, rice, corn—just like we do in life. Haven't you seen my mother [Eva]? She's always bringing containers of coffee and honey to the cemetery.

SK: So all those dead spirits made in wood, like the *machucador* [pestle] I photographed today, are all dead spirits?

M: Yes. Animals have spirits too.

SK: So when the shaman calls little devils, are these dead spirits of people and animals too?

M: Yes. That's why we want to take *pindé*, so we can see Grandfather. Last night we had a dream that we saw Grandfather. That's why Eva wants to sing [as a shaman]. Perhaps she will, but I don't know when. When I think of Grandfather's body already turning to earth, I am very sad. (−T/S)

Our conversation ended abruptly when the *bálsamo* (E. *pidókera*) tree we were watching glow with Easter's fire came crashing down toward the house. Miguel leaped off the platform house to the ground as I stared dumbly at the falling tower. It turned out to be quite a few feet away. The people sawed off all but the main trunk for firewood, and (in hunger and shame) Lucinda's children ate the baby parakeets that died when their nest fell in the fiery crash.

Reckoning

Sculptures of dead spirits are fabrications posed in counterpoint to life. They are tactile messages from Ancient Times. I think that humans make them to mark the boundary between living and dead, although if you ask, they will say that most are merely decoration. I have seen them not only as batons in shamanic ritual and household art (which evoke a more elaborate explanation) but as heads on a variety of tools such as *tumé* (ladder and boundary marker of home), pestle *(machucador),* and laundry beater *(makudo)* and as a child's doll and necklace. Given the repetition of their form in everyday as well as ritual contexts, my hunch is that sculpted spirits may serve to protect the living by warning the dead away from areas of human settlement and to remind the living of the immanence of their own death. Kin do not necessarily leave the landscape of life, or so the accounts of Grandfather suggest, especially when they have unfinished business. A name like Onofre has power still in this emotional geography that his animate body was forced to abandon.

Among the living, a process of reckoning is taking place. This reckoning draws on settlement history, alliances, and disputes among kin involving resources, politics, and unacceptable forms of exchange. (I do not repeat the specific charges that were being made until I know the case has been settled.) Into this discursive web the icons of the ancestral otherworld operate. Honed to cultural conception, the wooden faces repeat themselves, their stares vacant, inward and wordless under heavy brows. They are impersonal relations of the loincloth, string, bottle of rum, cup, and

Figure 14. Pestle.

knife on Grandfather's grave: objects that confirm the gap and continuing tension between past and present. They stand fixed in the cross-currents of interpretation, accusation, and doubt — sure signs that the wrongdoer will reveal himself in time. For in all this, one thing seems sure: discourse, carefully directed, can excite the impulse for crime's revelation. And so Onofre's family continues to circulate theories about the murder, patient that one will eventually catch the murderer in its net.

I watch Grandmother take the long strands of *pikiwa* vine, stiff as wicker when dry, out from under the river rocks that hold them soaking and bring them into the house. There she uncoils them. Holding each in turn between the big toe and the next, the knife in her hands scrapes off the bark, revealing the thinnest of lines in green, then orange, that lie beside the vine's smooth cream-colored core. These colors are the signs one looks for in the forest to know which of the myriad kinds of vines is *pikiwa*. Once scraped clean, she chooses the longest and strongest for the heart of the basket, perhaps eight strands. Of these eight, half are laid side by side; the others are woven under and over in an open pattern that is copied step by step from another basket, already old from use. Working outward from the center, she weaves in the rest of the strands till she reaches the top, where she closes off the rim with a band of tight weave.

In the landscape of everyday life, the people remain thinking. Their creations replicate, producing results that approximate their desire more closely; their questions steep, producing theories that distract the order of desire and dismay the observer.

five

Techno-Magic (Canoe Construction)

he 1984 rains tore a giant wild cashew tree (E. *kalkolí*) out of Pre-ciada's upper banks. With each rising, the waters took hold, impel-ling the tree further downstream. By rains' end, the tree reached the river's mouth where it flows into the Tupisa not far above Tamarinbó. Dzoshua saw it first and marked it as his own "so that no one would touch it." He will turn the tree into a canoe (E. *hampá*, S. *piragua*). He waits. The waters recede, stranding the tree high up on a rocky beach. Then he saws off its ends, paying standard wage of US$8 per day to a man from the neighboring village of Promesa to take up the other end of the long, saw-toothed blade. Back and forth they work it until the trunk breaks away from roots and branches. A day's work done, Dzoshua and his female kin, the Promesa man, a friend from the United States who is visiting me, and I walk single file across the mouth of the Preciada, following the shallow areas across the Tupisa, past the COPFA station, and along the earthen path down to the village. We meet a young black man who had just accomp-plished the arduous journey across the mountains from the Chocó in three days. An Evangelical agriculturist looking for work, he tells how years of travel through Venezuela and Ecuador have kept him in good physical shape. Like other migrants who pass briefly through this first human settle-ment on the Panamanian side, he is given a day's food in exchange for a day's work and heads off downriver to highway and city.

When we get back, Dzoshua has a bath and meal before returning to the beach to fix his little canoe (S. *canalete*) with tar he bought in Yaviza. As he works, he considers the big project upon which he has just embarked, calculating carrying capacity and dollar value. He has another canoe made of *pino amarillo (Lafoensia punicifolia)* that holds up to one thousand plantains. That one is still worth $100, even with the ends rotting. The canoe he has just begun will be worth no more, even though it will probably hold three thousand plantains. Wild cashew wood doesn't last as long. The canoe will not be perfect anyway, as the heartwood doesn't run straight. Cambium will have to be incorporated, but Dzoshua didn't wait to cut till the waning moon, a precaution that discourages cambium-eating organisms causing wood rot.

Later, swinging in a hammock in the shade of his house, Dzoshua takes time to answer the questions my friend and I have about the importance of the canoe in Emberá culture.[1]

Dz: Since my youth, the canoe has always been very important. In Ancient Times when I was raised, my father told me that he who does not know how to make a *piragua* or *canalete* or *batea* [large wooden tray for winnowing rice], he who is without this knowledge, would never be able to catch a woman. If you were in a big river, what would you cross in? How would you kill fish? How could you cut plantains? Or carry maize and rice? If you don't have one, you will have to borrow. No! you cannot borrow. I must do it alone. I look for no one. It must be me that does it. I can sell it if I want and with the money buy a *paruma* [S. wrap-around skirt] or plate for the woman. I can go downriver to Yaviza, El Real, La Palma—but you can't go to Panama City like a dog. Auw! It is for this that the *cholo* does it. It holds up to 15, 20, 100 *quintal* [1 *quintal* = 100 lb. load]. And you need the canoe to take plantain root cuttings to a new place! If you don't have one, you won't cross. Like a car, or boat, 5,000, 6,000, up to 15,000 plantains.

SK: But were canoes so big in Ancient Times?

Dz: Smaller, maybe of 6,000. Before we did not sell plantains, so the canoes used for traveling were about 2,000.

SK: And to cross the river with plantain cuttings to transplant, 2,000 was enough?

Dz: Yes, from 500 to 1,000. Now when the people are buying, now that we're going downriver, now we need 6,000, 8,000, 10,000, up to 20,000. (T/S)

Figure 15. Dzoshua wielding ax. Drawing by E. Goitein, from photo by L. Stoller.

The canoe is fundamental to riverine tropical forest subsistence. It carries Emberá between established settlements and orchards, to hunt and fish, and to resettle new regions. It has not lost its usefulness in contemporary times. Indeed, as Dzoshua explains, many of the changes taking place with development are indexed in the canoe's design. As households concentrate into villages and intensify agricultural production for market, men expand the size of their canoes. According to tradition, the canoe is also fundamental to Emberá masculine identity. It is an icon of a man's share of family labor and a reminder of his troubled relation to God. The canoe figures in a story from Ancient Times that pretends to explain why it is the Emberá race must work so hard to survive. Dzoshua tells one of many variants drawing on the theme of the Garden of Eden and a fall from grace.

God has thought: "I will make a canoe." So he goes to the forest, finds a tree, and tells Son: "I will labor. I will labor. Tomorrow go and see it." The next day Son went to see it. There it was, pure heart, standing straight up in the air. (If this were me, would I mess this up? No. "It's just fine," I'd say; "I want this, yes Papa." Aha. But nooo. It's not this way, no.) Son goes to look and says, "I'm a man. I'll do it too." Po, po, po, po, PUM! He felled it. It was ruined. When God came to see, Ooooph! Son has felled it, see? And when Son comes to the house, God said to him: "So you want it this way? Well, with force you will do it." And there we remain. "I will not help anymore." And so with thought and force we do it. And so we have the ax, all kinds of tools. If he had not felled it. Pride, see? "I am a man." For that reason exactly the people labor the canoe this way. (−T/S)

If the man was not driven to act on what was already in a process of becoming, the outer cask of the tree would have given way, leaving a standing canoe of pure heart, to be picked like fruit. Human intervention (a natural enough inclination for a parent to expect from a son) is an affront to the biblical God, who ends creation's ease, turning human inclination for action into the necessity of labor. The canoe becomes a cultural product to be paid for in sweat and money. To build it, a man must trade obligations, call in debts, and promise future return. All helpers expect to benefit from the canoe in proportion to the amount of labor invested.

It takes Dzoshua several days to organize enough people to roll the heartwood into position, the second stage of construction. By the time I arrive, Dzoshua's wife, Norma, his daughters Inez and Ritali, Inez's husband, Dalas, Dzoshua's cousin Anton and his wife are already relaxing. The task is accomplished. Dzoshua has $24 left, enough money to pay for three more days of hired labor. Anxious to get ax work underway, he hires Noke, a skilled elder from the next river who happened to be passing through visiting his cousin and looking for wage labor. After this, Dzoshua will have to rely on his family's help to finish, and not everyone is willing to help.

In the time of his youth in Colombia, Dzoshua explains, younger men learned by helping older men. In this way, a young man could eventually own his own canoe and, becoming a canoe owner, become qualified to live with a woman. Not only the size of canoes has changed in today's times, but also the value youth place on learning traditional skills. None of Tamarinbó's young men showed interest in the project. As the importance of cash grows, the acquisition of rainforest survival skills seems to be diminishing.

Dz: Before we almost never used canoes, [we used mostly] smaller *canaletes*. There were some that had. When the river was big, there were always some that had. The ones that knew how to labor, the old ones. He who did not know, did not have.

SK: So in Ancient Times it was not each man that had a canoe. That is more modern, in the time of now.

Dz: Yes. And now, for this, the people buy. He who does not know how to labor, even here, has to buy in order to have a canoe.

SK: It was not all men who knew how to do it.

Dz: Yes.

SK: So it was not all fathers who taught their sons. Only some knew.

Dz: If the boy accompanied, he too would know. If not—well, he doesn't know.

SK: So is this a secret?

Dz: No.

SK: Anybody can learn?

Dz: Anybody can learn.

SK: But it wasn't everybody that wanted to learn. . . .

Dz: Anton, for example, his father knew how to labor well, but this one never accompanied, so he does not know how to labor.

SK: I was thinking the other day that all the men there [at the construction site] already knew how to do it. Here there are many youths, but not one of them was there.

Dz: Well. My son Edi didn't help me. He didn't. . . . For this, the *cholo,* we, are not like you *kampuniá,* no. See, I spent the money [for hired labor]. If I had not spent the money, it still would not be done. They don't help. Not son, not grandson, not anyone. No help. For this, they don't know. Well, it was like this for us too in Ancient Times. (T/S)

Dzoshua tempers his disappointment with tolerance and imagines vaguely that perhaps non-Indian families are more responsible to each other. In fact, as this account shows, everyone in his family does help in one way or another. The extra helpers who came to roll the trunk leave after they partake of the sweet plantain drink (E. *sukula*) that Dzoshua's daughters Inez and Ritali hand around. Dzoshua, Noke, and Inez's husband, Dalas, begin the ax work, taking turns with two axes. This next step is called "taking off the top." Vertical cuts in series are made down to the level of what will become the canoe's top in such a way that large chunks from the rounded trunk break off, eventually leaving a long, flat top. Inez and Ritali sit around a cooking fire on the beach, watching the children and the three ax-wielding men. Most of the top got taken off that day.

Figure 16. Food staple: plantains. Photo by L. Stoller.

Dzoshua returned alone the next two days to finish the ax work, then he smoothed the top and sides with a plane. Then he went upriver for two days to hunt with his family, something the Emberá do a great deal of in the dry season, when traveling is easier and animals can be surprised at the riverside more frequently.

The hunt failed. Dzoshua has no meat to offer workers. He starts again using the last of his money to pay Noke. The next stage, also done with axes, is called *detripando* in Spanish, meaning taking out the log's innards (tripe). Repeated measurements are taken to assure the proper width of sides and bottom. A weekend interrupts construction, after which Dzoshua returns with two sons-in-law, Dalas and Adeba. Each takes turns with the ax. When the tripe is nearly out, Dzoshua goes over to the fire, where the women are cooking (as usual) and comes back to the tree/canoe chewing plantains in an exaggerated manner. First he walks to the tail end and spits little pieces of plantain onto it, then he goes to the nose end and repeats the food-spitting behavior. My face must have betrayed my astonishment. Dzoshua turns to me and explains: "That is how the canoe eats. You have to do this before the *detripando* is finished. The dead one,

77

Figure 17. Food staple: fish (*humpé* and S. *sábalo*). Photo by L. Stoller.

the tree, must be fed before. If left hungry, the dead tree will cause a disease. This disease is called *chankla,* and one gets it from sitting on the canoe. [It was the sitting areas that he spat on.] In this sickness a little beast [S. *bicho*] eats the inside of one's body, making a hole inside, and blood comes out in the urine." When I try to identify the disease, everybody gets in the act. Someone says it's gonorrhea, but Dzoshua says that it isn't, but like gonorrhea, it can be cured with a plant. "Now the tree is dead, and the canoe is alive. You must do this first."

The canoe's parts are analogous to the human body and divided by sex, I now learn. While the man navigates the canoe from the "nose," the wom-

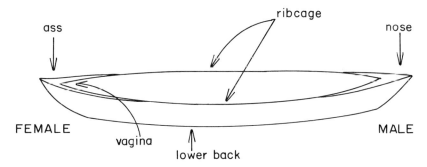

Figure 18. Body parts of a canoe.

an's place is in the "ass." The bottom of the canoe is the "lower back," and the sides are "ribs." And there's the part that no one can talk about: with much laughing and embarrassment, I learn that the V that forms the inner edge of the ass is the "vagina." (Actually, Dzoshua explains later, everything but the ass and vagina are male.) The analogy between canoe and human body inscribes this object of utility with added social significance. In a way that seems perfectly natural, the canoe is made to reflect the social organization of difference; along with bodies and things, it carries implicit social meaning. It is a masculine icon that incorporates the order of relations characteristic of traditional heterosexual marriage. Slipping through the landscape with a man and woman in their sexually linked positions, each passage is an elegant affirmation of unified but separate relation, the basic principle of Emberá social structure.[2]

Back in the quiet shade of Dzoshua's house, I try to find out more about this business of feeding the tree.

SK: When you were taking out the tripe, before the end, the tree was about to die. You gave food to the tree so that the tree spirit wouldn't be angry? Was it that way?

Dz: When I was doing that, it was to not catch *pete* [S. range of diseases from dog's mange to tuberculosis]. So that worms don't fall, or better said, it has worms inside.

SK: Worms in the canoe?

Dz: Yes. It has worms, and it passes them to us.

SK: Are there other things you have to do for the spirit of the canoe, or is this the only thing?
Dz: The only thing.
SK: Does the canoe also have a spirit like the tree?
Dz: Yes it has a spirit, yes.
SK: When the canoe dies, when it is already old. . . .
Dz: This I don't know. This is not noticed, how it thinks, no. As she doesn't speak, or anything, no.
SK: But the tree doesn't speak either.
Dz: No [laughs], I don't know if it talks. They say, this way, in Ancient Times when you are working, when I'm taking off the top, then comes the devil there inside, to shit inside. So, one is to die, the woman or you. So you have to put the cross all the time. When you leave for the house, you have to put the cross of sticks.
SK: When you're taking off the top?
Dz: So the devil doesn't come.
SK: When you've already taken off the top?
Dz: When you're finishing, it's already nothing. When you're there working, you have to have the cross right there all the time.
SK: I didn't see the cross there.
Dz: There it was.
SK: That thing you used to measure?
Dz: That's the same. God the Father said to us, "You have to put this way, this way, this way."
SK: Before the people used to do more than this and have forgotten?
Dz: No, they have not forgotten. Everybody in this country knows. (T/S)

The process of canoe construction involves a crucial step of transformation—in this case from tree as natural object to canoe as cultural object. In the moment of transformation the object is neither tree nor canoe, neither nature nor culture, a dangerous conceptual anomaly (cf. Leach 1964; Douglas 1966). According to Emberá cosmology, danger is intensified by the tendency of transformation to attract other concurrent transformations, a combinatory event that is powerfully creative and unpredictable.[3] Construction is coded linguistically and magically as a sequence of stages that inform the builder when to enact symbolic controls. The moment preceding the completion of transformation from tree to canoe (i.e., the end of *detripando*) is recognized by feeding the tree. In magical terms, recognition of the dying tree spirit allows the builders to pass safely through the moment of transformation. If the danger of this moment goes unrecognized, builders (and users) may be subject to negative effects of co-occurring transformation, here conceived as a dynamic of natural disease (wood rot) going awry in the sexually assigned seats of culture *(pete)*. Furthermore, according to Emberá cosmology, transformation is also dangerous because it attracts otherworld intruders (devils), contact with whom brings death. The entire period in which innards are being removed *(detripando)* is therefore ritually marked. As Dzoshua explains, before going home after a day's work, a cross of sticks is left on the top of the tree/canoe to prevent the devil from shitting in it, poisoning one of the spouses whose identity is connected to it.

What seems remarkable to me about the incident in which I saw Dzoshua perform magic is not so much what I saw but what I didn't see. Not only did I not see the cross, which was made of two pieces of reed, one slipped through a slit in the other, but I picked it up thinking it was a child's toy, took it apart, threw one part aside, and proceeded to measure the length of the canoe! Later on, as I observed the meticulous series of measurements that Dzoshua carried out with the interlocked reeds, ascertaining the amount of woodwork needed to assure proper dimensions, I realized that its practical function obscured its magical function. Because of the fusion of magic and measure, symbol and carpenter's tool, in the form of a single object, I would have assumed that the significance of this object lay fully within the realm of practical function. Had I not been otherwise informed, my empirical bias would have led me to be perfectly satisfied with a unidimensional view of things. It was a good lesson in awareness, leading to the development of a kind of double vision, something I needed in order to perceive what "everybody in this country knows."

Dzoshua worked alone for two days and then stopped completely for four, a long weekend. Early on the fifth day, he and Dalas are working when Inez spots a deer followed by two dogs across the river. Because they are Dante's dogs, no one else can go after the deer. She and Norma walk over to Dante's house, at a dispersed site not far from the work site, but no one is home. The deer vanishes. That news is related to the large group of helpers who eventually assemble to turn the canoe bottom-side up after the walls are done. Reaching the end of the holes that have been bored into the trunk from the top to indicate proper depth, Dzoshua finishes taking out the tripe and begins the next two stages. These involve different operations that may overlap in time: stripping off the outer bark and cambium and the more precise thinning of walls. Reaching the depth holes reminds Dzoshua of the magic an axman needs for acquiring force: "You get a *sorré* [the large male woodpecker with a red head, called carpenter *(carpintero)* in Spanish]. That one can make a hole in a large, hard tree by going fast and precisely with his beak. This bird will go and go, and if the hole is still not done, he will keep going until it is finished." The woodpecker's accuracy and endurance are behavioral features that lend themselves to ritual. Dzoshua continues: So you kill a *sorré*, grate its beak, and mix the powder with *jagua* (S. black dye from fruit of *Genipa americana*). Then while you paint it on your hands and lower arms, quickly stroking up and down first one then the other to apply the powdered dye, you chant (he says something to the effect of "leave me strong like you" over and over, issuing sounds in that mumbling undertone reserved for talk with extraordinary beings). This is done when the moon is full, above the earth at four or five in the morning, and just about to wane. (This is the same time a tree should be felled to discourage wood-boring insects, as they are least abundant in this phase.) The ritual is done four times in a man's life, at no specific age. The first time can take place in boyhood (Dzoshua points to his six- and eight-year-old sons), but it cannot be done more than four times because then you become too strong. Too much strength is no good. You can ruin a canoe like that. When used correctly, this magic makes a man stronger and better at wielding an ax. If you put him side by side with a man who has not done it, the one with magic wins any contest of strength. He can finish taking out the innards of a log by noon. When the *sorré* makes a hole, its cry is "Trrrrrrrrr-ke-ke-ke-ke," just like people when they are working. (When Emberá men are working most intensely with machete or ax, they cry out.)

Dalas, Tikebo (Dzoshua's first cousin's son-in-law), and Dzoshua switch off on the ax. Dzoshua works the walls, and the other two remove the last large hunks of wood off the outside of the two ends, tapering them. Finishing up thinning a section of wall, Dzoshua hits the side with the back of his ax, makes a noise like a woodpecker, and says: "*Sorré* says it's done." He explains to me: "In Ancient Times *Sorré* was *gente* [S. people]. It was later that God left him animal." Then he patted the walls of the canoe, listening for the sound his hands made against the wood, estimating thickness by pitch. He also measured the walls along the top edge and from top to bottom using finger widths as standards: he finds the top edge to be 2 fingers thick, midwall 3 fingers, and bottom wall 4 fingers. The walls needed to be worked till they measured 1½, 2½, and 3½ fingers respectively. Pausing again, Dzoshua explains, "*Ochorró*, the horned lizard [probably *Banisteriopsis banisteriopsis*], the one with the ax on his head, used to be a person too. It was when he was wielding the ax around his head in a great circle that the world changed, and there the ax stayed, right on top of his head. He can't run very far on water, as his ax weighs him down. It happened as the world was changing." When I asked Dzoshua about *Sorré* in a later conversation, he remembered: "I've got a thought," he said. "WAIT. There was a *cholo*, like us, in Ancient Times. He learned to labor with *Chicharra* [dragonfly]. *Chicharra* was from the forest . . . and when you've just taken off the top, it's there inside. This was the laborer of the canoe. With this — you kill it with a stick — PAH! — [here Dzoshua produces unwritable noises, then chants something under his breath] — THE EYES! 'Before like you, before.' As you wash [demonstrates eye-washing movements] WELL. 'I will stay like you were before, that way.' And so I rub my eyes like this so they see WELL. You just smash it and put it on." Dzoshua demonstrates the chant: "I stay like you, I stay like you, I stay like you. . . . In Ancient Times, this was the laborer of canoes. For this reason he teaches the people."

As the axmen leisurely thin the walls, I sit around the cooking fire by the water's edge with Dzoshua's daughter and wife (the former older than the latter), Inez and Norma. Inez begins to tell me her version of village conflicts concerning past attempts to start a cooperative store in the village, the tenor and structure of which contrasted markedly with the cooperative endeavor upon which we were presently embarked.[4] Everybody's just hanging out, waiting for more people to arrive so that the next stage, turning over the canoe, can be done. Dzoshua's son Edi and his wife, Melani, show up at the site. Trying to deflect Dzoshua's annoyance at his lack of participation, Edi announces that he is almost finished clearing the underbrush out of a piece of forest (the first step in slash-and-burn agricultural work) but won't start felling trees until everything is totally dry. (It has been raining the past couple of days, and people are worried that the dry season will be too wet, like it was the year before. It turned out to be overly long and hot, however.) Attuned to my favorite interest, Inez remembers: "Dzoshua told a great story last night. He heard it when he went downriver to sell plantains to Condoto, and he remembered it. Pow! [She and Norma laugh, remembering the punch line.] He heard it from Condoto's brother-in-law, and he's going to tell it again." By 1:00 P.M. the sides were finished. Noke and Omar, Norma's father, have wandered up. Dzoshua calls everyone together, announcing that he's going to tell a story. He's in fine form, enriching the words with pantomime and sound effects. Using the large pile of wood chips surrounding the length of the emerging canoe as a stage, he kindly tells the story in Spanish so that I too can understand. This is what I wrote down later from my notes:

Many kinds of ants have little houses. *Tra* [E. leaf cutters], the woodcutters of Ancient Times who now, after the world changed, must work day and night; Kapupudu [little black ants Dalas points out crawling around in the pile of wood chips]; *Dríbibidí;* and *Hëinsrä-torró* [E. Campenotus]. They were all there living in their little houses when *Imamá* [E. jaguar] comes by and asks *Hëinsrä:* "Who built this great highway here?" *Hëinsrä* replies: "The highway belongs to a giant called *Hombre* [S. man]. This giant is so big and heavy that he steps on us ants and kills us. Just like that! We may bite, but he's so big it does nothing." Then *Imamá* asks, "So where is this *Hombre?* I want to meet him." And *Hëinsrä* replies, "He passes this way every day on his way to work upriver." (He has a rice field upriver.)

The next day *Imamá* returns and asks, "So where is this *Hombre?*" But the ants reply, "Oh, you've missed him. He's already gone past on his way to work, but he'll be back. Why don't you wait for him?" *Imamá* waited and waited. Getting impatient, he asks again, only to be told, "He'll come by." *Imamá* got tired of waiting and decided to go up the road and look for himself. He went and went, and went and went. [Dzoshua strides up and down along the length of the canoe looking into the distance.] He climbed a hill, and then another, and there on the path before him he sees one of these giants and asks, "Are you *Hombre?*" And the giant replies, "No, I'm *Wëra* [E. woman]." And so he keeps going, going. Finally he sees another giant and asks again, "Are you *Hombre?*" "Yes," says *Hombre.* And *Imamá* says, "Let's fight!" [Dalas interjects: "They wanted to fight just like those two boys who were fighting here before," referring to Dzoshua's sons who'd been rolling around pummeling each other.] And *Hombre* says, "Sure, just let me put down my heavy load and smoke my pipe." [In slow motion, Dzoshua pantomimes the man putting down his load.] *Imamá* waits while *Hombre* has his smoke. Smoking, smoking, smoking, smoking, and suddenly, *Hombre,* POW! He shoots *Imamá* with a shotgun, all at once. Right in the face! *Imamá* fled, his face all bloody (but he didn't die, as this is a story). He went back to the ants and said "*Tío Ormiguita* [S. Uncle Little-Ant], you were right. This *Hombre* is terrible, deadly." And that's how it stayed, *Imamá* fleeing from man always, his face spotted. (−T/S)

Unaware and destructive, this folktale giant on his daily round of agricultural labor is a metaphoric figure of contemporary humanity, pushing back the last small pieces of rainforest on earth and annihilating diverse species of plants and animals, some of which are not even known to him. From the ants in their intricate niches to the formidable power of jaguars, all are defeated by Man. You can read this same folktale into the story of Darién, the biggest little piece of forest left in Central America.

Deceit is normal. But the combination of deceit and technology gives Man terrible power, allowing him to destroy the jaguar, natural contender and shaman's ally. With the shotgun is heard the Spanish name *Hombre*: the official language of state places masculinity in the domain of technology; whereas *Wëra*, Emberá name for woman, registers no challenge. The ascription of technology to the man overlays and reinforces traditional sexual divisions, although sometimes there are confusing reversals. Take motors, for example: if a couple owns a motor, it is the man who sits with it in the ass end, reversing the traditional position of the woman's body. Requiring ass-end positioning to function, the machine introduces its own logic, overriding the traditional semiotic. The power generated by the motor exceeds the power of human musculature, and the social significance accorded to its owner exceeds that of confronting the world with a pole from the canoe's nose. So while the woman's seat changes from back to front, her position in the social order does not change. This is a somewhat confusing effect. For if body position is indeed symbolically important, the change of woman's position from back to front should, but under these circumstances does not, signify her release from this benign form of traditional subordination. The apparent contradictions of the introduction of the motor into Emberá life may be clarified using Haraway's (1992) ecocybernetic model. Rather than understanding man, woman, canoe, poles, and motor as individual autonomous sentient beings and things, we can think of them as one thing composed of various human-technological elements. Together these elements constitute a particular functional relation to the environment. This analytic shift allows us to understand how, despite apparent contradiction, the patriarchal order of the whole—one human/technological interface—remains constant.

In the scene at the mouth of the Preciada River, the story is a vehicle for enjoyment and laughter, passing with the moment. Everyone is having a good time: with Inez's help, Dzoshua told some more tales with Iguana as trickster and tricked, and Dalas, the practical joker, said there was something crawling in the woodpile, which made the gringa (me) jump off her seat. Inez and Norma fed the entire assembly, numbering ten adults by now, with dumplings (fried flour dough), plantains, fish, and coffee with sugar. After the meal we got ready in great silliness to turn over the canoe, the beginning of the next-to-last stage.

A pole is cut and lashed across the top of the canoe, and a *makwá* vine rope is tied to one end. Dzoshua collected the *makwá* vine from the forest a few days earlier. To make its fibers more flexible, he pounds it with rocks, releasing the attractive sweet-smell used in love magic. First the women line up on the lower ground to pull on the rope, while the men push the long edge of the canoe from higher ground. It seems like the women are doing most of the work, then it looks like the pole is going to break. Skinny old Omar, groaning to make sure everyone noticed his displeasure at being chosen for this task, goes off to cut another pole. The pulling and pushing, still with much goofiness, begins again. As it becomes apparent that it is the pulling and not the pushing that is actually turning the canoe, the men come one by one over to the women's side. All at once it flips back side up with a thump.

Already late in the afternoon, everybody was leaving to go back to the village when Dante's son came by with his two hunting dogs. He explained why he wasn't with his dogs in the morning when the deer ran by. The dogs were tracking a white-lipped peccary (E. *bidó*) through the forest, when suddenly they disappeared. They had gone after the deer (E. *begí*) instead, but he didn't know it. He ended up catching neither prey.

The next morning, Dzoshua worked alone, taking off the outer wood on the canoe's underside, making the bottom flat. That afternoon he went hunting with his wife, Dalas's brother, and his wife. Dzoshua's dog was still learning how to hunt deer, and although the dog chased one down almost to the village, he lost it in the end. So they came back with nothing to eat. Dzoshua figured that with help, the canoe could be ready to be put in the river anyway, the final stage. Early the following morning, before he left the village, he went around to the people in their homes and informed them that the canoe would be ready to be moved into the river by noon. By the time I got there at 11:00 A.M., he and Dalas were chopping weakly at the bottom. They had eaten nothing that day but plantains, and Dalas, who was sick with flu, should have been in bed. But Dzoshua is anxious to get the project done (he started on January 9, and now it is the thirtieth). He wants to get to the stage where the canoe could be floated downriver to a work site closer to home.

Dzoshua was dragging; Dalas kept up the ax work. The last sips of coffee cream liqueur left over from my birthday celebration revived them a bit. Every once in a while Dzoshua's son Edi and his wife, Melani, would pass by with their children. Spearing fish from a *canalete,* they annoyed both Dzoshua and Inez with their thoughtlessness (although they did eventually come around to help). By 2:00 P.M. people begin to arrive from the village. Dalas's brother comes with his stepfather, and they take over the axes from Dzoshua and Dalas. Daniel, a man who is from the village but not directly related to Dzoshua, wanders by and also puts in a couple of hours' work. The two axes are now in constant motion, fresh men replacing tired. Lucinda's husband, Felipe, a newcomer to the village, also not related to Dzoshua, had just come from fishing upriver and is hanging out. With all the people coming around (a third of the male village household heads are now present), it turns once more into a fun occasion. Someone spots a toucan (E. *kewará,* S. *pico, Ramphastos swainsonii*), a favorite and once-common game bird, high up in a tree on the forest edge. There is a rush for rifles and bullets, but it is too far away to get a good line of sight. At risk of losing a bullet for naught, they leave the toucan alone.

Omar is here too, but he's acting tired from having to cut that extra pole the day before yesterday, reinforcing his reputation for not liking work, which goes along with his reputation for running after young women who never want him. (Omar, who had no direct relations in Tamarinbó when he came to settle, "gave" his daughter Norma to Dzoshua to marry. In exchange, Dzoshua was supposed to give Omar his younger daughter. But Dzoshua's daughter said it was out of the question, and that was the end of it. Hence the source of the jokes.) While all this activity is going on, Omar just sits by the fire, head resting on knees. Exhausted. Inez explains to everyone that Omar is just sitting around feeling bad today because last night he went catting in Promesa. When the girl's mother caught him going after her daughter, she hit him over the head with a stick. And not only that, teased Dalas, but Omar and Daniel are mad at each other today because yesterday Daniel was walking upriver and saw Omar hiding on the riverbank, secretly watching some girl bathing.

The sun beats down hard on the axmen, and they switch off every ten to fifteen minutes. Daniel does some fancy finishing work on the side wall: precise diagonal cuts in series along the top edge of the wall, then reversing direction, a row of cross diagonals (like cross-stitches), then reversing direction again; a third series of cuts leaves a nice, long, smooth area of wall. Then Felipe takes the ax and begins hacking unskillfully at this same place. We can all hear the erring sounds of small pieces being torn out. It is obvious even to me that although he is willing to try, this man raised by *kam-*

puniá in the cities of Colombia does not know how to work the ax. Not more than five minutes later another man politely relieves him.

At 4:15 P.M. it is time to put the canoe in the water. There are plenty of people. Thinking about the alternative directions the canoe might be carried, Dzoshua asks for a few opinions. Then we all get around, and—one, two, three—we heave it over to the river's edge. It slides smoothly into the water, the bow dipping low and taking in some. In a flash, everyone gets into canoes and heads off downstream. Dzoshua is in the stern, proud and serious, observing carefully how the work would hold up, Dalas is in front, Inez, Norma, the children, my friend, and I in the middle. We ride down to where the Preciada flows into the Tupisa and pick up Omar with four large heavy pieces of rubber tree (E. *huéporo,* S. *caucho*) that he cut for his sister Zelda to make sleeping mats out of the inner bark. So the canoe ends up getting a heavy try-out on the first run down, getting stuck a number of times in the rocky sections of rapids. We bring it down to the small beach in front of Dzoshua's orchard, across and a bit upriver from the village. After this, Dzoshua got really sick and didn't leave the house again for several days. Then he began to work on it again, doing the final smoothing out. He finished it by early February: it took a month from start to finish.

With the right luck, season, and place, and the willingness of workers skilled with the ax, the cooking pot, and the hunt, Dzoshua's canoe is constructed. Somehow reciprocity among kin and other villagers is elicited, overcoming the resistance to most cooperative projects (especially where money or food is involved) that stems from the Emberá's fierce attachment to household autonomy. Perhaps it is only a man such as Dzoshua who could call forth such cooperation, although it is not in every kind of project that he is so treated. Perhaps the people are called by the magic, stories, metaphors, and merriment that turn labor into celebration. Perhaps it is the mobility promised by the canoe itself.

The dugout canoe is a ticket to survival, taking one in search of food and materials to build shelter, in search of adventure upriver and money markets downriver. The archetypal example of what every Emberá man should know, a form of knowledge passed down from elder to younger, canoe construction is part of a tradition that continues in the context of changing historical conditions, persisting and transforming according to varying definitions of competence, function, and value. (Would there have been at least one young man present to learn this skill, the future might appear more promising.) Canoe construction is an accomplishment that demands qualities of workmanship and an awareness of and respect for the magical plane of experience that is invisible yet intereffective with the one we see. If there is ever a history of Emberá life written, it would have to include descriptions of special events such as these. The history of a people who tend toward egalitarian and peaceful ways, numbering only in the thousands, simple in technology and rich in material design, should be written on a human scale. It would be a history interwoven with myth, wherein rulers and superpowers would find their place only in the margins.

six

Misfortune's Hat

Misfortune calls forth interpretive forms that are appropriate to context and event. Mysterious misfortune, that which happens for no apparent reason, elicits shamanic interpretation. As used in classic ethnography, the study of shaman-ism tends to focus on shamans and their rituals. This has tended to restrict and exoticize the understanding of how shamanism structures imaginative discourse in a far more pervasive way. Among the Emberá, shamanic discourse is not limited to use by specialists in ritual contexts. In most cases of mysterious misfortune, for example, the interpretive process is an end in itself, one that stops short of ritual.

Hai (E. spirit[s]/devil[s]) is the elemental principle that binds cause and effect in shamanic discourse. The presence of *hai* is implicit in all interpretations of inexplicable misfortune. Moving among humans and animals, whose bodies are transparent to their vision and permeable to their passage, *hai* effect reversals of life and death, cure and curse. *Hai* borrow biological forms for appearance's sake, but they ignore biological limits. Immeasurable and lacking in intention, *hai* may not even feel the need to survive. Neutral, they can be swayed by song, dance, and perfume and can be captured and controlled by shamans. Empty, they are the essential vehicles of unnatural transformation, the means by which human and de-

Figure 19. Postmortem of hunting dog in plantain orchard.

monic intentions are enacted. In the scenes to follow, shamanic discourse engages the forces of history with those of spirit to analyze problematic circumstances surrounding cases of misfortune.

Only the Hat Remained

Antumiá is the demonic messenger of the shaman. When shamans battle, they send Antumiá to kill. Like the snake, Antumiá has its own *hai*. The bird that lives below the earth, the faceless black humanoid who comes up out of the river to drown people, the ancient *Madre de Agua* (Mother of Waters) named also in Maroon oral histories (Price 1983:70) — these are the forms associated with the *hai* of this demon, the attributions humans lend to sensations of invisible animosity.[1] When that bird's eerie descending sequence of minor notes echoes through night's dark wall, first here, then there, impossible to record before it retreats again, the Emberá say, "It is Antumiá." Dzoshua said he encountered Antumiá twice in Sambu and once around Yaviza loading plantains with his friend Gomez. They heard "Cheeeeeee" from downriver, "Cheeeeeee" from upriver, and they knew it was two Antumiás fighting hard. Then finally, they heard one "Cheeeeeee" from the victor. Once I was traveling downriver to Yaviza with Dzoshua and his wife, Norma. We passed a black-*kampuniá* house with two young boys and a couple of adults sitting at the water's edge. We continued on without greeting them when suddenly one of the boys, about fourteen years old and naked as the day he was born, started running in the low river in our direction. Dzoshua told Norma to row faster and then turned to me and said "Antumiá!" with half-joking unease. The boy seemed to enjoy the chase as if he knew he was frightening them. I told him to go home, but he said he was running an errand. Sure enough, when we rounded the next bend, there were some other *kampuniá*, from whom he retrieved a hoe.

Antumiá can appear as *hai* in different forms, or it can kill with an invisible hand. When they had to explain the disappearance of a corpse to the Guard, Isadora's family told them it was Antumiá. This explanation was accepted. Isadora, now an old woman, relates her account of the events as she experienced them with her mother, father, and father's nephew (her uncle) many years ago.[2]

I will tell a story of Antumiá to the white woman.

That Antumiá, we, as that is a story, I will tell already, how we have passed thus.

There was a sick person.

We took him.

That Emberá, "Colombia," he was called.

Then [now] deceased Heronomo was sick.

And then, we were going there to Pirré. We went to get him cured because he was sick.

Then in Yaviza we were sleeping.

Then we, we were already leaving, the sky was dawn blue, and we were going downriver.

Then we were arriving at Isleta [a place where the river divides in two, leaving an island in the middle].

Then I, as close as I am to you.

So near, I had my son.

Then sloooooooooow, that Emberá Colombia paddled the little canoe.

Slooooooooowly paddling, then, here thus it happened.

He fell in the water.

"Ai! Mama, my uncle fell in the water."

Now yes, I grabbed the oar.

Then, thus the whirlpool rose up, took him.

Then I grabbed the oar, the little canoe, now yes, put [hand down to touch]:

The bottom was dry.

"Ai! my mother, that one that was this way," it is said.

Ai *kau!* My companion, that animal, the animal it was that caught him, animal, it is said.

Antumiá caught him.

Now yes, my mother cried.

Thus we were, there was [something] off the back end of the little canoe.

We grabbed the floating hat.

My mother grabbed that, that which belonged to the deceased.

I, now yes, my old man was going to die.

In this way the shaman will have killed him. [TN: The teller assumes that the listener knows that her mother was distraught because she was thinking that a shaman (not present) wanted to kill her husband, Heronomo, who was also a shaman. They were fighting with each other (for unspecified reasons), and so the absent shaman sent Antumiá to kill Heronomo. But it was Heronomo's nephew, the deceased Colombia, whom Antumiá took.]

Now yes, we returned again upriver, again for Yaviza.

We returned. Antumiá took him in the river.

Then truth, we were arriving.

My [now] deceased mother, right there, went to the [government] office.

From the office she came.

Ai! Antumiá took him, took Colombia.

Now yes, The Guard gathered all the Emberá to go search.

To look for that dead one.

Searching, downriver from Yaviza, there searching, searching, searching, searching.

93

Upriver also, the people searched.

They didn't see him in that day's search.

The next day, as it was midnight, Antumiá cried out.

EEEEEEEEEEEEEEEEEEEEE!

In that moment the [now] deceased Heronomo that was there said [in his dream]:

"Ai old woman, they have killed my nephew today.

Antumiá has killed him," it is said, "has killed him," it is said.

"Early tomorrow morning I will go meet him," it is said.

"Here below the dead [cemetery] below.

There I am going to meet him," it is said.

"They already killed my nephew," it is said.

Antumiá.

[interruption on tape]

Then, then, he met him, right there, now yes.

They met, truth, the dead people, already dead.

They met, now yes, once again, in Erara [El Real].[3]

Now yes, we took him to the Guard in El Real, to give the declaration.

They took him to El Real.

Then they brought the dead one too, Colombia it was, to El Real to bury him.[4]

Now yes, we went inside the office.

We who did not kill.

We were in the office. [TN: The teller is identifying her group as those who did not kill, because she says that according to local judicial practice, the people who bring in a dead body are automatically accused of being the killers.]

Myself, as I was at his side.

They took me inside first.

I spoke.

We, truth, brought him downriver.

In order to see/cure, in order to go.

Then truth Antumiá caught him, truth.

I was close in the river, he fell, truth.

Then truth, a little whirlpool appeared [as if something entered the water from] above.

I caught the little canoe.

Inside put [my hand], it was dry.

Then again, my mother, who was behind, grabbed the hat.

"Ai Antumiá, killed my *compadre*," it is said.

"Killed my *compadre*, truth."

In that moment, that Emberá took us to the office,

When we were there, the man spoke again.

And it was that way exactly, the truth was spoken.

And it was that way exactly, the declaration said.

The same, that way exactly.

We left, he held the wake in El Real, that man.

Dead.

That dusk we buried him EEeeee!

Then, he was little, he had become laaaaaarge.[5]

Until here went my story. (T/E)

Whisked out of reality without so much as a splash, a man taking his sick uncle to another river for a cure disappears. Only his hat remained: a sign of impossible denotation, dangling, nagging for placement. (Unlike the inch of candle out of place, which served as a piece of a puzzle connecting Grandfather's corpse to his murderer [Chap. 4], the hat pointed to naught.) The uncle's wife grabbed the hat. She knew this death missed her husband, the sick and embattled shaman, and killed the nephew instead. Whether the death was deflected by chance or by design was not stated, but in any case, she was frightened. Emberá gathered to fish out the body, to decipher, witness. The Guard must be given an appropriate explanation: will someone be blamed?

The incident provokes tense instability, tipping the balance between continuity and chaos. A struggle to reassume human mastery ensues. A shamanic narrative is produced, creating a discursive field of opposed forces linking this human event to the otherworld. Antumiá is identified as agent, evil messenger in a battle between shamans, one of whom is seriously weakened, seeking help from a third. The messenger (its *hai*) is sent to the canoe, taking not the shaman but his kin. The people compose a narrative to fill the gap between reality's appearance and the disruption caused by loss. Although the nephew's death could not have been predicted, the narrative leaves no loose ends. After all, outside the range of comprehension it provides, nothing happened. The Guard, probably all non-Indian in those times, defer to the Indian's special knowledge and accept their explanation. Here one minute, gone the next; perhaps the soldier-scribe entered "accidental" next to "cause" on the official form.

The people project the shamans' inscrutable methods onto the wider geopolitical field, where they resolve things with the military government without identifying a guilty soul for punishment.

A Macheteyed Monkey

For most Panamanians, Darién is out of sight and out of mind. The mostly black and "Spanish" (Latino-white) government workers who go there are the few who get to know Emberá lowland forest culture. They motor up and down the rivers with regularity (or at least it was regular at the time I did fieldwork), visiting each settlement site to carry out specific functions of state—the COPFA folks who control hoof-and-mouth disease and guard the border, RENARE folks who regulate renewable resources, SNEM folks who spray DDT for malaria control.[6] The workers also assist with transporting people upriver and downriver, act as messengers and godfathers of Emberá children, and tell exotic tales of their experiences with the Indians. A RENARE worker named Gordo told me a story about superstition in Union-Chocó, the largest of all the Emberá villages, home of the first cacique, whom I had met in my initial quest for permission to do fieldwork (see Chap. 1). Gordo had gone up there for a political congress, but the cacique hadn't yet arrived. He happened to come at an awkward time. As tape-recorded in Spanish on October 30, 1984, Gordo told this story:

> Someone had found a dead monkey slashed by a machete on a path outside the village that day. It was a distant mountain species not usually seen in the lowlands. It was slashed strangely: three big gashes and the corpse left lying there. The news terrified the villagers. They took the macheteyed monkey as a sure sign of *brujería* [sorcery], a sign that someone was to be killed. They came down from their houses and stayed awake on the ground talking all night.
>
> The next day the Emberá village head and the *corregidor* [S. magistrate] went to examine the monkey. There it was, still bleeding three days after death. This was horrible. The people did not sleep for yet another night. They looked for an explanation. Somebody must have done something wrong to evoke this. Everybody was cross-examined. Finally one man

broke down. He confessed that it must have been his deed that brought this on. It was the time he went downriver entrusted with a canoe-load of maize to sell for someone. Well, he did sell it, but he spent the evening afterward drinking up the proceeds, leaving the next day without ever paying the person his due. The people in Union generally agreed that this must be the action behind the sign and that this man should get the money and give it to the rightful owner at all costs. Now the danger of being killed was focused on this man and his family; tensions abated somewhat, although the villagers were still too frightened to sleep. They spent yet another night awake on the ground, with only women ascending to prepare food quickly and descending again. After three nights of agitated sleeplessness the cacique finally arrived. The villagers were all standing along the bank, watching his canoe draw near. They began recounting the situation as he reached. The cacique listened and said, "What's all this hocus-pocus stuff? We've gone beyond this kind of superstition. A monkey can come down from the mountains. They move around just like people. Somebody must have seen it and killed it. So what?" In this way he calmed everybody down. And that was the end of the excitement. (T/S)

Unlike Grandfather's corpse, the macheteyed monkey did not belong in this locale and was brutalized more than necessary even for a kill. The killer just discarded his grotesque prey—surely this is not the act of an ordinary hunter. Why does the monkey journey so far from the mountains, and how could it bleed so long after the death? To the people of Union, the macheteyed monkey is a forecast of some future horror to be carried out by someone of malign intent. This prediction follows from the Emberá shamanic code, in which someone with malicious intention can (with training) make use of invisible otherworld forces, extending the bounds of human agency beyond the empirical through the use of *hai*. Abandoning their unprotected homes for the ground, they sift through the arguments, trickeries, and mistakes of the villagers, searching for an event that could be responsible for precipitating vengeance, an event that fits the requirements of narrative resolution. They find it when a man confesses to a mishap over money. His confession, probably one in a number of guilty self-reports, becomes an object of consensus (at least as it was represented to Gordo, the government worker who, like myself, would understand only the Spanish mixed into Emberá speech). The confession that suits consensus locates the source of conflict outside where Indians are more susceptible to failure, and away from the group of decipherers, who under the circumstances present themselves to each other as allies. Deflection of the cause of evil outside of kindred's domain is a symbolic strategy characteristic of Emberá shamanic interpretation. The scenario is not unfamiliar: downriver, in the *kampuniá* town of Yaviza, the Union man sells another man's maize but never pays him his money. Nor does he buy the kerosene, cloth, salt, machetes, oil, pots, and pigtails that would be useful back home. He just blows it on booze. The misdeed calls for a simple reversal — he should pay back the money.

But in this case, narrative resolution is inconclusive. Danger is still imminent. Although a guilty man and his family are identified, the people must all be sifting through the wrongs and misunderstandings of their own past, each one wondering if he or she is not, after all responsible. Like the nephew who caught the death of his uncle in the story of Antumiá, there is no guarantee that the killer's lust is specific or his aim infallible. After three days of sleepless disruption, the cacique arrives and presides. In his wisdom, he brushes aside the web of anxious discourse by abolishing its premise: *it is not a sign.* It's just your usual macheteyed monkey, he says, and this is just superstitious thinking. Glossing over the gruesome details, he lifts the stereotype of superstition that many *kampuniá* (like the man who tells the story) have of Emberá systems of interpretation and uses it in an intracultural context. The strategic borrowing succeeds in corralling the villagers' anxieties, putting them to rest. Submerged, the forecast of malign intent waits . . . for next time.

True to his leadership role linking indigenous tradition to nation-state, the cacique appropriates a derisive *kampuniá* label in order to de-escalate Emberá fear of misfortune. *If* the guilty man were able to pay back the money immediately, *if* his misdeed were indeed the cause of the sign's malign intent, and *if* the act of retribution hit its target exactly — only *then* might the village return to normal. The cacique's resolution is much more powerful. With a fragment of mirror he carries with him from the outside world, he erases everyone's paranoia in one stroke.

Ethnographer's Nightmare

El Viejo (Old One) is a withered old brown stick of a man who wears Western clothes with a hard safari hat and carries a walking stick. He lives in the village between river and highway that is half Waunan and half Emberá where I carried out preliminary research. The village head is his son. In my first meeting with the son, he told me that his old man knew about plants. I met him. We sat on a log. I told him that I was interested in medicinal plants, and he told me he could cure cancer, snakebite, and other things and that each plant cost $50. I tried to explain that I didn't have that kind of money for plants and that anyway, I wanted to learn in general. I would meet him at dawn the next morning.

El Viejo lives on the Emberá side of the village, but he is Waunan (which I didn't discover till later, when he told his stories into my tape recorder). He was the region's first settler. He found the site in the early 1940s and went back and got his relatives from the Chocó. He married an Emberá woman. She was the first of his three wives. Field note excerpts from my first days as anthropologist follow:

[June 19, 1983] I got to the house El Viejo shared with his first wife early early. She was making fried bread and coffee. She served me first, then everyone else around. I waited about two hours, while the old man treated a young campesino with oozing lesions who said he was from the Gulfo Balbao. El Viejo gave him a bath and some bottles of stuff. It was all very secretive. There were two travelers there too. I asked them some questions, but they wouldn't answer. The old man asked them for an exact list of names of everyone in their family and the name of some other woman. Sounded like sorcery to me. Afterward, as we left, I asked the old man if he did orations, but he said no, he only cured with plants.

We walked out to the highway. We sat down at the thatch bus stop. He asked me again what I wanted. He came down in his price to $25 for each plant brew. I told him I wanted to understand their culture and that I would carry plants for him and not ask any questions. This seemed to satisfy him temporarily. We crossed the road, a rice field, and went into the forest. Nicking the bark of several trees in one small area, he found a branch he was looking for and cut a piece about four feet long. I didn't write or ask questions. We stopped to rest beside a pool, the remnants of a river. He was still trying to figure out what I wanted. He decided it was sex, after asking me if I was married or had any children, etc., saying—when I played dumb—"You know, it's like the desire to have something to eat." Then he made the old in-out gesture with his hands. I denied this adamantly. The old crow!

We head back. As we were about to enter the open field again, we stopped, ostensibly waiting for the sun to pass behind the clouds. He turned to me and asked how much a woman charged for sexual services. He wanted to trade! I told him I was sure I didn't know. He told me the story of a *colono* woman who could not be cured by the dispensary and came to him. She wanted to pay him with her body because she had no money. He didn't want to, but he did it anyway. He really must not understand. He tried to sell me a good luck potion and collected some cinnamon bark *(yerba canela)* for tea. I decided I'd better not go to the forest alone with him again.

Later that night a Waunan man came to talk to me. He was the father of my friend Salome. He showed me two pieces of *raizilla* (S. little root, *Ipecacuana harabes*).[7] He says he knows all about plants. This one is for stomach pain and snakebite. Take a little piece, crush it, and drink it with water. It comes from a small bush with round leaves. He wants to come to the United States to cure my family and wants me to take Salome along.

[June 20] El Viejo's younger son, with whom I was making Emberá phonology tapes, told me that his father wouldn't teach me without money. I told the youth that I had no problem with that, but thought it was important that the old man pass on his knowledge to someone.

[June 22] [Finished the detailed village map I'd been pacing out since I arrived.] From a distance, I observed a constant flow of patients coming and going to El Viejo's house. None was an Indian. They were all blacks or campesinos. I was invited there to record stories. He told me three, the first in Waunan, second in Spanish, and third in Emberá. A young black woman from a nearby town was lying in a hammock with her feet wrapped in leaves, tied on to hold medicine inside. She was waiting for the medicine to dry. She said she had fungus and because she didn't take care of it and walked in dirt, the medical doctor in the clinic said her sores could turn into cancer. So she came to El Viejo.

[June 23] [Surveyed family names of male and female household heads corresponding to map.] The little girl that was teaching me how to cook on the hearth told me that El Viejo ate (i.e., killed) a little boy. No Emberá or Waunan goes to him.

[June 28] [In the morning, the whole village gathered in one house to have a meeting with a representative of the renewable resources agency (RENARE) about the cooperative agricultural project the village is doing. At twilight, the representative left, and the Emberá talked among themselves about various issues, e.g., how payments would be made in proportion to hours worked, sick pay, saving money, accountability of officers. People were curious about my furious scribbling as I tried to keep up. (The talk was mostly in Spanish, both because it is the language of development and finance and because it is the language most Emberá and Waunan held in common.)[8] Sometime during the long sultry afternoon I talked to a woman about the age to which old people live. She said there were few (only two) old people here because the others were all killed off by sorcery, by *häïmbaná*. She explained no further.

[June 29] Last night I had a nightmare. Startled, I awoke just as a woman of indefinable nationality with long straight hair was about to slice through my collarbone with a metal instrument like a hacksaw. First she hid it inside my books or things, so that when I went through them, I would feel a sharp slice. Then she came after me. I was running up a misty mountain road like the ones in old movies about trying to escape out of World War II Germany. My hope was sparked by the sight of a uniformed woman standing on the road beside a guard post. But when I reached to ask for help, she was like air, or it was as if I were invisible. I went to the little building, where there was a second guard. I felt terror when I realized that my attacker could just ignore the guards. She set upon me, trapped in the corner of that little space, and with this silver tool, was about to slice. . . . I awoke, wide awake.

My first thoughts were of El Viejo, and the possibility that he might be giving me signs to keep me away, or more frightening, that he was performing witchcraft on me already. This thought got me really scared, because the terror in the dream occurred when I realized that authorities of "the real," symbolized by the uniformed guard, could offer no protection. They could not even *see* me or my pursuer. I thought how easily I could go crazy, driven by bad dreams and thoughts. I decided not to take the motorized canoe trip from this village on the highway further into the interior that I'd been planning with my Waunan neighbor and his wife (who also happened to be El Viejo's daughter). (It turned out that I did go, but because of high gas prices, taking the bus down the highway was much more economical.)

OK. That is one side, I say to myself. The basis for nightmarish consequences happening to me are unlikely by rational standards. It's probably my own mind creating the dream in vivid response to the strangeness of the environment, the hearsay that I'd been told, and my discomfort about the intrusions of mapping and census data collection. Under the circumstances, I'll have to abide by this second interpretation and leave the rest to fate. But I'll be wary. Never before in my life do I remember having a nightmare. And since I'd been in Cueva, my dreams until this point had remained unconscious.

The campesinos and blacks who come to see El Viejo pay him for his knowledge in dealing with specific problems; for me, he was just one possible source in my pilgrimage of human science. Directed to him, I was directly put off. Avoiding him (at least insofar as his curing expertise), I went about the business of collecting demographic data, taping stories, and learning the language. But the contact had been made, and somehow I had been included within the scope of negative influence he seemed to hold over many on the Waunan side of the village (where I stayed). My first time out in the field, I was also realizing the threatening aspect of my larger project of "studying culture" (which could, after all, mean anything), as for example when the wife of the village head refused to tell me her family name. However, I felt secure in my good intentions, was made comfortable by people who seemed to enjoy having me around, and kept what I thought was an objective distance from shamanic affairs. So it did not occur to me that my contact with the old man or the intrusive aspects of my work would make me subject to any kind of attack (to sudden misfortune) — until the nightmare, when I awoke to my (possibly imaginary) vulnerability. And so I became positioned as a discursive subject within a web of shamanic allegation (cf. Favret-Saada 1980). My actions (interviewing, mapping, etc.) were operating on a level of which I was not aware, involving me in things beyond my conscious intention. Caught.

The experience shifts the ground of my realist sense. Caught in the paranoid strands of shamanic retribution, my unconscious pulls out scenes from old movies, composing bits of memory to send me a personalized message. *It was only a dream.* I do for myself what the cacique does for Union: I pull out a fragment of mirror (rationality) and fix my sense of the real, reasserting the illusion of stability and easing the fear of misfortune.

The Possession of Young Girls

When fear of misfortune arises suddenly out of a particular historical conjuncture, there is no single sign that points to an instance of malign intent (as in only the hat remained and the macheteyed monkey). There is instead an overabundance of interrelated signs signifying major shifts in general conditions with unknown effects. The complexity of issues involved may overload the traditional system of narrative interpretation used to decipher probable cause and possible cure. This effect is exacerbated when terms of interpretation are replaced by the dominant terms of the nation-state and negotiations of change are moved to official arenas that submerge and marginalize forms of shamanic interpretation. At such times, the traditional system of interpretation may shift gears, supplementing discourse with sounds of the spirit.

While working in Cueva, I used to take breaks and go to the nearby town of Santa Fe. There I met a *kampuniú* medical doctor doing his required internship in the field, who told me a story that he never quite figured out how to think about. It had been two years earlier, in 1981, at the Twenty-fifth General Congress of the Emberá and Waunan. The first draft of a bill stipulating the functions of leadership and political "organisms" was presented—a historic step in the establishment of the proposed *comarca* ("Carta orgánica" 1970, in Herlihy 1986:185). The doctor was with all the congress participants in the schoolhouse in the center of the village. All of a sudden they all heard wild screaming. It came from a house nearby. He went to look. The screaming came from a young girl jumping about the house as if she were having an epileptic fit. Or so he first surmised. As he was examining her, however, he heard another scream. It came from a few houses away. And then another, and another. A consecutive chorus of girl's voices traveled around the village, tracing an arc around the schoolhouse. Later, the village head explained to the doctor: "The first young girl to scream brought a spirit with her from the Membrillo River. This spirit was passing among the girls."

The voice of a spirit *(hai)* brought by the body of a young girl—is that what everyone heard? And/or was it the voice of the people in the name of the spirit, who protested the official political event through the young girls, the class of community members most marginalized by the proceedings?[9] Where there is no narrative to fit the breadth of historical misfortune, interpretation winds around the center with a scream that everyone hears but no one owns.

Conclusion

The scenes described in this chapter show how nonspecialist Emberá use shamanic discourse to locate misfortune in terms of their broader experience. They experiment with interpretation to find the one that fits an unnatural or uncanny occurrence, one that can patch a break in the continuity of everyday life. Extending discernment into that which cannot be sensed directly, Emberá compose narratives using *hai,* the capricious spirit-mediators of history. The method avoids direct blame, lest misfortune be perpetuated in a cycle of retribution. The aim is to discover the path of peaceful restoration, the right reversal. The process of interpretation may not always work, but it always does give the Emberá the means to respond — and that in itself can be a cure. At times, shamanic interpretation tends to run away with itself or is too tentative to be reliable. It is then that interpreters can take advantage of coexistent systems of interpretation; then that Euramerican rationality can be pulled, like a white rabbit, out of the conceptual bag, diverting discussion. If misfortune does not recur, things usually correct themselves one way or another.

A hat shakes loose from the mundane, pointing only to lack, posing questions of the imagination. And from the imagination, the people's questions return, cured, mysterious and magical as ever. Renewed, the questions keep wait with hope, ready to seek sense in death's unpredictable desire — the next time.

seven

Scale of Sentient Beings
(Political Economy of Race and Gender)

Cultural identity is reproduced in a landscape of difference; for its part, difference defines the edges of the real. Consider the hearth the center of the universe; home, the place most familiar and safe. Moving outward from one's personal center, one finds others with whom one identifies: Emberá, the most fully human of all sentient beings. But Emberá fill only a small part of the world; they mark off that part as theirs, unifying it by repeating the particular patterns of the Emberá Way. Where there is juxtaposition with those who are different, boundaries are constructed. Using salient features of race, wildness, and tangibility, the landscape of experience is coded. These features also code the narratives that tell of Emberá interactions with those who are different. From these, a scale of sentient beings can be abstracted. Open and negotiable, the scale is a succession of qualitative difference that begins in the center and is ordered in relation to home (see Fig. 20).

Upriver is where the stories of Ancient Times figure the unknown, the territory of animals, like the axmen Woodpecker and Horned Lizard, who had speech and technical skill before the world changed (Chap. 2). Just beyond areas cleared for daily rounds of human activity, the forests upriver border an otherworld. There the devils *(hai),* those beings whose spirits are not anchored to form, slip into reality most readily. Tricky, they

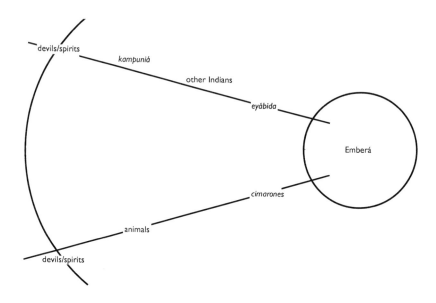

Figure 20. Scale of sentient beings.

appear as the image of one's sensual passion. Excitement and pleasure make one forget one's sense; reaching out, one is overcome with whirling dizziness. In the conceptual space between humans and animal/devils, the *cimarones* can be located. Those Emberá forced by the Conquest to resume a state of wildness, the *cimarones* shun contact with the outside world. They have even given up obtaining salt to cure their game, a key feature that distinguishes human from animal. Their feet, which have a neat slice cut in the tender part of the arch, carry them as swiftly as deer in the upriver forests of Darién, they say. Their tracks are seen still.[1]

Conquest fractured the upriver forest location of the unknown. Word of Spanish kings and queens and New York City skyscrapers provokes a radical departure from Ancient Time geography. Yet devils may also slip in from these new unknowns. Entering through market towns like Yaviza, post-Conquest devils may take the form of *kampuniá* (non-Indians) in order to disguise the sensation of strangeness they bear from the realm of death. In the moment before deadly embrace, devils may assume the figure of another race, combining the ambiguity of strangeness with the energy of taboo. In the brief instant between the time a human acquiesces to pleasure's attraction and the time the mistake is realized, death is touched, and in the devil slips. (There's little margin for error in desire. Suspicion must be both intense and constant.) On the scale of human difference, *kampuniá* humans, because they may hide devils, mark the edges of the real.

Sentience is feeling or sensation, as distinguished from perception and thought. Humans share sentience with animals, *cimarones, kampuniá,* and devils. By lending human order to difference, the scale of sentient beings interposes distance between familiarity and the unknown, life and death. I'm not sure whether ghosts are sentient. (They may be without feeling, given more to perception and thought.) Ghosts confound the scale; searching for what coexistence denied them, ghosts track the living right through quotidian experience. They haunt the center of the real, the key to their sensation's memory. So even as you and your kindred construct difference among the sentient so that you can live in similarity's safe haven (differences' reverse), the deaths of kin create dread paradox in the most intimate part of the real.

With devils and animals, the ghosts of ancestors animate the conceptual space that borders on death and the otherworld. As Emberá distance themselves from home, the loss of familiarity is a loss in the capacity for discernment. It becomes increasingly difficult to discern real world beings and otherworld beings. The symbolic significance of black-*kampuniá* is best understood in this context. As political economic mediators between Emberá and the outside world, black-*kampuniá* are located between Emberá and all other *kampuniá* (outsiders who have power to condition everyday life, despite their physical absence). As symbolic mediators between Emberá and the otherworld (outside as unknown), black-*kampuniá* are located between Emberá and devils/animals/*hai,* who may take on *kampuniá* guise. The duality of their roles is conflated in practice, making much social interaction with black-*kampuniá* a paradoxical combination of appreciation and fear for Emberá.

The scenes to follow, drawn from contemporary narratives of personal experience, focus on interactions between Emberá and others. Apropos of interracial boundaries, dialogue focuses on the production and resolution of fear — not because there are not also positively cheerful interchanges that happen at interracial boundaries, but because it is the dynamic of fear that is most easily exploited in the alienation of ethnic identities, one from another, in the creation of interest groups by a (militarized) democracy.

Figure 21. Emberá and gringa with peccary and dog. Photo by J. Benson.

Tracking interactions along the scale of sentient beings, first outward, then inward toward home, this chapter is a border zone pastiche that ties Darién's magical real to the politics of the nation-state.

Her Face Is a Sieve

Tuli Vieja is a an intricate image who walks the boundary on the edge of the real, in streams. She's a *kampuniá* devil, a post-Conquest personage at life's extreme. An old devil, she's an animal with breasts hanging down to her waists. Tuli Vieja's face is covered with little holes. Her long hair falls to the front, hiding the sieve face that sucks out the life from an unprotected human glance. She is called on to explain mysterious disappearances of children in personal-experience narratives. She calls for the magical reenactment of parental save-the-day Christian magic formulas. The credo *Our father who art in heaven,* spoken by a godparent of the stolen child, compels her to relinquish it. Emberá have seen her, as the following personal experi-

ence narrative recorded in Palo Blanco testifies. Abebaiba, the brother of a
man who saved a child from Tuli Vieja in Colombia, told it to me.

This happened to my brother.

My brother was the godfather.

The godfather, my brother.

So a *kampuniá*-woman woke up early.

She came.

Like our mother, "Let's go son."

And right then she pulled him by the hand.

The Tuli Vieja, they noticed.

Right then the father knew an animal had carried him off.

The father knew.

Then, on the other side [of the river], the deceased Kurichi, the godfather.

It is the godfather that can get him out by praying.

Praying well, the Our Father.

The old man went to find him.

And he got there, truth, about three in the afternoon.

He went up well above, the godfather.

He saw the boy's leg from above.

He went along the path.

Going then, on the edge of the mountain.

On the [river]bank, he had been taken.

The stream Hampávadó, it was called, it was in Colombia.

Then, then, he heard the scream. "Aiiiiiii!" Screaming.

And there went the godfather.

He was praying, the Tuli Vieja.

Maria Rosaria, she was called.

[SK: "She was named?"]

Yes, it was this she was named, Maria Rosaria.

Then, the godfather said thus:

"Maria Rosaria, that son, bring him here.

We're going to pray the Credo."

"Aiiiiiii!" she cried, Tuli Vieja.

She did not like that prayer.

Meanwhile, the old man was praying over there.

Then, truth, he found the son, he was standing.

Covered with the filth of Tuli Vieja.

He had fallen.

Tuli Vieja had put on a blue *paruma*.

The *paruma* is blue, blue. The face,

Is like a colander, a colander for *chicha,* a gourd with holes, thus.

This, it was here like this [miming her hair falling forward on her face].

Covered, so that her face is unseen.

It is the face that scares us. That [pointing his finger at his face]: little hole,
  little hole, little hole, like this.

Full of little holes like this.

One's entire face, like this, all.

This one, she covers it so that it cannot be seen.

Covers her face with hair so that it cannot be seen.

Truth, the godfather took the boy.

Took, brought, the old man.

It is the godfather that takes back the son when Tuli Vieja carries him off,
  the son.

And so it happens; Tuli Vieja, it is she who carries off children. (T/E)

Tuli Vieja's surreal ambivalence rides the crest of diffuse fears of difference mixed with unavoidable dependencies on *kampuniá*. With Tuli Vieja the terrors of Conquest are conjured for ritual reenactment. She is all the horrible excess that accompanies "civilization's" ideals. The power of lies, the awkward juxtaposition of race can be defeated with its own credo: icons of Spanish-*kampuniá* vanquished with Spanish-*kampuniá* logic. The magic words *Our Father* recall this Tuli Vieja (Maria Rosaria) to her own strange origins. Flung like a lance, the missionaries' words of power can release an innocent child. Misfortune is averted.

Tuli Vieja looks ugly, but like a straw man, she allows her combatants success. You even have to feel sorry for this kidnapper, forever lonely, walking at the edge of fate. Tagged by the concept of *kampuniá*, she is a fragment of mirror into which no one must glance, reflecting and resolving ambivalence in history.

Zones of Race and Development

There are some rough convergences in the way the Spanish manipulated racial difference during the early years of Conquest and colonization and the way that contemporary Panamanian leadership—with much international advice—rationalizes the zoning of territory according to race ("ethnicity") in Darién. Echoes from the past cast suspicion on development's purist aims, suggesting that while they seem to be designed to make life a bit better for the locals, they also go a long way toward organizing things so that nation-states can assume institutional control. There is the paradox of "equality," for instance. Two years after Colombia's independence from Spain came the law of 1821 establishing the equality of Indians as a race. As a result, the Indians lost their protected status and the land reserves that the Crown had set aside in their name. For blacks born before independence, equality (freedom from slavery) was not granted until 1851. Freed into the lowland forest, already home to several generations of enslaved ancestors, the blacks had to move into territory inhabited by Emberá and Waunan, return to work for the Spanish as "freed" laborers (the *libres*), or get arrested on the basis of vagrancy laws that replaced slavery laws (Arocha 1992:29). The migration of freed blacks into territories inhabited by Emberá and Waunan divided their chains of dispersed settlements into small enclaves and pushed others further upriver into the more inaccessible and less fertile headwaters of the Chocó and Darién (Castrillón 1982:129, 156).[2] In general, there has been relatively little intermarriage between the races. For the most part, Emberá practice endogamy, marrying other Emberá, or related indigenous people who fall into their category of *eyábida,* including Waunan, their sister linguistic group, and Catio (but not Kuna or Guaymi, the other two major indigenous groups in Panama).

In Darién, as time passed, the blacks and Indians were left more or less to themselves. Together they have worked out a reciprocal system of survival without much interference from large plantation owners or corporations. Blacks living and working in the towns and lower reaches of the rivers have entered into trading, shopkeeping, government service, and farming. In buying the bulk of agricultural produce (plantains) from Emberá upriver, trading produce for goods in urban markets, and selling the goods to each other and to the Emberá, blacks have kept the local economy going. While this arrangement has allowed the blacks who have lived in downriver towns greater access to education, health care, and money, it has also allowed the Emberá to continue obtaining things that they themselves do not produce while living in relative isolation upriver. The bi-racial political economic agreement has been enhanced by social exchange in the context of trade, service and travel, as well as special relationships like god-parenthood, which recycle some of the blacks' wealth back to Emberá.[3]

However, Torrijos's interventions altered the conditions under which this biracial agreement has stood. Some months after the 1969 coup, when the general assumed full control over the Panamanian government, he declared: "Having finished with the oligarchy, the Panamanian has his own worth independent of his origin, his cradle, or where he was born." And so a proclamation of (male) equality, just like the one applied to Indians in the 1821 Colombian law, is restated 150 years later. Once again, the apparently positive moral creed is shaded with ambivalence when its specific effects are considered. While Torrijos's "revolutionary government" has led to the institutionalization of Emberá politics and the reorganization of people and territory into village and *comarca,* the same policy activated a dormant agrarian reform program that built the highway and moved in land-hungry *colono* farmers and ranchers. To my knowledge, there has been no effort of this magnitude to enhance the rights and resources of the blacks in Darién, who made up a regional majority according to the 1972 census (OAS 1978:247).[4]

In 1972, the Torrijos government rewrote the national constitution, instituting a system of local representation by districts. Polling booths were set up in all new Emberá villages upriver and in all new *colono* villages on the highway. The electoral power the blacks held over the region began to diminish. The loss of their control over regional elections, competition for the cargo boat trade brought by the highway, and challenges to their customary property rights both within and without the proposed *comarca* are new conditions that undermine the traditional dominance held by local blacks in Darién. In direct contradiction with the proclamation of everybody's "own worth independent of origin," the actions of the Torrijos and later the Noriega governments had differential effects on the races/ethnicities of Darién. These differential effects, and the tensions between Indians and blacks that have resulted, may be no accident. Centuries before, Spanish colonial administrators also found that antagonistic relations between blacks and Indians were an aid to controlling the colony. They imposed rigid legal separation, phrased in the religious terms of the times (protecting the Indians' faith), to support this antagonism (Pavy 1967:116). In that time, the Spanish failed to get the Indians to move into villages; in his time, Torrijos succeeded. In the late twentieth century, the structure of dominance continues to shift toward distant incorporative systems of control. As the region becomes more integrated into nation-state and world markets, the ideology that accompanies military force in the production of wealth for foreigners has changed from organized religion to secular humanism. What has not changed is the reliance on race as the basis for social and economic division.

In sum, there are some odd consistencies between early Conquest and colonization and contemporary development strategies. These include the differential application of the idea of equality, the concentration of populations within racially homogeneous but distinct areas, and the cultivation of antagonism between groups divided by race and territory. In this context, the system of signification (cf. Comaroff 1985:4) that underlies the geography of race—the one I call the scale of sentient beings—maintains its relevance. Drawing on this mythico-geographic set of boundary markers, the Emberá renegotiate current events. As the prefixes *post-* and *neo-* before colonialism are inserted with the times, changes and repetitions are registered in their narratives of everyday and official life.

The dominance the blacks have enjoyed over the Indians has not occurred without some resentment. As the blacks voted themselves in as authorities of state, they have taken advantage. The nonlocal black-*kampuniá* chief of the U.S. antimalarial program (SNEM) offered a hypothetical situation as an example: An Indian would ask $10 for a pig, and the *libre* would say, "Forget it, I'll give you $8." Then he would just take the pig, and the Indian wouldn't say anything. Or, says a Colombian black who lives among the Emberá: In the time before Torrijos, when Indians got down to Yaviza, they were forced to work at assorted tasks like clearing someone else's yard or hauling. And if they didn't want to do it, they'd have to pay to get out of it. In their capacity as representing the law of the nation, black-*kampuniá* also mediated disputes that occurred between Emberá. Eva's husband, the village head of Tamarinbó, told me one story about a dispute over pigs and how it got resolved with a black authority of local renown. He remembered it from his youth in Sambu, before the time his father took him *paseando* (traveling) up the Tupisa River to find a wife. Sambu is the region of the Emberá *comarca* that lies along the Pacific coast. Most accessible to the Chocó, it is the part of Darién that the Emberá settled first and most densely.

> Manawa's pigs were eating my father's corn. (I was away in school at Gara-
> chiné at the time [1950s?].) My father gave him four warnings, but he took
> no care. Finally, my father put bullets in his rifle, shot three of the pigs, and

caught the fourth. He informed Manawa, then went down to town to the magistrate. At this time the magistrate was named Juan Duaya, a black-*kampuniá* who is now dead. Juan Duaya was a fearsome man. My father brought the pig as proof and told his story. Juan Duaya called Manawa down. Manawa said, "I want this man to pay for the pigs he killed." But Duaya said, "No, he will not pay. And what's more," and he turns to my father and said, "How much do you want to charge for the corn eaten?" "Five dollars per *mazorca,* but I'll take fifty dollars for the lot," my father said. And Manawa had to pay right there. That man Duaya was a fearsome man! (T/E)

When Emberá come downriver to town, they are in the territory of others. They participate with caution, enjoying some things (like basketball) and shunning others (like cockfights). The following scene, excerpted from my field notes, sketches holiday events in Yaviza.

Fiesta for San Francisco and the Official Opening of the Highway

On March 12, 1985, I fly into Yaviza, arriving on the third day of a four-day celebration. I've never seen the town so lively. The highway extension isn't actually complete, but in honor of the official opening, cars are allowed through. Vendors from everywhere are selling their wares. Music is blaring from inside the *cantinas;* tables of frying foods are lined up on the sidewalk. *Cholos* are down from the rivers, *libres* in from all the regional towns, *colonos* from the highway, and government workers and politicians from Panama City. The milling crowd is intoxicated by alcohol and the feverish atmosphere of cockfighting. I join a crowd of all ages and ethnicities watching the games at the basketball court. Organized by home town or village, the teams strut in their bright, cigarette-sponsored uniforms. The largest Emberá village, Union-Chocó, coached by the president of the Emberá Teacher's Association, loses against Pinogana (*cholos* vs. *libres*). (The *cholos* have been practicing in their courts upriver, but their average height puts them at a distinct disadvantage against the *libres*.) Yaviza is dazzling against Chepigana (*libres* vs. *libres*). Tucked away in shady backyard spots, politicians and government officials sit around, with plenty of booze, cigarettes, and food on plastic-covered tables to smooth their transactions. Big shots talk while little shots try to get their two cents in (e.g., a *colono* comes up and asks about his grazing land that falls within the domain of the wildlife park). The man from MIDA (agency that regulates swine and cattle) tells him it depends whether he can follow the rules, which are made by COPFA (agency that monitors hoof-and-mouth disease). Everybody is dressed up and gay; those who have neither money nor enthusiasm stay away from the central streets.

The gallery reserved for cockfighting events has been outfitted with a new wall. Fights have been going on continuously since Saturday, intensity mounting. Between fights, the men stand outside holding their cocks, discussing and placing bets. The *colonos,* easy to identify in their Panama hats, make a strong showing for the highway; *libres* represent the various towns. Emberá are scarce. As you go in, a man says something like, "Give something for the saint," and you're supposed to pay a quarter. Earlier that day, before I arrive for a peek in, one guy didn't want to pay a quarter, and a big fight broke out. He grabbed a knife and then a hammer that had been lying around. The crowd packed inside moved back out on to the street. When the guard moved in with rubber hoses, the fight stopped. People squeeze in the gallery until it's packed shoulder to shoulder. It's a circular arena with about four or five tiers. The owners of the cocks stand below with the big bettors around the edge. Thrown abruptly into the ring, the cocks peck at each other with spurred feet (no razors). The fight I see is agonizingly slow: peck, peck, peck, slowly necks cover with blood, agony. The crowd loses patience, longing for a quick, exciting fight. People are shouting, changing bets at every turn. The captain of the cargo boat *Surpresa* is down in the center holding a fistful of dollars. Everybody is waving bills around. The level of aggression is superhigh.

Like basketball teams, cocks represent particular communities. Depending on the cock owner, the fight represents a battle of ethnic groups (*libre*-town vs. *colono*-highway) or community (*libre*-Chepigana vs. *libre*-Yaviza)—at least the macho side of ethnicity and community. Betting is structured accordingly: if you live in El Real, you better bet El Real. All the bets go down on a list. People are supposed to be honest about reporting bets they place with each other and on each cock; apparently the cock owner gets a percentage of the take. As anyone can bet on any cock at any point in the game, I'm not sure how the system functions. In any case, it looks like many thousands of dollars get passed around. I suppose the money circulates from primary sources like owners of big cargo boats and stores to various bettors with less access to capital and, if some is left over after the partying, back to women and children in home communities.

Bred for spectacle, and read as social text, the cocks imbue men's bets with bloody passion; the fierce pain of the cocks tracks the course of men's poverty and wealth; the cocks' bravery or loss enlarges men's pride or shame (cf. Geertz 1973:412–54). The Emberá are not generally attracted to this spectacle; they stand outside the cockfight as social text. The equation of money, masculinity, and blood that seems to motivate it does not jibe with their cultural dispositions and habits (cf. Bourdieu 1985:72).[5] If an Emberá man has a lot of money, the last thing he will do is publicize the fact. If Emberá display wealth at all, it is only after cash has been exchanged for material goods (e.g., I notice that Dante's son has a new red shirt, some new gold teeth, a pair of running shoes, and a waterproof watch) — and even this might be done with some trepidation. An egalitarian ethic, a pervasive lack of money and material goods, fear of shamanic retribution, and nervousness about entering an aggressive arena with racial others are factors that dampen the gambling spirit of Emberá in this context. As the new highway widens the provincial scope of Yaviza Town, they approach public life in their own distinctive way.

National Context of *Comarca* Politics

The struggle for the proposed *comarca,* Emberá Drua, is the central metaphor in the politics of village formation. Asserting their rights in the landscape, the Emberá forestall *colono* invasion and retake some of the local power their dispersion upriver once afforded the blacks. But Emberá involvement in the *comarca* process is also part of a larger process of reorganizing people, territory, and resources that exceeds Emberá interests. This larger process, framed in terms of modernization and development, redefines territory and resources as private, communal, or public property and replaces customary use and ownership practices that rely on verbal agreement with legal ownership based on written documentation. On the regional scale, territory is divided into zones for differential development. In plans for Darién (e.g., OAS 1978, 1984), differences in development correspond to differences in race and, in the case of the wildlife park, in species. Building on mythico-historical distinctions between the races, zoning tends to rigidify distinctions and test the limits of interracial reciprocity.

Ascriptions of race to upriver, downriver, and highway areas are generalizations that obscure the extent of mixing. Inconsistencies become nodes of potential conflict. For instance, there are Emberá and Waunan villages along the highway. Situated outside of the proposed *comarca,* the people who live in these villages identify with the new politics of the *co-marca* process as a unifying endeavor for the Emberá and Waunan people as indigenous group in a multiethnic nation. Territorially, however, they are peripheral to discussion. Not protected from *colono* incursion of their lands, villages along the highway like Cueva are becoming incipient sites of interracial confrontation.[6] In addition, there are blacks who have built farms in the mid reaches of the rivers, some of which fall within proposed *comarca* bounds. They worry about what rights they and their descendants will be granted in *comarca* legislation.

There is the case of Mejía, a prominent black man who owns plantain orchards up and down the Chico River. One of the closest rivers to Yaviza, trade links were established in the Chico early on. I first heard of Mejía when I was studying land use in Palo Blanco. He owns a large orchard abutting what has since become Palo Blanco, a relatively large village of forty households surrounded by a number of dispersed settlements. As the village grew, land good for growing plantains became scarce. There were already several households in the village that did not have any place to plant them. It was well into the dry season when I was there, and even people who did have orchards did not have enough plantains to eat, much less enough to sell. At village meetings, they discussed the problem that some people were taking plantains from other folks' orchards without permission. At times like these, it becomes apparent that despite all the changes accompanying village formation, one fundamental thing has not changed: the Emberá continue to rely on plantains for both cash and subsistence. Despite highway extension and agricultural development efforts to diversify markets and crops (to include rice, corn, and yams), plantains still provide the primary economic base for the Emberá. The same goes for the blacks in the towns, who depend on buying and transporting what the Emberá produce.

With unusual foresight and willingness to work out of town, Mejía built himself and his descendants a small empire of plantain orchards upstream. (He's well known for fathering many children of mixed race.) When I got to Yaviza, I interviewed him about his thoughts on the *comarca* and took down the following notes:

[July 10, 1985] Back around 1942, I had the only store in the area of Palo Blanco. It was I who built the paths upriver. [Actually, he sponsored work parties in which he gave Indians *guarapo* (fermented sugarcane) in exchange for their labor; they drank and worked.] The paths I built enabled the Indians in the area to come buy in my store and send their kids to school. The first school was there until 1955, when it moved to Marañon. I was born in Panama. [I'd heard from someone in Palo Blanco that he was a Colombian who came as a young man and married a Panamanian teacher.] In the 1940s, life was easy. We sold rubber and *raisilla* (ipecac), and of course there was raising pigs. During World War II, it got difficult to buy oil, but in the hill in front of Palo Blanco there was lots of *trupa* (a palm, E. *uruta*), from which we got all the oil we needed. And of course, at the time one could always kill thirty or forty toucans to eat, whatever.

[SK: What do you think about the *comarca*?] Of course, I'm worried. Listen to this story: I had a friend in the Tuquesa [River]. All of a sudden, he turned a cold shoulder on me and said that all *libres* should be thrown out of the *comarca*. Well, I got him drunk, and finally he told me why the about-face. Apparently his daughter married the son of the head of the big village downriver, who was also first cacique at this time. The cacique promised his new in-law my farm when the *comarca* comes through!

[SK: What about the fact that you hold a large proportion of a growing Emberá community's land base? Do you think that some sort of tax might compensate?] I've been working hard in the region for forty or fifty years, and for the first twelve years there were no motors. We had to do all traveling by pole. [This is still the case for most Emberá.] And, this I've explained over and over again to the Indians. Although I own twenty-eight *kabuyas* of land, I have twenty-eight children. [SK: It is said you own much more land than this, all along the river.] Well actually, I am the administrator of several other orchards [whose owners are also *libres*]. You know, the Indian is not a worker. It was the Colombians, coming in search of rifles, shotguns, and merchandise, who stayed two years and then went home, who did most of the labor in the orchards. But, you know, the Colombians of good custom have since gone home to stay. The National Guard treats Colombians so badly that only the bad ones stay. Anyway, it is these peons who developed the orchards of Darién to be what they are today.

But you know, the Indians basically like and respect me because I led the first strike to raise plantain prices from twenty-five cents per hundred. This was about twenty years ago. Everybody got in on the strike. But the National Guard zoned in on me as the head, and they were going to beat the shit out of me when a bunch of *libres* barged into the jail saying: "What are you doing with Mejía?" After that there was a meeting and the biggies came from Panama and the price went up. This was way before *Jumarasó*.[7] Then came Torrijos. I ran against the Emberá (L. Lino) for legislator in the party of Arnulfo Arias this year. And I won. I had Yaviza and the highway behind me. But they threw the ballot box in the water. The Indians didn't vote for me because the government put it in their heads that if Arnulfo wins, he'll bring all the other *interianos (colonos)* to settle in Darién. But this wouldn't happen. (−T/S)

Some Emberá did fear that if the opposition parties were to come to power, they would lose everything they had gained by cooperating with the military government. At the very least they feared they would be once again ignored, made to suffer in scorned isolation as they were before Torrijos. Whether or not it was best to vote as a unified group siding with the military party (PRD) was a matter for sideline dispute among a few Emberá when I did fieldwork. The debate intensified as the legitimacy of Noriega's government was challenged by the United States.[8] As a representative of the opposition party, Mejía brushed aside the Indians' concerns. And like many who still perceive Darién to be a vast untapped forest, he thinks it unnecessary to reserve Indian land. Leaving stereotypes and contradictions aside, Mejía's sentiment about the *comarca* is shared by some Emberá, mostly those who still live in dispersed sites and/or who own rights to substantial property. One Emberá elder, one of the first to settle in the Tupisa River, secure in his landholdings, thinks that the *comarca* is not that good of an idea because it increases the difference and the tensions between two ethnic groups that have always been separate but interdependent economically. I heard his opinion secondhand from García, a part–North American Indian, Vietnam vet who lives at times in Yaviza and at times in the bush panning gold. In agreement, he quoted the Emberá elder referring to the blacks as saying: "We've always needed each other, why separate?"[9] While there are voices of dissent among the Emberá, it must be emphasized that the majority do voice support for the *comarca*. Although antagonism with black neighbors and tradespersons is generally considered undesirable, the *comarca* represents a double hope (1) that sufficient forest resources will be reserved to allow the Emberá and Waunan to live a good and healthy life as agriculturists, hunters and gatherers within Darién; and (2) that organizing themselves as a political body will allow them to participate in the progressive aspects of modernization in greater Panama.

Party-based political opposition, such as Mejía represents, challenged Noriega's regime through the ballot box. But the people of Darién also represented a different kind of threat. The strong alliance that blacks and Indians formed with each other in remote isolation is oriented toward the Chocó of Colombia—a strong reminder that drawing an international boundary on a map does not in itself constitute a break in cultural and historical continuity. The military regime would not gain dominance here merely by throwing ballot boxes in the water. They needed to split the interracial alliance and its eastward orientation. By instituting change differentially by race, as in the case of the *comarca* process, the regime could set the conditions that would lead to increasing tensions between Indians and blacks in the context of everyday social interaction. They could also take advantage of the fears resulting from senseless acts of violence that have been accompanying transnational capitalization and migration. The military regime used the intensification of tension in these troubled times for its own insidious advantage.

A Double Chocoano Murder and an Indian's Land

The Tupisa River is one of the many minor routes migrants use to cross the mountains between Panama and Colombia. Tamarinbó, just past the COPFA guard post, is the first village people find coming down into the lowlands. The American dollar in Panama draws the black Colombians from the Chocó (called Chocoanos or *libres*), who go back and forth between home and wage labor. There is quite a bit of interchange between the black Chocoanos who live permanently in Yaviza and those in the Chocó. Many Yaviseños still identify as Chocoano, even though they were born in Darién after it became Panama. Friendships arise between the Emberá and Chocoanos who are regular migrants, traders in town, or farmers in the lower and middle reaches of the rivers. But the ones who are strangers, preceded by bad reputation, are cause for concern. A personal-experience narrative that Eva told me illustrates the tense mixture of violence and vulnerability that sometimes shatters the peace of the upriver forests.

Late March, on our trip upriver to get wild foods to bring home for Easter, we passed the place called *chorromai kampuniá peútumá* — the waterfall where the Chocoanos were killed. Dark green vines grew down, clinging to the sides of the watery rock face. Eva told me the story as we pushed the canoe upstream. It went like this:

> The two Chocoanos were working for an Emberá man, one of Eva's uncles.
> The men decided to go home to Colombia to spend Easter with their
> wives and then come back again after the holiday. Eva's uncle had not paid
> them yet. They were to receive the money owed them upon return. But the

Chocoana Laura, who lived in the dispersed site upriver where Dante lives now, did not know that they hadn't gotten paid. She figured they had a lot of money. She and the man who worked for her plotted to kill them. The man went after the two with a rifle. He shot the first one, who was walking behind the other, in front of the waterfall. His body was found on the beach. The second one heard the shots and started running, but he couldn't climb the steep cliff that edges the bend. He climbed the wild cashew tree, and it was there, from across the river, that the other blew him away. It turned out they had nothing but a plastic for sleeping on, a pot, and some plantains. They were going to fish on their way.

At the same time, the people from the Emberá villages of Natal, Promesa, and Tamarinbó—many people—were traveling up to Tambó for the pre-Easter week of *monteando*. First they saw one body on the beach—bloated, in a long-sleeved red shirt, arms stuck straight up in the air. [Eva mimes.] Both bodies were already rotting badly. The people sent a little paper down to the Law in Yaviza, and the National Guard came up. Even a doctor came to do a postmortem, what kind of bullets, rifle, etc. Then they found the rifle in the Chocoana's house. But somehow the culprits had a chance to escape. They went back to Colombia. The Law remained silent for some time. The two figured it was all forgotten about and came back to the Chocoana's house. As soon as the Law sensed them, they picked them up and put them in prison. [I asked Eva why they didn't send a little paper to the Law when her father was killed. First, she said, one needed a lot of money for that. When I protested, she said that her brother remains silent, and as he's the *barón* (male), she does nothing.] (−T/S)

Incidents of senseless brutality fuel fear. The Emberá observe with anxiety the Chocoanos' murdering each other.[10] For nothing the men were killed, they had nothing but a plastic for sleeping and a pot and some plantains. Someone thought they were paid some dollars for their labor before they left; that was what brought death. One must proceed through life with great personal secrecy. For this, the Emberá prefer to place their families at least a bend apart even from other Emberá. Vision accords certain power. It is best to reduce the likelihood that someone can watch you while you are unaware. Anybody. This feeling is intensified in relation to those with whom you share less, those whose skin is darker and who have soft crinkly hair and put otter in their stew—unless you know them, or they have been become godparents of Indian children.

The formation of villages contradicts this tendency toward protective isolation; at the same time, the formation of villages provides greater security from unexpected violence. The Noriega government exploited these fears, drawing support from the Emberá in exchange for gestures of protection.

The Oppressor Is Also the Protector: Dealing with the Guard

Six years after the Guard came and took the Chocoana to prison for murder, they came back. The bush had grown up on the place, and they said the folks round here wanted some Indian to take over the place, not a Chocoana. So Dante, an Emberá man kin to the Tamarinbó folks (one of Grandfather Onofre's nephews who came from the Baudó River in the Chocó via Sambu), agreed to settle his family on the spot the Chocoana lived, which was just upriver from the village.[11]

Customary ownership practices are based on use. If you work a piece of forest, clearing and planting, or inheriting or buying it from someone and tending for it, it is rightfully yours. But if you abandon it, after six or seven years generally, someone else can come and lay claim to it.[12] There is some ambiguity and conflict inherent in taking over abandoned land, for one isn't sure whether the original owners will return. But Dante had the backing of the national military, in whose interest it is to secure Darién as a resource base drawing revenues for Panama, at the same time using the forest as a barrier to Colombia (and as was confirmed by Noriega's trial, as a hidden place to process cocaine). To control back-and-forth migration — in the context of international development and conservation programs — the zoning plans for the Darién map the gap according to race, such that the remote border zone is inhabited by allied Indians and wildlife. Military and development strategy is not inconsistent with the perspective of many Emberá, who fear the violence that some migrants bring from Colombia.

In the Darién of 1985, Noriega was still riding out the popular paternalism of the Torrijos regime. And the Emberá were feeling the protective as well as oppressive aspects of military dictatorship. Once retreat upriver became a strategy with no future, the Emberá held out their hands and signed their names in the hope that advantage would tilt to them. Many became soldiers in the Guard. To the frustration of Panama's opposition forces, most voted PRD. In the meantime, the state exploited cultural distances encoded in the scale of sentient beings, formalizing differences into boundaries between zones of race.

I took the following notes at a regional congress in the Chico River, village of Corona (the same one in which I was seeking permission to work, see Chap. 1). A not atypical series of requests show how the Emberá tried to make their votes yield protective services from the Guard. The requests reveal not only the fear Emberá have of outsiders but also the mistrust Emberá have of their own chosen leaders. It is apparent that resistance to political economic organization above the level of household has by no means disappeared with village formation. The meeting fell between May 1984, when Noriega was said to have fixed the election that put President Barletta in power, and late 1985, when Hugo Spadafora's headless body was found in a mailbag on the Costa Rican border. Even as "the democratic cloak over Noriega's violent rule was being stripped away (La Feber 1989:196–97)," things seemed to be going more or less well toward establishment of the Emberá *comarca*.[13]

[September 17, 1984, first morning session, parliamentary procedure in force] Big claps for the Forces of Defense [new name for the National Guard]. The major in charge of the Darién region, headquartered in La Palma, wanted to know of any difficulties they were having. Only men spoke: the Emberá Legislative Representative (L. Lino) brought up the problem raised earlier about the Guard coming to the villages and sending Emberá to work in Yaviza. Lino explained judiciously that it was not like the old days, when anybody could grab an *indígena* and make him work like a slave. Various other problems were mentioned. The third cacique, whose jurisdiction is Sambu, asked the major to tell the sergeant in Sambu to help him. (The cacique hopes the military will bolster his authority.) The head of the Emberá Teachers Union got up to say there were Colombianos running around Union-Puente (the black village adjoining Union-Chocó) scaring people. A village head presents a case, going on for several years, of one man owing another man $600 or their value in plantains. The same village head wants the army to do something about Sorgano, a sharp bend in the Chico River with a dangerous whirlpool, where people say the mythical river serpent Hëi lived (or where they used to believe he lived) [see Fig. 7]. The major said he'd present the case to the proper authorities — maybe they could help dynamite the river bend. The legislative representative (L. Lino) asked that the Guard help protect the *comarca* from marauding Colombianos and foreign gold-diggers. The Guard said they might assign a guard to the border area in question. Another man said there were eighty-eight Colombianos digging gold, not in the *comarca*, but near enough so that if an *indígena* goes hunting, they would kill him. More about illegal entry. . . . The head of Palo Blanco has problems with an Emberá in his village who won't cooperate with group work projects, and he'd like outside help, or advice. The head of the village we're in wants a soldier stationed in his own community. [Most villages did not have soldiers in them, but if they did, they were usually Emberá themselves.]

Violence of the few feeds paranoia to subjects of the state, undermining the positive bases for relationship between Emberá and blacks in Darién, upon which local peace has been achieved. To name the people you can trust, your system demands more divisive distinction. Whom can you talk to without feeling danger? Colombiano from old or Colombiano from now; *libres;* Chocoanas; Darienitas: all the same American-born people of African ancestry who cross over between the lowland forest on either side of a not very high range of mountains. Yet there is some truth to the idea that their ways have been shaped by different balances of brutality and compassion. The question arises the moment you cross their path.

Panama City Bar Scene

Day to day, things usually proceed in a lighter vein. Going by a row of black *kampuniá* poling the river in canoes, familiar greetings are called out: *hermano, tío, primo, compa* (brother, uncle, cousin, Godfather [from S. *compadre*]). Then, soon as they round the bend, some comment is spoken that brings attention to race. Acknowledgment is transient, just long enough to pole in opposite directions in the river or make a trade or present a case or ask for a place to sleep the night. Exchange among familiar strangers is expected and respected with curious restraint. Because they are much rarer, exchanges with gringo *kampuniá* can be more suspicious. They have their own strange origin and history further from the everyday real. (In Darién, *gringo* refers to any Caucasian of European descent, except for Spanish.) The white gringo *kampuniá* who stay for a time in Darién are few, usually a smattering of priests, missionaries, gold-diggers, and, more recently, conservationists and scholars. As representatives of the centers of transnational powers, they are somewhat awful (in both senses of the word). The myth of incredible riches and God's grace does not cancel strangeness, for assuming alluring image is just play for devils. Here's a personal-experience narrative about interracial communication among a twenty-five-year-old Emberá from Palo Blanco, Río Chico, his black friend from the Caribbean community of Panama City, and a gringa whom they met in a bar. The Emberá told me:

> I was working construction in Panama [City], earning about $1.50 an hour. This was quite good. [In 1985, minimum wage for unskilled labor was 70 cents an hour.] Every week I saved $50.00 with the owner of the company, and took $40.00 to spend. [Note that he must have been working ten hours a day, six days a week, to bring this home.] I had a black [*chombo*] friend that spoke English, and we'd go to a bar together, where people from all countries went, gringos too. It was expensive: $1.00 for a soda, $2.00 for a rum and milk. I'd buy one drink and sip it real slow while I watched the women. There was a gringa who seemed to be attracted to me. My friend would translate for me, and she knew Spanish too. But I was afraid. I'd never been with a gringa before, although I've been with some Chiricanas [women of Spanish descent from Chiriqui]. I thought maybe she would kill me. . . . I didn't know. . . .
>
> This went on for some time. Each weekend my friend and I went to the bar, until one time, she sat on my lap and started kissing me. Well, you know it's expensive to go with a gringa, $25.00 an hour. I did go with her, and it was just the same as the Chiricanas. And after this, I used to go with gringas a lot. I even had an *oficial* [official (girlfriend)] who lived in the Zone. I used to give her money from my paycheck. We used to go out together and do all kinds of things; we'd go *paseando* [cruising] in a car. My brother married a gringa who lives in Panama City. I don't know why my brother didn't press me to marry the one I had. [He was so wistful. I asked: But you're here now; are you married to an Emberá woman?] Yes. [SK: Kids?] Only one little girl. It's all the same. (−T/S)

Sexual desires bounce off culture's strangeness scale, but, after repeated chances, transcend culture's artifice. Gone off to the city, this young man broke through the fears that prop up social categories designating acceptable and unacceptable sexual partners to find the edge of fear a fiction. It's all the same with one of another race, he learns, caught up and advantaged by a cash economy that drives its own dynamics, prevailing over a sexual economy that is, for many still, defined more neatly by endogamous code. But most Emberá still stay among their own, where there are fewer contexts for social interaction to develop between races and where sexual distance is more natural. This man's story was unusual anyway. Most of the stories that return from the big city confirm, not dispel, anxieties of interracial contact.

Upriver with Eva

Tupisa is one route migrants may take when they cross the mountains to Colombia. From there, they may go straight downriver, or cross westward through the forest to Tuquesa. Taking that river down, they reach the highway past Yaviza and avoid military review. Remote as it may seem, experience in the upriver forests is not untouched by transnational economic differentials that induce labor migration. When Emberá traverse their domain in daily food-gathering activities, meetings with strangers are not uncommon.

Eva and I set off about 8:00 A.M. one day, following her son Gregorio, who had gone on ahead. He was going hunting with Ivan, the *libre* COPFA official who lived at the post, built where the Preciada flows into the Tupisa. The hunters were to take the straighter path through the forest with the dog. Eva and I were to go around in the river, hauling the big COPFA canoe. We would meet them where the path comes out of the forest and would give them a lift back. While we waited for Gregorio, who, finding Ivan with bullets to spare, had gone back to the village to get his rifle, Eva and I crossed the river to check a beach a little ways up the Preciada. There in the sand we saw footprints of paca (E. *përöwära*). When Gregorio came back, he was with a friend from Promesa, and both were riding horses. Eva and I set out upriver to cut *guineo* (banana) in orchards adjoining abandoned house sites.

First we stop at the orchard of Eva's Aunt Beatriz on the left bank. It was overgrown, and *sicatoca,* the disease RENARE has been warning about, had struck. Most of the *guineos* were not producing. We loaded only one small bunch in the canoe before continuing upriver. We were walking the canoe over a rocky section of white water when suddenly we came upon two figures sitting on the left bank. Before they saw us, Eva says in a hushed voice: "Should we beat it downriver?" Me with my great eyesight didn't know what was going on. I figured they were the teenage Emberá couple who had passed us before going upriver to collect firewood. She whispers again: "Let's go down [river]." And I thought, jeez, after lugging the canoe all the way uphill already, what's the big deal (figuring she was being overly sensitive about lovers' privacy or something)? Finally I caught on, but so did the figures in the distance. They'd seen us and were gesturing wildly from the bank. Signaling—five days—six days—no food—help! They were two *paisas* from Colombia, another couple of poor souls to wander down to Tamarinbó half-dead from the perilous journey across the mountains. The problem for us was what people say, that sometimes these guys are real desperadoes, murderous criminals escaping justice in their own country, capable of anything. So naturally, as two unarmed women alone, we were, to say the least, hesitant to go near. So there we stood for a full five minutes holding the canoe steady in the middle of the river. Eva says again: "Let's go down?" I didn't know what to do, and she said with her usual deference: "It's you who know." What the hell. I've never been here before, but how can you turn away? So we pulled over to the beach, and they came round the bank to meet us. They'd been walking six days, the last two with no food. They even tried to eat plantains green. We were the first people they'd seen since their guide, taking a watch in payment, took them over the pass and told them Panama was two days down, that way. One was Peruvian, the other Colombian. They both had passports, but the Colombian didn't want to pass by the post. They asked us for food, but we had none. We told them they were almost to the village. As we parted, who comes out of the bush but Eva's husband, Rubén, the village head, with fishing spear and goggles. He looked over their papers.

After that incident, the three of us went on together. The next stop was Aunt Beatriz's orchard on the right bank. The old previllage house was there, all fallen. We looked for some sugarcane to suck, but someone had already eaten all the mature stalks. Since no one was cleaning up here, most of it hadn't grown back edible. The pineapples grew large but didn't flower or have spines. We did find two nice bunches of *guineos* high up. Eva made deep vertical cuts in the trunk with her machete until the tree creaked juicily over, away from its neighbors. Then she hacked through the fallen tree, pulling out the bunch, watching out for the clear liquid that gushes from the trunk and stains clothing. We left these bunches sitting half in the river to be picked up on our way back down. As we left, Eva said gaily: "The canoe is the horse of the Emberá. This way we transport cargo, plantains. Everything." While we were busy on land, Rubén was sailing facedown in the current trying to catch *humpé* and *koromá* (armored catfish), the staple protein source eaten with green plantains or *guineos*.

Next stop upriver was the orchard of Aunt Beatriz's son. When we walked in, we heard grunting! *Kuriwa* (agouti). We found what it had been gobbling: *ëräka,* a large wild palm tree with clusters of red (unripe) and black (ripe) fruit at the base. (The outside of this fruit is filled with red dye that can be scraped to use for body and basketry paint. The many little seeds inside can be ground and cooked with plantains.) There were lots of other fruit trees as well: cacao, mango, *guineo*. After leaving there, we went upriver to reach the meeting place of the hunters. It was beautiful there. We waited a short time, but they didn't come. (Gregorio didn't get home till dark and never caught anything.) I took some compass readings as we went downriver fast and easy with the current.

Postscript: I talked to the *paisas* the next day. They'd spent the day swinging machetes in exchange for meals. Their bodies seem to be recovering, but their minds were definitely blown. They'd seen skeletons propped up against trees and clothes strewn all along (wet clothes rub skin raw). Since they didn't know the way, they'd come straight down the river, steep, forceful, rocky. They were scared out of their minds, especially at night, when they slept on little dry islands in the river: they might easily have been swept away by *creciente* (rising current). The Colombian was upset because he had left his city shoes out to dry on the floor of the house and somebody swiped them. The village head said he couldn't do anything about it. (I guess *paisa* border crossers are fair game.)

Home

In contrast to *kampuniá* border zones, it is not dramatic events that lend character to the home but the repetition of the uneventful. The mundane pattern of everyday life is reality's center, the Emberá Way.

To enter an Emberá house, one climbs a *tumé,* a log into which comfortably spaced notches have been cut. The bottom end fits in a hollow worn into the ground; the top end leans into a corner formed by the floor and a jutting support beam. In addition to providing stable ascent, the *tumé* politely signals the receptiveness of house residents. When residents are home and guests are welcome, the *tumé* is up with notches facing outward; when residents go out briefly or for some reason do not want guests or dogs climbing up, notches face inward; when people leave for an extended period, out on a day's hunt perhaps, the *tumé* is taken down and laid under the house.

Tightly woven palm thatch, either circular or rectangular in shape, extends low around the house sides. Underneath, there's a shady, dry place to rest from tropical extremes. The most traditional and still most common houses have minimal or no walls. Fresh breezes sweep through the open

Figure 22. Rectangular roof under construction.

Figure 23. Circular roof under construction. Photo by L. Stoller.

space, cooling the skin and enlivening the hearth's fire. The eye is free to gaze out onto activities in the open space between houses, river, and jungle edge. In the old days, the first settlers like to say, a man could hunt wild peccary from his house. Animals would wander right into the dooryard garden, and poom! Lunch. Now, except for small birds, wild animals keep their distance from human settlements.

The house has sections, divided by type of material and level. In Tamarinbó, most floors are made of the light, strong, and flexible outer bark of the stilt palm *ebá-bákiri* (S. *jira, Socratea durissima*). Once fibrous innards are removed from the stilt palm, the outer bark develops narrow slits when pressed flat to make the flooring. The slits allow liquid waste to be washed through to the ground below. Hardwoods, sawed by hand into wide, smooth boards, may be used to construct the central living space and sleeping platform. Small open squares are cut around house posts for waste disposal (e.g., for infants to eliminate). The houses generally have three levels, each a few inches higher or lower in relation to the others. The kitchen, on the lowest level, is dominated by the hearth; the central living space is usually the middle and largest; the highest level, for sleeping and clothing storage, is most protected from dirt tracked in during the day. Except for an occasional bench or hammock, a rare table and chair, there is no furniture. A platform higher than the next becomes a bench for sitting; a double row of bamboo poles encircling the platform's outer rim provides a backrest for those sitting on the floor facing inward.

Spaces are filled with all sorts of things. High on the outer beams hang *parumas* (E. *wa*), the brightly colored lengths of imported cloth that women wrap tightly around their bodies from waist to knee. Freshly washed banners in the wind, parumas, imported from China by Panama City stores and stocked in Yaviza, display the worldly gifts of man to woman. Dry *parumas,* clean and ready to wear, and old ones, sewn together to make sleeping tents, are stored with sleeping mats made of plastic tarp, Taiwanese woven reed, or the beaten inner bark of the rubber tree (E. *huéporo*). At daybreak, fluffy seed pillows of the balsa tree (E. *mohópono*) and small pieces of wood sculpted to fit comfortably in a neck's curve also find their way to the corners of the sleeping platform, where the roof comes down low. Here too, on hanging shelves or tucked between beam and thatch, are baskets: *petá,* its oblong body and tight-fitting lid made of the striped surface of the long stalks of the *joropo* palm (E. *pärärä*); *hamará,* its close weave forming a large body with straight sides and a big, wide-open mouth. Inside these, the rest of the shorts, pants, loincloths, T-shirts, and special-occasion brassieres that make up the family wardrobe are stored, along with schoolbooks and cigarette packs that a woman of the household might be selling. The smallest baskets with rounded bottoms and narrowing tops (E. *üchuburri*) contain matches, needle and thread, and a woman's collection of plastic beads in solid strands of primary colors, large *(kirrima)* and small *(neta)*. If a woman has them, these little baskets contain her necklace of coins *(parata kada)*. Collected from Panama now and Panama when it was still Nueva Granada, from the canal-building times of France and the United States, from Colombia, Ecuador, Chile, Peru, and Venezuela, the overlapping coins are tied together in series and handed down from mother to daughter.[14] Some coins are so old that they are smooth from wear; dates begin to appear in the nineteenth century. Gathered from many foreign systems of exchange, the coins have been inserted, refashioned, and kept in this indigenous culture. Coin necklaces testify to the enduring bonds between generations of Emberá and to the long and wide-ranging contact Emberá have had with foreigners.

It is to these corners of the house that the children run to change in and out of their white-topped, blue-bottomed uniforms and into their *parumas,* shorts, or loincloths on each break from the village schoolroom. Slipped into the thatch above their heads may be the old batons of a deceased relative who was once a shaman, or the batons sculpted for play or fright, similarly composed of human figures with heavy brows, closed eyes, and silent mouth, in communion with animal familiars who sit solemnly on their heads or backs. Things that do not require easy access like stored grains, old shoes and books in plastic buckets, boxes and baskets, and extra heads of green plantains may be tied to beams or set on shelves built across beams in the dark, dry space enclosed by the roof.

There is variation in the construction and use of house platforms. For example, a hearth may be located within the central living space, and people may sleep there when there's not enough room on the sleeping platform. Multifunctionality of house spaces, especially the central living platform, is managed throughout the day by repeated sweepings by women and girls. With leaves of the broom tree (E. *nulpa*) tied in a bunch, messes from eating and weaving are cleared away to make space for rest and socializing. After the final evening meal, the floor is swept one last time before the sleeping mats are unrolled in their customary spots, and the tents strung up from the rafters. The small flame of a kerosene lamp, made out of a baking soda can and a rag, lights up the colorful wraps of sleepers and the faces of talkers and storytellers. The flame glows softly through the night to keep away blood-sucking bats from the dogs and sends out a steady signal of reassuring presence to neighbors in the distant blackness.

The hearth (E. *itarrá*) is framed by a three foot by three foot wooden square on the floor, lined first with large green *platanillo* leaves (*Heliconia* sp.) and insulated with packed dirt. Upon this is placed three large, slow-burning logs (E. *tibi*) pointing toward the center, their ends adjusted in and out to accommodate large or small pots. As he does for most of the heavier tasks done nowadays, the man takes responsibility for bringing in large logs. He might bring one home from the *monte* where the family is working or might make special trips out, depending on availability. A fourth log of fast-burning wood, to be chopped into small pieces for kindling by man, woman, or youth, is left on the ground below. Hung above the hearth is usually a rack for smoking meat and fish, a fan (E. *pepena*) woven of *joropo* palm, and long prongs (S. *teneza*) made from a folded piece of palm (E. *chachagaráiri*) to grab hot pots. Along the edge of the hearth frame, between the long logs, sit one or two comfortably broad benches (E. *ambugé*) for women to sit on while they cook. These are often carved in the shape of animals such as turtle or deer. To the side of the hearth is an area of preparation where food brought in from the orchards and forest is left. (An extra *tumé* is often kept back there for the climb up.) In normal times, there's at least one giant head of plantains, probably some *guineos,* and a couple of machetes occupying this space. The area contains utensils such as aluminum and steel pots; a wooden stirring paddle (E. *kamísusú*), companion of the giant steel pot (E. *kugurú*) used for large gatherings; plastic and glass mugs and bowls; calabashes (E. *säö*, S. *totuma*) for holding grains and liquids (often engraved with animal and plant designs); a calabash with many little holes that functions as a sieve (E. *sambirruka*) and the wooden holder upon which it rests (E. *anhó*) for separating the liquid from fibers of palm fruits; spoons, forks, knives; chocolate beaters made from sections of woody stem with multiple branches on one end; a metal hand grinder. Utensils are placed along one side of the kitchen area on a shelf, on hanging equipment made of tree parts with convenient configurations of outstretched branches, and in baskets of all sizes and weaves. Large work baskets (E. *ë*, S. *chiles*), their sides called "ribs," handles "ears," and bottom "heart" (where the first strands of *pikiwa* vine are bound together), are also kept in this area along with plastic buckets filled with river water for cooking, cleaning, and drinking.

Men usually take primary responsibility for building the house itself

Figure 24. Dyeing palm stems for basket weaving. Note *tumé* in upper right corner.

and the canoe. They also make the longer-lasting wooden objects for their wives such as *ambugé, kamísusú, anhó,* mortar and pestle, mallet for beating clothes, and mallet for cracking nuts. Women usually make the objects that tend to wear more frequently such as gourds, *pepena, teneza,* brooms, and baskets. That each person learns to make and use objects appropriate to his or her sex is an important part of Emberá youth education, part of what one must know in order to catch a mate. The large mortar and pestle used for pounding rice, corn, palm fruits, coffee beans, and fish poison is left on the ground. There in the shade beside the house, a woman, usually with another woman, but sometimes with her husband, takes the rice stored in its seed case and pounds enough for a meal. Stretching arms high above their heads, each pounder comes down in turn on the pile of rice. In an even, forceful tempo, the husks are broken off the seed, and every few rounds the whole lot is removed and placed on to a large round wooden tray, the *batea,* for winnowing. The rice is thrown high up off the tray, seeds falling back down and light broken husks settling out into the air. Winnowing goes faster in a breeze. Like other acts of separation, a bit of magic might be used. (There's a winnowing chant sung in Spanish about

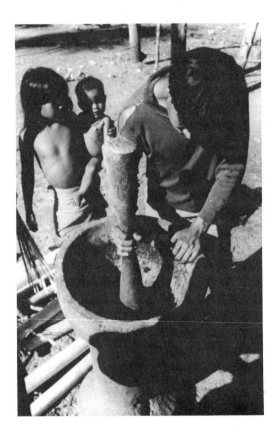

Figure 25. Mashing *dokán* leaves for fish poisoning. Photo by L. Stoller.

wind and a dog with a lopped-off ear.) As the movements are repeated between mortar and winnowing tray, the rice gets whiter and more uniform. Occasionally, a few red seeds appear, vestige of the days when many more varieties were cultivated. Between pounding and winnowing, there is time for talk. Activity attracts passersby. Children gather about, and chickens scrabble for stray grain. When it is done, if the owner of the rice is working with a woman of another household, she measures out an oval-shaped sardine can full from the pile and gives it to the other in exchange for her labor.

Mɨa namá trɨanya eterré trɨanbita.
Man trɨánbira diápeda ɨnándrɨbɨrɨde trɨánwata.

Figure 26. Chicken house.
Photo by J. Benson.

Wërarä, wërarä, eterrera bírusíma.
Wërarä, wërarä, píradɨ kuádaduma.
Wërarä, eterrera ya bírusíma.

Wërarä, wërarä, pátachúma dzude zesedátuma.
Wërarä, wërarä, eterrera bírusíma ansábodóma ya.
Daídu wa kuadátua.

Wërarä, wërarä, ya eterré bírusímana píradɨ kuadátuma.
Wërarä, wërarä.
Wërarä, ya.

(Here I will sing the chicken song.
The song is sung early when it is dawning.

135

Women, women, the chickens have sung.
Women, women rise all.
Women, the chickens have called already.

Women, women, come and cook hot plantains.
Women, women, the chickens have sung, it is already dawning.
Go to bathe in the river.

Women, women, the chickens have sung, rise all.
Women, women.
Women, done.)

The eldest woman in the household usually is the first to rise with the day. Arising with the chicken's first song, she awakes before dawn to bathe and to prepare the family breakfast. Grown daughters and daughters-in-law may rise a bit later and come to collect embers. If a woman is without an infant to care for, on most days she goes off with the working family members to the fields, orchards, or woods.[15] Unless the work site is so far that they will cook out, the family returns in the middle of the day for a meal. At such times, a woman may carry over a hundred pounds of plantains in her *chile*. ("Like a horse" and "Keeps one in shape for childbearing," says Celestina wryly.) Washing off their sweat and dirt in the river, women refill the household water buckets. If kindling is not already chopped, she'll get the embers to ignite again, first blowing, then fanning with the *pepena*. While the rest of the family relaxes in the shade of the thatch roof, the woman head of household first begins to prepare a family meal. That women are obliged to constantly to take care of others whether or not they are tired makes work at cooking, cleaning, and carrying as hard as the more intensive but discontinuous masculine labor. Emberá men acknowledge this.

Once the fire is going and the water brought to a boil, the woman cuts off a hand of green plantains. Slicing off the tip of each long fruit from its base, slitting it down the center, peeling off the thick, sticky rind, she'll slip the white fruits whole into the boiling pot, and the meal is on its way. Ideally, a good meal contains some fish and some meat of deer, peccary, agouti, paca, chicken, or wild bird in addition to plantains, but at least there are usually plantains.[16] Most commonly, boiled plantains are accompanied by catfish soup, made from *humpé* (S. *guacuco, Chaetostomus* sp.) caught while traveling back and forth from the work site. While plantains are cooking, these protein packets in heavy, slimy armor are gutted, washed, and boiled with fresh coriander, garlic, and oregano. Once the fish is in the pot, a woman can relax with the rest of her family gathered round. This is the time for talk and laughter. When it's ready, people and plates counted, the woman gently ladles out the now-delicate, many-boned fish with some soup in a bowl and hands it out with a side dish of boiled plantains. Men and guests who are eating are served first, then women and children, a mother usually sharing what she has left in a cooking pot with her youngest. Rarely are there seconds, except for plantains. If not eaten, extra plantains go with fish bones to the dogs. When everyone's done, people leave their dishes near the washing area, scoop out some water from the fresh water bucket with cup or calabash to rinse hands and mouth, and lay down to rest. Dirty dishes are washed in the river by one of the women or girls when again the family rises for action later in the day.

Describing a meal on an ordinary day actually overemphasizes the foods available from rivers, forests, and local crops in most villages. The time when Emberá lived purely on wild and cultivated foods is beyond recent memory. Even in distant villages like Tamarinbó, which has no store, several food items are brought in from outside. Regularly brought in are cooking oil and sugar (substituting for wild palm oil and cultivated sugarcane, the processing of which is labor intensive), salt (a substance that virtually separates Emberá as cultural beings from their wild relatives the *cimarones* but that is unavailable locally), flour (an imported luxury food), kerosene, and matches (which have replaced flint). In larger, more established villages where local wild game and fish supplies are disappearing, people have become increasingly reliant on expensive cans of low-grade tuna and Spam.

As reliance on subsistence products declines and reliance on bought food increases, women depend more on their male kin. Buying alternative food products may reduce women's work load, especially in regard to processing products like oil and sugarcane. But these alternative products must be bought with money earned from increased agricultural labor, making it unclear whether women's lives are actually made easier. The politics of changing gender roles should be taken into account here as well. Because men are the ones traditionally responsible for dealing with the outside money economy, the replacement of wild and locally cultivated products with products of foreign manufacture may diminish women's power and authority within the home.

In the range of humankind, the distances and identities encoded in the scale of sentient beings are constructed on the basis of race: the Emberá rely on a different race, the black-*kampuniá,* to supply them with goods from the outside world so they can keep their own way of life in the forest. To create a center, a locus of identity, that depends on the outside world for its constituent elements (e.g., salt), internal differences are organized on the basis of sex/gender. Situating Emberá identity and sense of self on the scale of sentient beings depends on intraracial division. Women and men are trained to be responsible for different aspects of reproducing the everyday reality that is home. Through repetition of materials and routines, heterosexual partners manifest the core concept of Emberá as fully human. Women, however, are more restricted in their identification with home. Symbolically, this identification with Emberá reality as distinct from animal and *kampuniá* realities weighs more heavily on women. When they go out into the world beyond Emberá settlement, they take the back seat in the canoe (unless they have a motor) and play the silent partner in transactions with *kampuniá.* Money, the quintessential sign of *kampuniá* exchange, falls into the domain of masculine adventure and responsibility. Traditionally, a man uses money to buy a woman objects she can use in the home. When he gives her silver coins, she strings them side by side in a distinctive arrangement, the Emberá Way, and keeps them in a small basket to wear for special occasions.[17]

Conclusion

Communion with people whose features you transcode as strange, acknowledged unfamiliarity sparks ambiguity and taboo. Telltale signs of inscrutable, potentially horror-provoking seduction rise in the clear, cool current of the river, diffracting and distracting the air on blazing rockstone beaches (or submerged), edging dark green purple brown hush of bush. Once you are face to face, the devils' subtle weirdnesses must be broached head on, but they are damn hard to discern. (They are always in another, never in you except as illness introjected.) Dizzying murk, chains of signifiers like cobwebs in a vampire's abandoned lair, sparks firing off so nervously they take on a spin, jumping impulses form strong-featured monsters lustrously guarding culture's boundaries. Would you be so bold as to risk becoming myth-making fodder just for temptation's sake?

Encounters imbued with the danger and lost promise of rainforest crossing are now a matter of transnational contention. Across the mountains, the lowland bush is Medellín's backyard, home to M-19 guerrillas, cocaine cartel, shamans burned for suspected murder, malaria, hoof-and-mouth disease — and kin one left behind, rivers of your youth, and myths of your dreams. As ugly as Tuli Vieja is, she is a medicine for disembodied boundary feelings. Her hand plucks little children out of the real, to keep her company I guess, and in so doing, she marks the holes in the scale of sentient beings, lots of little holes, in what should be a human face.

Mysteries of coexistence invoke attraction and horror on a sliding scale of sentient beings. Culture's sliding scale (interpolated by warlike states who fight to claim the names on the maps) cue your powers of discernment, align the features of chaos according to some phenomenological order, guide you back from the otherworld to the center of the real, enchanted and safe.

Humans share existence with all sentient beings. Emberá principles of causality derive from this encompassing, interpenetrating view of spirit and matter. Training this awareness to the repetitions of history, Emberá create images of difference in relation to which they (provisionally) orient their selves. Into this, walk the foreign colonizers and developers with all the mixed intentions of their business. Observing which human differences are meaningful locally, outsiders use them to build a new order, disrupting that which came before. In their hubris, they turn a blind eye to the wider scope of being and cause, never imagining the folly of their ways. In their guilt, they try to correct the follies of the past (e.g., with indigenous reserves and wildlife parks), only to work their way deeper into the contradictions between legal proposal and cultural praxis.

eight

Shaman's Song

The wood carvings, animal familiars and rhythms and melodies of Emberá and Waunan shamans bear an uncanny resemblance to those brought by the Siberians some forty thousand years ago when they crossed the Bering land bridge into the Americas (e.g., see Brodsky, Danesewich, and Johnson 1977). With time, it appears that these ancient ritual means reached distant and diverse geographies, where they continue to be used in enacting the passage from everyday — whatever distinctive place-time that might be — to other worlds, however they are culturally conceived. With these symbols, shamans call cosmology into the quotidian, engaging the phenomenal beauty of life for healing — whatever the nature of current illnesses and misfortunes, the condition of nations and histories, or the manners of pleasure. Some say the most powerful shamans are those withdrawn most deeply into what's left of the dense lowland forests. But no matter how far shamans withdraw, they cannot heal effectively if they isolate their vision. The pain and suffering the people bring them in these times must be read against the grain of a world-system rationality that stakes its truth on objectivity, splitting religion from medicine, spirit from matter, factor from factor. In the paradoxical progress of colonialism and development, the practice of shamanism has become a thing of magic empowered by scorn (Taussig 1987).[1] Indigenous exchange, white-*kampuniá* Conquest, slavery, missionization, democratization, zonation — it all gets played out again and again in the insistent repetition of ritual healing.

Acquiring Vision

The possibility of acquiring shamanic power is open to all Emberá and Waunan. Any man or woman willing to pay may learn to cure/sing.[2] Becoming a shaman requires meeting the shaman-teacher — the *patrón,* or master — in an encounter removed from everyday experience. Children whose parents or grandparents are shamans are more likely to become shamans themselves. Not only do they assist in ritual work, but they may also be chosen to inherit the shamans' batons, the wooden scepters that house each shaman's particular spirit/animal familiars. However, even if a shaman is your parent, when he or she becomes your teacher, there is no guarantee that his or her otherworld form will be consistent with one familiar to you. The following text, recorded by Vasco (1985:36) in the Cauca Valley of Colombia, vividly communicates the kind of danger involved in learning to become a *häïmbaná.*[3]

> He said he learned with his father, that it was this that he left as inheritance. In the learning "my father was an evil heart, and he nearly killed me in dreams. In dream I saw pure fire; after it was taken and put out; I climbed up a tree, and the fire calmed down. I was given fire; then it was taken there and put out. Thus it happened many times. Finally, I climbed down from the tree after it was put out and went to look. There was like an animal. I fought, dragged it by the tail, and brought it to father. 'Father, what is this for? I caught it.' And father said: 'Ah, you've beat me; take it there above to my office [in the forest], close it in there, and it will stay for always. Already you will not fall sick, already you will not fall; now you can cure.'" (my translation from Spanish)

As the Colombian texts describe, a student is challenged by animal spirits, which must be conquered in the learning process. If this is achieved, rather than getting sick from the contact (as an unsuspecting person would), you become their owners, turning them into helpers whose extraordinary abilities of sight and movement are bent to tasks motivated by your intent. When this process of learning was explained to me in Darién, more emphasis was placed on acquiring knowledge of song. In these terms, building up a repertoire of song — or, better said, investing *the* song with more and more power — is the condition for gaining control over spirits. If you want to become a powerful shaman, you experience such encounters with several different shamans. The more you experience, the more knowledge, power, and vision you acquire, and the more precise becomes your discernment of good and evil intentions in each shaman's heart. You have greater control over the learning process as it proceeds; your skills of discernment allow you to be a better judge of whether or not it is worth risking new student-master relationships. The importance of such relationships extends beyond initial learning encounters. Even after a master's death, you may call upon those who have taught you in order to assist in a cure.

Each shaman builds up his or her own storehouse of power by capturing spirits who have the power to see into bodies. But just as animals can be let out of a corral, spirits can be let loose and trapped again by someone else, or they may be trapped while on a mission. A shaman who cures may capture the spirits causing the sickness that were sent by another shaman. Thus curing, while requiring spirits, also provides a means to gain control over more spirits. As you acquire more spirits, you assume greater responsibility. In order to maintain control, the shaman must keep "feeding" the spirits by holding a song event periodically. In this sense, shamans are dependent on patients to provide financial means to stage songs that are their cure. Without patients, shamans either have to sustain the considerable cost of making *chicha* or buying liquor for "feedings" themselves or find that the power that is the basis of their practice recedes dangerously.

Knowledge and power circulate among shamans and are sustained by a population of patients. Together, all practicing shamans constitute a net-like organization that extends throughout the demographic range of Emberá and Waunan populations. Any person hooking into the net of shamanic encounters becomes a vehicle of power. By maintaining a personal store of this circulating power and by manipulating it in song, the shaman can either heal or kill. The former effect of power is sought by people with sickness, the latter form is what they seek to reverse.

While shamans are strongly linked in service to their own family groups, the reputations of great shamans are spread by word of mouth, attracting people from great distances. Discourse about shamanism is a discourse of journeys. Long journeys to meet shamans of powerful repute are undertaken by those who want to tap their power, either because they want to learn how to become shamans themselves or because they search for a cure — endeavors that are often one and the same. Journeys give narrative form to a patient-student's search and to the actual curing event itself. Journeys bring a patient-student to the homes of shamans, and from the ritually marked spaces in the central platforms, the shamans use their songs to call spirits to come and lend vision.

Short of Breath

From Panama to Ecuador, those searching for cures and knowledge will hear of Emberá and Waunan Chocó shamans, the lowland healers of great renown.[4] The particular Emberá shaman whose work is presented here, however, is not a man of great renown. His ritual practice is neither the most elaborate nor the most traditional (in the sense that it adheres most strictly to preselected codes). Of the various shamans I met, however, he was most concerned to articulate the place of his practice as he conceived it in the context of an outside world that came to him through missionaries, moviemakers, and medical doctors. As well he might, he took the ethnographer's presence in his ritual practice as an occasion to represent his profession to *kampuniá*. His explanations to me stand out, not for the way they elucidate the mechanism and logic of shamanic practice, but, instead, for the way they show his strategic positioning of shamanic practice in respect to foreign *kampuniá* terms. He reinterprets the unspoken but ever-present Euramerican perspective, forestalling judgments that contradict the truth-value of his knowledge. As is expected with a code that is secret and dangerous, and a professional doctor-patient relationship that is confidential, he sets clear limits to the knowledge that he is willing to share. His discourse does not flow directly from his knowledge to mine; instead, it is his knowledge filtered through and reflected off the ideas that he the shaman thinks that I the listener have of him the shaman. The full logic that underlies the power of shamanism, if it is at all possible to conceive of one, cannot be communicated.[5] Instead, a glimpse of ritual healing is presented with an interpretation that focuses on the vulnerability and power of shamanism in history.

It is January and well into the dry season, so it is easy to wade across the Tupisa River without getting my pants all wet. The crossing is right above the place where Gabriel, the man in search of a cure, grew up. But he has little to do with the place now that his father took a second wife and has a second set of children. In fact, he barely talks to his father and stepmother any more. When things got bad between them all, he, his sister Carolina, her husband, and some other Tamarinbó folk picked up her house piece by piece and moved it upriver into the village.[6] And now when Gabriel is around, he lives in the village with them, working in his sister's orchards and receiving cooked meals in return. But being a bachelor in search of a cure, he's not around that much.

The walk from Tamarinbó to Promesa, the next village downstream, takes me a bit over an hour. I hurry as dusk approaches, going along the river path, passing orchards and houses that are familiar yet cryptic, signs that recollect stories of strange encounters like Ako's fright (Chap. 4). Eventually I come to the place where the path turns away from the river, short-cutting the big bend right above Promesa. I cross the little stream that veers off from the main river, edging my way across a slippery log while holding on to a pole that a helpful passerby has stuck upright in the mud. The path follows a steep rise. Hoofprints from Promesa's horses have dried deep in the mud, forming a firm, if uneven, walking surface. Nearing the top of the hill, I turn and look back out over the lush green, broad-leafed orchards that brighten the lowland plain and beyond to the mountain border, the slate-blue silhouette of Colombia.

Over the rise, the village that is my destination slips into view. I'm prepared to spend the night in the house of Gabriel's father's brother, the *brujo* (S. shaman) who is trying to cure his trouble. Although Gabriel has had this condition he calls *tadzi iña-bákara-numua* (I/we cannot–breathe–state of being) for a year already, he has only begun treatment with his uncle after going three times to the doctors in Yaviza. Each time he was told that they could do nothing—a classic rationalization of the need for magical cure. Two weeks before this, Gabriel had gone downriver to sell a canoeload of plantains and buy rum and other items necessary for the *chicha,* or song, a ritual intensification of the course of treatment he has been undergoing.[7] This morning, upon his return, he stopped by to let me know that tonight would be the night. He was anxious and still could not draw a deep breath. These symptoms led me to give him some of the inhalant asthma medicine I had in my kit, but to no effect. Gabriel was contemplating the loss of his breath and the essential, yet oddly ephemeral, place of breath in life. The only solace remaining to him was his confidence that his uncle was a good *brujo;* he had already cured two other boys in his care, and they were almost ready to be sent home.

As I come down into the village, I experience the shyness that Emberá feel when they enter another turf, intensified by the other strangeness that being a gringa means. But I have been here a few times before, to talk to the Emberá teacher, the village head, and a wood sculptor whose work I admire. Walking on the path toward the open space in the village center, I come across a group of men sitting on some logs under the trees and ask them where I can find the house of Gabriel's uncle, Joaquín. He happens to be sitting among them; I am surprised by the youth and handsomeness of his face, for all the other *brujos* I have met were old and shriveled. He shows me to his house himself, making sure I wash my feet in the bucket of perfumed plant water placed next to the ladder before I enter. Joaquín informs the women by the fire about my presence and then goes back out to his companions.

Gabriel and Carolina have come earlier in the day but are not in the house now. There is at least one familiar face though. Januario, another Tamarinbó resident, is here visiting his wife, who has been staying with her family because she is "sick" (she is Joaquín's wife's daughter by a previous marriage). Later someone told me that her sickness was due to the fact that Januario, an intelligent and usually calm person, had flown into a rage and beat her up. The two of them seem to be getting along well enough now, however, and are relaxing in their corner of the sleeping platform. There are various other people mulling around, doing whatever needs to be done in the remaining hour or so of light. The floor, newly washed with the same sweet-smelling infusion used for our feet, is just about dry. People are beginning to organize their sleeping accommodations. The higher-level sleeping platform is reserved for resident family members, and soon most of the main platform is staked out. Bedding is neatly arranged around its borders until the only space left open in the house is in the center, where the *brujo* and patient will sit through the night, the edge near the door, and the busy area immediately around the hearth, which is at the far end of the main platform. I am shown a place on that end to set up my sleeping tent, a small rectangle of floor between an old grandmother and the kitchen. I'm not especially happy about the spot, because the cockroaches usually abound on that end of the house as soon as it gets dark—if they even wait for that—but I grin and bear it, tucking the edges of my tent carefully under the mat. I reassure myself that this time I'm going to stay awake through the whole night with the *brujo,* so it won't matter (although I never could successfully fight the spell of thirty or forty sleepers in one room).

As it gets darker, the house gets busier. Everyone is coming in and must be fed. In addition to the large family that lives here regularly, there are a number of patients who, together with the relatives brought along to care for them, are on extended stays in Joaquin's "hospital." The cooks take turns at the fire. Someone asks if I will cook, and I pull out the bag of sweet plantains that I have fried earlier and brought along. That gets me an approving glance. Once they are sure my basic needs have been met, everybody just forgets about me for a while.

When Gabriel returns, he comes over and tells me about the various patients. There's the boy who caught the heat of the devil (E. *hirua-numua* = heat of the spirit-state of being) one night while walking in the forest. The heat of the devil is dangerous; the boy could kill his mother by spreading it to her. Another boy has lost his spirit in the river (E. *tadzi häüre doedá-besia,* our spirit in river-stayed). One day his mother had left him in the canoe while she was diving for fish, and he fell in. She rescued him from about forty feet away. Since then he has had a chronic case of diarrhea. They are from Ansabidá, a village downriver that has no resident shaman. In serious emergency cases the people there call the shaman from the Río Chucunaque, a woman renowned for her curing abilities. But this time the boy was brought to Joaquín, and according to Gabriel, his treatment has been successful. There is also a woman named Adela from a village on Tuquesa, the next river over. She's on the rebound from the Yaviza clinic, where, I learned in a subsequent conversation with her, she was given a bunch of different kinds of pills for tuberculosis all at once. She got dizzy, and she's been dizzy ever since. Taking an alternate route back home in order to stop and see relatives in Tamarinbó, Adela has stopped here along with her teenage son and daughter, her caregivers. Joaquín told her that perhaps someone had given her something to drink, maybe water from the headwaters (a substance with a magical potency that can be applied either to harm or to heal) or perhaps some other form of poison. In this way, he uses a shift in language to legitimate his methods for treating Adela, changing the cause of illness from natural (the wrong pills) to unnatural (poison-devil) according to a logic that he will explain to me later this night. She ends up staying with him one month, but to no avail. Tonight she is somber, but she is wont to make light of her illness. She has been spending her days talking and laughing, cooking and sharing the piles of fish her kids catch for her.

Gabriel tells me that he will live here a while after tonight's song, the second one that Joaquín has performed for him. He'll stay at least until he's feeling better and Joaquín tells him he's cured. Then he will pay money for one more song. The darker it gets, the more nervous Gabriel gets. By

Figure 27. Baton.

8:00 P.M., blackness becomes the walls of the house. Everybody has eaten and has begun to settle down. There's still a lot of talking going on as some women prepare the coffee with sugar I've brought along as an offering. Joaquín joins Gabriel and me by the hearth's corner, and we each get a cupful.

I tell Joaquín that when I first saw him, I was surprised to find him such a young man. He says nonchalantly that kids start learning when they are eight or nine years old, little by little, and then continue seeking more teachers as they get older. Someone told me later that Joaquin's father was also a *brujo* and that Joaquín had inherited all the batons from him — and he had quite a bunch, maybe ten. Batons, called *barra* in Emberá, are pieces of carved wood in which human and animal figures are sculpted, often one on top of the other. Some take the form of lances or arrows. My favorite is a snake with a curving smile on the side of a heart-shaped head. They say that the little animals (S. *animalitos*) stay in the batons as if it were their house and that the shaman who is the owner (S. *dueño*) of the batons is the owner of the *animalitos* that live inside.

As with other symbols associated with shamanism, the meaning and use of the baton varies with person and place. One time a friend of mine told me that his grandfather who was a shaman made a personal baton for everyone in his family, and these were used whenever they were sick. On the basis of this idea, it seemed that anyone could have a baton made for himself or herself. And so when I went to meet a shaman of great repute who lived in Yaviza (right next door to the state hospital), I figured I'd ask him to make one for me (it's always better for a stranger to arrive with a specific request), only to discover later that most people think that if you ask a shaman to make a baton, it is because you want to become a shaman yourself (which I was not then and still am not prepared to do). In any case, the Yaviza shaman made me a set of four small ones — two human figures I call *espirito muertos* (S. dead spirits), a spear, and the smiling snake. I have not activated them with song.

When I ask Joaquín for permission to tape his song, he wants to know what I am going to do with the recording, and I explain how the song is an important part of Emberá culture and that therefore it should be included in my study. He said, "Oh, to listen to, no more," but was not entirely satisfied. He reminds me that *brujos* are professionals who are paid by both patients and students, and then launches into one of the more popular themes of Emberá conversation — how gringos make more money. To emphasize the latter point he brings up cases of missionaries with fat salaries and people who come to Darién to make movies (I had heard another report of this last event), two types who do not share their earnings with the Emberá. I feel that although Joaquin's argument is justified, I nevertheless decide to stick to the position that I have sustained in all my dealings with shamans so far — that I do not fit into the category of paying patient or student because I am neither sick nor have any plans of setting up a shamanic practice of my own. I have decided upon this policy because, in terms of my work, the recording of a song has no more or less monetary value than a story that someone tells or a genealogy or, for that matter, measurements of agricultural work. And if I were to pay for all these things, even if I could afford it, I would be turned into a central exchange bank instead of a person. I also think that I should not vary this policy just because one *brujo* is more convincing than another. But I still feel the issue of money is unresolved. How can my work that speaks of but does not create shamanic effects, an academic parasite on a magical host, avoid participating in the terms of the system it studies? The issue of whether or not I can justifiably stand outside the system of payment that binds a shaman's student is further complicated by the role that money plays in the ritual itself. In the context of the song the patient pays the shaman's spirit helpers. As you will see in the case of Gabriel, monetary payment pressures the spirits to come to human aid; it is this same payment that eventually goes to the shaman (although outside the ritual context there may be another fee paid directly to the shaman, especially if the shaman is approached by a person not related as kin). Thus money, operating simultaneously on both symbolic and material planes, is an essential element in the production of magical effects.[8]

Joaquín goes off, only to reappear in the space in the center of the room, where a girl nine or ten years old has been sprinkling perfumed water every once in a while at least since the time I arrived. Adela, the women suffering from dizziness, is sitting there alone, legs bent around close to her torso, shoulders slumped. A leafy crown transforms the figure of Joaquín as he strides across the room with two large hoops of the woody *matamba* vine grasped in his hands. Tall and swift, he crosses the space toward her and swings the hoops down in circles at her sides; her body slides momentarily into the double frame of circles. Then he strides back, then forth, back then forth, back then forth; the leafy hoops are shaking, and sounds come out of his mouth. His hands release one end; the hoops become leafy, spiny whips. The woman sits low, the *brujo* stands tall; his wrist flicks overhand, the whips slap the floor; he backs away then forth again the whips slap the floor; he backs away then forth with a sudden jerk the whips crack, and his voice does too in that guttural, pressured way that is spirit-talk.

He leads her to the far corner of the room. Flames from the kerosene lamp shed barely enough light to see. He sits in front and above her on the edge of the sleeping platform, their faces close, deep drags on his cigarette, streams blowing into her face and round her head. In the streams are the words of spirit-talk, drags deep then blows of talk, pieces of song filter between, drags deep then blows of talk. Done.

The little girl enters the center to set up the stage for the evening's song. She is dressed for enchantment. Her body is painted in black, rings and diamond patterns decorate her face, arms, chest, and legs; she wears a pretty *paruma* and many strands of beads designed to beckon. And so too the perfumed water she sprinkles over the space of song, round and round, under the watchful gaze of Joaquin's wife, a woman so old I thought perhaps she was his mother. She lays down two large, broad *vijado* leaves, the "table" upon which *chicha* is served. Eight cups of various foreign manufacture follow in a double line along the outer edge of one leaf. Gabriel, who bought the bottle of rum in Yaviza, opens it and hands it to the girl. Then he's sent out into the dark to cut some more leaves. Carefully following the wife's instructions, the girl pours a little rum into each cup, making sure each one has about the same amount without using up more than half the bottle. Then she covers them with another *vijado* leaf. When Gabriel returns with the two smaller ones he manages to find, she lays them on top of the other, then on top of that, a cloth of green cotton, then another big leaf. The "table" is almost set.

A little bench (E. *ambugé*), a manifestation of the transformative power of the mythical serpent called Hëï (Vasco 1985:56), the shaman's otherworld connection, is placed at one end of the table. According to my interpretation of the Emberá model of ritual curing, the shaman places himself or herself at the boundary between everyday and otherworld by sitting on the bench in the ritual space. The patient's illness is conceptualized either as an invasion of invisible beings or qualities from the other-world into the patient's body or as a loss of a patient's spirit. In position, the shaman uses the song to call his or her spirit helpers, the devils or *animalitos* who see. In this, the shaman opens up his or her own body not only to spirit allies but to the illness-causing spirits as well and, through them, to another shaman who may be directing the spirits causing illness. The interjection of the shaman into the circuit of power in which the patient is caught and the act of seeing the cause of sickness are two basic components of the mechanism of cure. According to this model, then, the aim of the cure is to break harmful contact between patient and other-world, placing him or her firmly and safely back in everyday life. As such, the song event is a ritual enactment of myth for practical ends. It is also a personal instantiation of a particular set of social and symbolic relationships that converge in one moment of a patient's life history.

Gabriel will sit on a mat, on the end opposite from the shaman's bench. Joaquin's batons are placed in front of it on top of the layered leaves, parallel to the cups underneath. Joaquin's wife corrects any mistakes; it is important that everything be as it should be. She is also making the *brujo's* "drum," stripping off the lower fronds of several fan shaped *pärärä* leaves and tying their stiff stems together.

The most extraordinary aspect of this ritual setting is its simplicity. The two other shaman's songs/curing events that I have attended both prepared a more elaborate construction entailing a little house (S. *ranchito*) in which a patient or "table" with *chicha* sit. But apparently the placement of leaves on the floor is sufficient for Joaquín's symbolic purposes. After all, he is running quite a large "hospital" in his house. Nearing the end of the preparations, the girl empties a pack of cigarettes onto a little plate and then places a few of Gabriel's bills underneath them like a doily. He illuminates this activity with my flashlight. All the sleepers are in their places. Finally, the leaf drum is placed within easy reach of the *brujo's* bench. Gabriel mentions the time. (It's clear that he thinks Joaquín ought to be getting to work.) Joaquín tells him that it is exactly 9:00 P.M., just the time they're supposed to start. Gabriel comes across the room to ask me the time—my watch says 9:17.

The little kerosene lamp is put in a plastic bucket over by the now-vacant hearth, its light muted to a dull glow. The *brujo* sits in the center of the room before the ritual table. The girl comes over and hands him a little bottle of perfume. He puts some on and returns it to her. She continues around the room giving and receiving the bottle from everyone in turn.

Some anoint themselves with a bit on a fingertip, others tilt the bottle up onto their necks and chests. Gabriel is walking around right behind the girl supervising. There's still some talk and a few jokes as the night settles into the house.

Tooooooo. toooouoo. tonooooooooouuo. . . . tootonotootootoo-toouooooooooo.

A conch shell calls out softly from the upriver end of the village. It announces the beginning of another shaman's song, that of the father of Melani of Tamarinbó. A pack of cigarettes is passed around and then, more slowly, some matches. Joaquín lights one and calls me over to the center. (I had told Gabriel I couldn't see from the corner.) Again he asks me what I want, and again I tell him. He said OK, bring your sleeping mat and lay down here, motioning to the space parallel to the table. Until 1:00 A.M. I stay there sitting or lying between *brujo* and patient, an audience of one who can imagine but not envision the *hai* as they come and go on smoke and sleepers' breath.

Tooooooo. toooooo. tooooooooooooo. . . . tootoootootootoo-tooooooooooo.

Joaquín calls on the conch, he shakes the dried leaves of his drum sharply, then, batons in hand, he passes them up and down the front of his body, arms over his head. 9:30. Joaquín swigs from the bottle and then one by one empties the teacups, searching under the layers of cloth and leaves, offering some to Gabriel, "Are you sure there's no more? Where's the flashlight?" Peeking under, no they're definitely empty. He'll only sing until 2:30 instead of until dawn at 3:00 or 4:00. Then Joaquín says, "The government doesn't recognize Emberá *brujos,* even though they heal a lot of people." "You know one has to buy 60, 80, 100 dollars a night to make these batons work." "Gabriel," he says, "you're going to spend maybe 30, 40, or up to 60 dollars for the curing; you will spend money, but it will always come back to you. To be well is most important."

The song is a waterfall flowing into the night air full of possibility. Calling the spirits, froglets, bird, cicada, all the *hai* to come and drink together, it's a party. As we drink, that which is false falls away, and the truth is revealed. To reveal the truth is to cure. Send all evil away on the insistent beat of the many-fingered leaves of the drum tapping faster, oh much faster, than the heart beats.

In and out of song, Joaquín (J) is never possessed; he is the chief. He speaks to Gabriel (G) in Emberá, to me (SK) in Spanish, and to the spirits in spirit-talk and song.[9]

J to SK: Well, always drinking liquor you know.

SK: Uh-huh.

J: Yes, every singer—how should I say?—every time you sing, you drink liquor. Then you are able to see the illness more, to see which illness you have. It's exactly like this, see? Nobody is seeing here, no one is seeing, no?

SK: Uh-huh.

J: We are not even seeing a shadow-ghost. You are there, and the other, and the other. They're awake, no? They are not seeing a thing, truth.

SK: Uh-huh.

J: We say yes, we are in the dark. We say, I, he that sings, I am here, say that yes, therefore something happens. We say this is like a table at a canteen. Then they arrive, arrive . . . bring . . . all this. Than that same one says, "Money." We say, you see how they . . . well, you've been to theater, right?

SK: Uh-huh.

J: The same way seen, manifest, one sees clearly, the spirit goes, it brings the devil, it. . . . Already one sees the illness he has su-perclear. If he has an illness of the *brujos,* or we say, an illness that is a devil-thing. Then they already see you. Then one is . . . , they say, we say, if he has nothing of the devil of *brujería,* you say he has nothing. Then already one knows more or less, no? the thing already. It's of the *médico,* the doctor of Yaviza. Understand?

SK: Uh-huh.

J: Then it's just as I say, no? If he has nothing, I tell him, "You have no illness of *brujería* a devil-thing." I can send him to Yaviza al-ready. Then the *médicos,* the doctors of Yaviza, treat him on the basis of pills on the basis of injections on the basis of say, radiogra-phy. THERE one takes all this, no? There they also see WHICH ill-ness is happening to the patient at the time, understand?

SK: Uh-huh. But if it's a thing of the devil, then he says something?

J: No, here I say to him, no? We say, if it's a thing of the devil, I say, "Such is the sickness you have." Then that yes, I can do the opera-tions on him . . .

SK: Uh-huh. And from there you can cure?

J: Exactly. This thing is difficult too, yes? Because there are devils capable of screwing you up.

[Of all the things he could have talked about, Joaquín chooses to tell me about the relationship between Emberá shamanism and Euramerican allopathic ("Western") medicine. For one thing, it's clear that he wants non-Emberá to consider his practice from the point of view of medicine, rather than religion, which he does not mention. Regarding his practice from the former perspective, the effectiveness of his treatments testifies to his professional worth, while from the point of view of the latter, his practices are condemned as a thing of the devil—but a devil that has the capacity only for evil. The first comparison evokes legitimacy, the second only a Christian style of hell.

But he does more than frame his practice from the perspective of one set of institutionalized Euramerican practices rather than another. He divides the semantic domain that includes both shamanic and Euramerican allopathic healing practices in two: a domain of "natural illness" that has nothing to do with devils, and a domain of *"brujería"* that does. Thus he lays out a cooperative rather than competitive model of Emberá and Euramerican medicine based on the idea that there are two different but necessary kinds of practice corresponding to two kinds of disease, a division of labor of sorts. According to his model, his position is privileged by his power to see into the patient, thus allowing him to diagnose when patients should be sent to the Yaviza clinic—a power the doctors there lack. If the doctors in Yaviza cannot cure a patient—not unlike nonspecialist Emberá women whose botanical treatments of natural illness among family members sometimes do not succeed[10]—they do not know if their failures are because they are trying to cure a thing of the devil or not. If they are, their lack of vision might cause them to persist in treatment programs that Joaquín would already recognize as futile. So in this way, he makes a specific place for himself in the contemporary world; at the same time, he provides a way to think about the relationship between Emberá *brujos* and Euramerican-trained doctors without getting stymied in contradictions.]

Side A of the tape ends. Joaquín explains to me that if he messes up, he could catch Gabriel's disease. Then he turns to Gabriel and talks to him in Emberá. I pick it up again on Side B.

J to G: Down there by the path where that Emberá Domingo lives. I look and he's thus, like an Emberá, quite young, no white hair. This is no ordinary youth. Anybody could mistake him for one though. Batons—I tell you he's got like two hundred batons. Well, yes, he's got them gathered together all in a big sack tied from the beams of his house. Ninety. José Manuel eyábida *häïmbaná* [= shaman of related Indian group].

"Greetings, how are you?" [Joaquín acts out a hypothetical approach to the eyábida *häïmbaná*.]

"Thus as I am sitting, Eyábida." Then, then it was, thus he said thus, "What's happening? He's no *häïmbaná*." You arrived in Colombia, but you didn't get there. Which *häïmbaná*? Which *häïmbaná* is great? [There are a great many people here in Panama who sing but are not true *häïmbaná*—they can't make the devil shout night and day or make snakes come into the house like the great ones can. But the journey to find a great *häïmbaná* in Colombia is difficult and uncertain.]

His son is here, that one named Chichuru. He's young like my brother Santiago. Young boy that he is. *Daúbaráda.* [*Daúbaráda*, from the root *daú* for eye, is another Emberá word for shaman. Joaquín is saying that the great shaman looks as young as Joaquín's nephew Chichuru and another local youth.]

Because he stays just this way, as if always at that stage of life. Thus they study. Well, actually he was old like you are. He's 30, or 35. He's already old and has had up to 30, 80, 100 *patrón*. 100 *patrón* that are.

That one, in the forest thus, he knows when they bring a sick one. "Tomorrow they'll bring one," he notices and tells them. Here there is no such thing. Here there is mockery.

Son, I have traveled. I never, I to the headwaters of Salakí-tree, Salado. There are many Waunan nearby. We are here, the owner arrives. Look there. *Chukal* [a plant] is eaten. Thus they told him, "You can't look at evil-face." Well, after this they asked. There that old man. Son that has a long path, that has, is. What do these words mean? [The shaman that Joaquín visited in the rivers of Colombia has extrasensory perception; he can see people coming to him through the forest before they get there; no one has that kind of power here in Panama.]

Joaquín switches to the pressed speech for talking to the spirits. After the spirit-talk, soft song phrases with intelligible words:

J: Bird cicada rub their wings together.
Our breath, that is what we are going to alleviate.

Thus you are needing.

[The verb for wings rubbing — *sönwända-numua* — is equivalent to the
   verb for drinking and curing; all are transformations of the same act.]

*Spirit-talk. J is calling the spirits, good and bad, to help cure; then he turns to me
in Spanish:*

J: Advise me when you get sleepy.

SK: Uh-huh.

J: You can sleep over there [pointing to where I sit], you can dawn right
    there, it's fine. This is all without problem. Then, we'll hear the re-
    cording in the morning, to see, what . . . [the recorder is giving me
    trouble fading in and out] . . . what happened. Caught well, or not.
    Then you'll go to Tamarinbó in the morning. It will function again
    there, well, so that you can listen, so that you can hear, no?

Leaf shake.

J: You have to catch EACH *brujería* with this recording, each *brujería*.

SK: That would be good.

Leaf shake, then spirit-talk.

J: Here, son, all the *hai* are arriving.
   Well, we're going to alleviate it all.
   All are going to alleviate as a man.
   Well, this that is in his body, we will alleviate.
   We'll turn it around at once.
   The *hai* that are here are hard, as are the ones that are going to be here.
   The *hai* that drink are here.

*The meaning of the next few lines is hidden by voice changes; the leaf drum stops
beating, and the spirit-talk continues:*

J: Thus how they drink, the *hai* that there are hard.
   We are going to make them cure our son, make them alleviate him at
      once.
   For that he is a man.
   Of all that know the clouds.
   Dreaming, that I will drink, all that is going to be.

Well, they'll alleviate our son, make them alleviate.

Joaquín beats the batons now on the floor, one two tap, then:

J: Whhuuuuuusssssshhhhhh. [A long rush of breath empties out, then song of vocables accompanied by soft leaf drum.]

Loud, long leaf shake. Again Joaquín begins to explain things to me in Spanish:

J: For this I tell you, no? We the Emberá have our doctor, ah? But Emberá—like this that I am here—we cure sickness, that which is happening to the patient here.
SK: Uh-huh.
J: This is what I'm singing. Arriving here are froglet, and froglet, and froglet, and froglet, lots of froglets. I say, I call the spirit of my devil froglet. Say, I am the devil's chief, understand? I am chief of the little devils. Then, they explain to me: Fulano has SUCH a sickness, or Fulano, with SUCH a little devil I can cure him.
SK: Uh-huh.
J: So they let me see, manifest. Then I myself, I tell him he himself, the owner of the sickness, no? "You, this is what's happening," and then make a balsa doll, done.
SK: They're like batons, or that's different?
J: The baton is that which I have in my hand. In this here is the little devil.
SK: Uh-huh.
J: I am like the chief of the little devil.
SK: Hmmm.
J: Then they, if possible I'm going to ask: "Fulano . . . SUCH sickness." If they say he hasn't got any sickness from *brujería*, we, what can we do? They can do NOTHING, if it's not a thing of the devil, a sickness of *brujería*. In that case, one can't make use of them. So I explain to the patient, "Man, this thing is not of *brujería*." Go to the *médico* in the town of Yaviza. But I say: NATURAL SICKNESS. That's what it is called. Natural sickness. It's not a thing of *brujería*.
SK: And what are the little devils saying about Gabriel?
J: That boy, he's a nephew of mine. He's the son of one of my brothers. So what happened to the boy, according to what I see, no?
SK: Hmmm.
J: The boy was in Darién, traveling around this province. Here, nothing

more, well, this AREA. When he came from there, he came back with that sickness. It happened there.

SK: There in Sambu?

J: For that, each *brujo* does not tell, does not explain, does not say publicly SUCH Fulano, such place, happened to you.

SK: Ah, you cannot.

J: No.

SK: It's a secret.

J: It's of the secret, exactly. Already you understand.

SK: Hmmm.

J: If it is that you are a student, you know a lot.

SK: Hmmm.

J: That I am seeing, if what I can do, if I can cut it. . . . I would make such a one tranquil. Without pain . . . I am a hospital also.

SK: Hmmm.

J: So if I don't accept all those froglets, the sickness will fall on me, myself.

SK: True?

J: Yes. Thus one has to accept all of them . . . all the froglets, whichever froglets, so many distinct devils, no? . . . to cure him. [I have reached the limit of what Joaquín will tell. I don't know what he actually does when the froglets come, and I cannot find out anything specific about what's wrong with Gabriel.]

Song of vocables, followed by spirit-talk, accompanied by leaf drum. Occasional emphasis is added with beats of medicine stick to words that mean:

J: The hard *hai* that are, that look well.

   At that which you are needing.

Joaquín shifts into Emberá to talk to Gabriel.

J: Distinct animals that are, are coming.

   You will see nothing, you, others, look well at brother.

   So speak, son.

   Silent as you are, yes you.

G: It is to you, Uncle, that I am speaking thus.

J: If you don't believe, if you don't believe, only you know this. Then if you are believing well, it's you who knows. [In other words, if you don't believe in what I'm doing, tell me now.]

157

Leaf shake.

J: Because I, thus if you don't believe my words, not me.
Today I am drunk, drunk.
I say to you thus, drunk to the top.
I like to speak all, truth, yes my word.
I like to speak of real things, true words.

Leaf shake.

J: Over there son, no more liquor?
I'll still keep singing.
So you it is that speaks.
My animals, my body thus are.
Thus you speak.
Thus you suffer, Aché.[11]

G: I don't want that suffering.
What I want is my breath, as I was.
For that I am paying.
For that I am believing the words of you all.

J: Thus that you spoke.
In truth you heard well.
I am speaking my words.

Leaf shake, followed by song of vocables and then song with words that mean:

J: I want to drink to see.
How I'm feeling, how I'm drinking son.
Always I, in order to heal.
As that still does not believe the truth.

Leaf shake, followed by song of vocables:

J: je ee e e eee
hai na e na ne
are-ra-re [refers to Nonameña, or Waunan person]

Then song with words that mean:

J: Life continues, *hai* that drink.

So already the *hai, hai* that are.

hai Nonameña.

The song continues softly with leaf drum accompanying Gabriel's talk to spirits.

G: True that you see me by this means.

True that I see you, drinks that are, cigarettes that are, money that is.

For this, you will alleviate my breath.

That you'll make me breathe, true.

That there is for this, that you know.

That I'm paying you all.

This suffering that I have I do not want.

True that you see me.

Thus as I am.

True, that you'll make me breathe well.

For this I am paying you.

There is liquor if you want to drink.

Song of vocables continues after he stops talking. Joaquín then moves into a song that combines the words and melody of a popular Spanish folk song with the vocable healing song of the Emberá.

J: Ai chinangito

Ai son de colores

Mi barquito va navegando

Madrugada qué bonito [throughout, for *bonita*]

Hai hombre hai

(Ai *chinangito*

Ai it's of colors

My boat goes navigating

Dawn how pretty

Hai, man, *hai*)

Ai chinangito

Ai son de colores

Mi barquito va navegando

Madrugada qué bonito

Hai hombre hai

Ai chinangito
Ai chinangito
Ai son de colores
Mi barquito va navegando
En la madrugada
Hai hombre hai

(Ai *chinangito*
Ai *chinangito*
Ai it's of colors
My boat goes navigating
In the dawn
Hai, man, *hai*)

Joaquín beats baton against the floor four times.

J: Hai de da di
Hai de da di da
Hai hombre hai

Ai chinangito
Ai son de colores
Mi barquito va navegando
En la madrugada
Qué bonito
Hai hombre hai
Hai de di da

[The melodic pattern of this song contrasts sharply with the traditional details that compose the surrounding ritual (e.g., construction and use of ritual space, song of vocables). When my neighbor Celestina heard the taped song back in Tamarinbó, she said, "Gabriel's wasting his money on this guy." Her reaction reflects audience constraints on creativity in shamanistic performance. But perhaps Joaquín's improvisation with traditional melodic form has a magical aim that is not so inconsistent with the rest of his performance after all. He may be attracting *hai* with the pretty musical and linguistic image of a boat of many colors riding on the sea. The image resonates with the story of the phantom gringo boat sent by otherworld spirits called Chämbera (see below and Chap. 9), suggesting that it may be a key metaphor in the language of cross-world attraction. In this scene, the

Spanish-*kampuniá* song may be inspired by this gringa-*kampuniá* visitor. Indeed, when Joaquín picks up the musical dialogue again after Gabriel finishes speaking to the spirits, he says that the *kampuniá hai* are here. This is not merely a sociable concession to my presence, for he speaks in Emberá to Gabriel and not to me. Joaquín is using my status as a gringa as a resource in his magic.][12]

Gabriel talks to the spirits again; Joaquín's boat song continues softly in pauses between each sentence:

G: That you look well at once you all, with what am I thus.

[song]

This sickness that I have thus, I do not want.

[song]

I am going to be right, that I say, for that there is liquor.

[song]

Money there is, for that.

[song]

I am paying for that.

[song]

Then Joaquín sings words softly:

J: The *hai* are hard.

Kampuniá hai are.

G: For that they are, for that they know, truth.

[Gabriel says he has provided money, liquor, cigarettes — all the ritual means necessary to invoke the spirits' aid. Payment is a condition of cure; it permits Gabriel to voice his worries and desires through the shaman's expertise. Money is exchanged for vision, and vision transforms the words describing symptoms into the words of cure. Gabriel cannot take a deep breath; he cannot live his life. Of what does his symptom speak? Searching, he sits across from his uncle, the *brujo,* and together they hold a party for invisible drunks. Time is measured in darkness, the many-fingered leaf-drum tapping as if wind-blown, but too regular, too synchronized to be less than human, hypnotic. Patient and curer are surrounded by sleepers' breath, somnolent cloud, media of transformation. Precisely, the home's center becomes a phantom's haven.

Gabriel seeks aid to fight that which grabs at his breath and undermines his days, making him feel less than fully human. He can only imagine the cause; this imagining enters into ritually magnetized social space to be re-shaped and returned. His emotions and his breath are gathered together and set forward on a path to well-being—after all, that's the least they can do.]

Again Joaquín sings:

J: Hai son de colores
    Mi barquito va navegando.
    Qué bonito hai ombe
    A di ba di ba di
    A di ba di ba di

   (*Hai* are of colors
    My little boat goes navigating.
    How pretty, *hai,* man
    A di ba di ba di
    A di ba di ba di)

[The song continues into the night, but my tape ends. Overcome by the sleepers' atmosphere, I go off to my corner next to the old grandmother and think no more about Gabriel.]

The next day Gabriel says that he doesn't feel any better yet, would stay another fifteen days, then go through another song. I wait till after-noon to talk to Joaquín, but he never wakes. I see them both again about a week later along the path between Tamarinbó and Promesa. Gabriel's been working for his uncle, clearing a piece of Joaquín's *monte virgen.* Joa-quín extracts labor from his nephew, a fair exchange of time and energy, agricultural labor for magical labor—not an imposition of power. Like Emberá and Waunan shamans generally, Joaquín's shamanic power does not extend into everyday life. He does agricultural work to support his family as everyone else does. He might make some extra money or get people to help him, but his magical power ends when the ritual song ends. His power is not over people but over spirits. And although he owns his spirit familiars as if they were pets, he must nevertheless entice them into helping him see. The shaman learns the art of seduction, rather than the rule of law.

Not long after I see Gabriel and Joaquín out working, news comes that Joaquín has left his wife for another woman and has had to leave Promesa in fear of revenge. Without household support, he is now vulnerable both magically and economically. He tries to reestablish himself in exile with his new woman, closer to him in age, and a few faithful male companions. I see him later in Yaviza, then in Tamarinbó, and then once again between, going downriver to sell a load of plantains with his brother, Gabriel's father.

Joaquín's life change has thrust him out on a journey. Homeless, he must give up his practice. His patients are abandoned. His state illustrates the precariousness of a shaman's status and (cf. Atkinson 1987) the importance of the relationship between shaman and community. His cure incomplete, Gabriel goes off to an Emberá settlement along the highway to seek treatment from Beatriz's brother-in-law (the *patrón* who taught Beatriz the song in haste after Tamarinbó's shaman Onofre was murdered). Adela comes upriver to Tamarinbó, where Legio treats her dizziness with plants. I don't know what happens to the other two boys. I see Gabriel again in July. He'd been mugged in Curundu, the shantytown bordering the Canal Zone that many Emberá live in when they go to the city. His money was stolen, and his hand was slashed by a knife. The doctors in the hospital there gave him some pills. They think there is something wrong with his heart.

Susceptibilities of Empowerment

When misfortune or illness occurs, the Emberá and Waunan produce an array of interpretations to explain the event and to identify a remedy. These interpretations draw from the set of images, categories, and models of processual relations that constitute the semantic field of shamanism. Some interpretations point directly to the need of shamanic curing ritual, as in specific forms of illness. If no adequate interpretation can be agreed upon, as in many cases of misfortune, or if remedies fail, as in chronic or repeated illness, a shaman may also be called upon. The shaman's task is to listen to the multilayered, open-ended contradictions and ambiguities in the discourse of illness and misfortune and enact a ritually focused movement toward closure and resolution: a timely spinning of the torn strips of experience into personal myth (cf. Lévi-Strauss 1967:161–80). Drawing from the shamanic field of meaning a set of images and relationships applicable to the specific set of symptoms and personal history of the troubled person, the shaman funnels anxieties and questions into the circuit of ritual power and returns them transformed. Through the agency of the shaman, the shamanic field acts on the patient's desire and pain, restructuring these in language and in the unconscious, altering the sense of self and reality, and, one by one, transforming the relation between Emberá and Waunan culture and the world.

In the search for cause and remedy, the interpretation of illness and misfortune may identify a misdeed (as in the case of the macheteyed monkey, Chap. 6), or it may invoke the figure of a shaman of evil heart/intent (as in the shamans' battle in the account of misfortune's hat, Chap. 6).[13] In practice, however, the evil shaman's figure seems to play no more than a shadow role in the discourse of tragedy. People are afraid of the power that shamans wield, but if particular evildoers are ever identified, they are usually outside the normal range of social intercourse. Cases to the contrary exist, of course. In the three villages that I got to know best, there were three cases in which the intention of shamans might be brought into question. It is difficult always to know, however, if negative attributions derive from their role as ritual or as social actors. The three shamans in question were all patriarchs, already deceased or the eldest generation alive. In addition to being shamans, they were the first to settle their extended families in the sites that were to become villages. As first settlers, they enjoyed a certain dominion over the land surrounding their settlement site. The authority of first settlers, however, is limited by the egalitarian orientation of Emberá culture and, in prior times or in small villages, by the abundance of unused forest. For those seeking aid from men who are first settlers and shamans (a combination that might be no coincidence), respect for dominion may be mixed with fear of magical power. A brief sketch of the three cases conveys how the dynamics of curing and killing in the shamanic field, and hence the kinds of interpretation of illness and misfortune produced, is informed by the character and acts that ritual specialists demonstrate in their roles as social actors. In this way, history sways the forces of magic.

Cueva

Cueva, the village along the highway where I did preliminary fieldwork in 1983, is half Waunan and half Emberá. The houses were distributed according to ethnicity on either side of a center path drawn roughly from the highway to the main port on the river. Each side included the home of a shaman. El Viejo, the shaman on the Emberá side, presented himself as Emberá but was actually a Waunan married to an Emberá woman. He was the first settler in the area; his son was village head. I was directed to him when I first arrived, and it was to him that I attributed my nightmare (Chap. 6). As far as I could see, he treated only campesinos and blacks who came from outside the village. He seemed to perform plant medicine (much of which is common knowledge among Emberá and Waunan) and Cauca Valley–style sorcery (a mixture of incantation and ritual accusation) to a greater extent than ritual song. No one within the village went to him for cure, for, as I learned from a Waunan girl and a woman, he was perceived as evil, as "killing" or "eating" children and old people — or as an Emberá man said, with condescension instead of fear, because "he used to know how to cure but can't do it anymore."

In contrast, Cicero was a shaman on the Waunan side who was generally thought of as having good intention. His son, who was married to Viejo's daughter, lent me the house of his father located next to his own. Cicero was staying in a dispersed dwelling in his garden down the highway in order to guard his crops from theft. I had seen him a number of times healing village persons with song (it was he who gave me the confounding explanation that he was getting out the devil, see Chap. 2). But I didn't realize the shaman was the owner of my house until he came in one day and discovered that I had been using his ritual bench, the seat of power that represents the mythical serpent named Hëï, as a pillow. Not knowing that the shelf hanging from the roof is considered private space, or the little wooden bench of any special significance, I had taken it down. He chastised me gently. I took comfort in knowing I lived under his roof. (When I visited a year later, the house had collapsed.)

While I was there, his grown daughter was visiting from another river with her family to sell plantains, bananas, and mangoes. She was suddenly stricken by an internal pain near her stomach. In the days that followed, people gathered around in sympathy as he sang and bathed her; she was brought back twice in a jeep from the clinic in a nearby town, sicker than ever. Eventually the family undertook preparations for an elaborate ritual song. Throughout the next week they gathered balsa and natural dyes with which they carved and painted a curing house and dolls, gathered golden palm fronds that they wove and hung from walls and ceiling, and gathered and prepared food. (Corn to make the alcoholic drink *chicha* was not in season, so store-bought rum was used.) Throughout these days and nights,

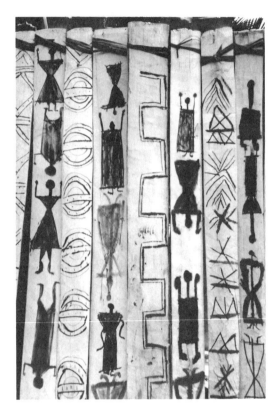

Figure 28. Waunan drawings on discarded curing house made for Cicero's daughter in Cueva.

I would intermittently hear the shaman's song and his daughter's infant's cries from the house next door. At the end of a week, at dusk, everyone came to sleep around the ritual space of cure, and the healing song event took place. The next morning the patient seemed better, and the baby stopped crying.

In the course of these activities I grew to sense a tense balance of power within the village from the perspective of the Waunan among whom I lived. This balance seemed to be embodied in the opposing figures of (symbolic killer) Viejo and (symbolic curer) Cicero. Particular cases of illness, in both indigenous and nonindigenous patients, were managed in accordance with, and were productive of, this balance of power. And in a larger sense, the balance of power seems to have been the result of, and a forum for negotiating, structural tensions that were inherent in a village divided in half by language and ethnicity, whose site lies between river (old ways) and highway (new ways), and whose land base was being increasingly challenged by campesino colonizers.[14]

Palo Blanco

Palo Blanco, the village on Río Chico, had no resident shaman at the time I did fieldwork, although an itinerant shaman frequently came through. Instead of two opposing shamans whose differences seemed to split aspects of good and evil in the village, in Palo Blanco, the split between curing and killing was constructed in opposing narratives about one shaman, a man who was the first settler and who had been dead many years. The narratives were told by two of the shaman's grandsons, Bernabe and Valentín, now two elders in the village. They each told me their versions of the story independently, for they interpreted Grandfather's actions differently. They also had different perspectives on the role that shamans should play in the new politics of village and *comarca*. The two cousins did agree on the circumstances that set this story in motion, however. The text I present here is a synthesis of the points upon which they agreed.[15]

The Phantom Gringo Boat

One Easter when Barnabe and Valentín were young boys, their grandfather the shaman took them to find a chest of gold that was buried in the Congo River, not far from the island of El Encanto [Enchantment]. They had been told exactly where it was and that it was buried by a Spanish store owner who made the gold in the lumber business. But they never reached the treasure. To get there, they had to canoe downriver and out into the expansive waters of the Gulf [in itself a frightening experience to boys accustomed only to river travel]. As they neared the Congo, they caught sight of what appeared to be a gringo boat. The boat was luminous and colorful. They tried to catch up, but it kept slipping away into the waters before them. Although they hauled and hauled, their canoe seemed to hardly move. They could smell the diesel fumes; it burned their eyes. When nightfall enveloped the boat in darkness, they heard things, like sounds of a barrel being thrown overboard. At dawn, the boat remained elusive. Grandfather took ill. He told the boys that the boat was a phantom, that it was *hai* sent in challenge to him the shaman from the Chämbëra, the non-human beings who live below the earth. Grandfather's throat closed up, he could barely speak, he had no strength. The boys, although young and frightened, managed to row to La Palma, the provincial capital at the mouth of the sea. There they paid a black-*kampuniá* cargo boat owner to take them to Yaviza, where they met close family members who had come down to town to sell plantains. Night fell. The next morning the family set off in haste poling upriver for home. Just below the cement gate built by the water company, seven cows crossed their field of vision. The cows were Grandfather's *hai*.

In Yaviza, they had bought the soda, *aguardiente* [white rum], cigarettes, and blue aniline dye necessary for the song. As soon as they reached home, they collected *pärärä* leaves for the ritual drum. They painted and perfumed their bodies and then set Grandfather down with ritual bench and batons at his side. Grandfather could not even sit up; little humming noises were all he could make. But his bodyguards, his *hai*, accompanied him. By the next morning he could talk a little. Grandfather bade his family members to bring everything necessary. Four young women—painted, perfumed, and wearing new *parumas*—set to work separating the corn kernels from the cob, then grinding the kernels and putting them in the big pots for making *chicha*. Others went out into forests and dooryard gardens to gather balsa wood and *achiote* [S. *Bixa orellana*], source of the red paint that contrasts with the aniline blue. With these materials, they sculpted and painted distinctive classes of animal dolls. They brought *makenke* for firewood to cook the *chicha*, *pärärä* palm fronds for braiding and hanging. They caught a horned lizard [E. *ochorró*], made it drink *chicha*, and tied it up with *patákoro* plantains for the *hai* to eat. They built a *ranchito* and set the table with the broad-leaf *hoja vijado*, then filled calabashes with *chicha* for the *hai* to drink.

Grandfather could see all the crew members of the boat. He made a model of it. He put in the captain with no head or neck and the crew member with no feet [see Fig. 1]. He built a boat with a roof and a plane on the top for the *hai* to go back to the other side. [These Chämbëras were prepared!] He placed this spirit boat on a shelf on top of the decorated *ranchito*, above the calabashes filled with *chicha*. When all the details were properly in place, Grandfather used his powers to bring the phantom gringo boat up from Yaviza. By means of his knowledge he made a tide to get the boat up to the village, a current that came from below, like a motor. Then he tied it up and caught its *hai*. In the process of curing himself, Grandfather acquired the power of the Chämbëra's familiars. He held this power in his batons: it made him larger than life. Over the years, he would share his power with no one who came to him for knowledge because, he said, it cost him too much. Eventually he died a slow and painful death. (T/E and −T/S)

Thirty years passed since the shaman-Grandfather died. The *hai* that he brought had scattered around the settlement that had since become Palo

Blanco, the village in which this gringa recorded the tale.[16] The gringo spirit crew wandered the village outskirts, and no one was in control. There had been a recent epidemic of spirit attacks, mostly among young women. When youth encountered a spirit in the forest, they were said to feel their bodies whirling. When they returned, they presented the villagers with a mad rush of spirit-talk. They suddenly saw and sang with the power of extraordinary vision appropriate to practiced shamans. Valentín's daughter was the first to suffer in the recent rash of attacks. She saw the boat. It was tied up there below the calabash tree next to Abebaiba's house. The traveling shaman that came through Palo Blanco could see it also.

Bernabe counted twenty-one cases of sickness in recent years. Fearful of spirit attacks and concerned that fear could trigger household dispersal regardless of development's progress, villagers agreed that they needed a shaman who could retake control. They collected money and hired a man from another river who was a relative of Grandfather, one who knew the same song Grandfather used to capture the spirits in the first place. This man tried to recapture the crew left behind, but he could not match Grandfather's power and met with only partial success.

The shamanic field pertaining to the village of Palo Blanco was out of balance. The double aspect of curing and killing was here merged in one figure, the deceased Emberá shaman-grandfather, who brought underworld spirits to the village and died, leaving no one in control. His grandsons interpreted his actions in opposing ways. The favored grandson, Bernabe, eldest son of the daughter who married an Emberá, inherited all Grandfather's plantain orchards to distribute among his siblings at his discretion. His education beyond grade school was financed by Grandfather, and his literacy qualified him as official village head, a position he kept for many years. Bernabe thought Grandfather had to bring the spirits up to the village in order to cure himself. He placed responsibility for the loose spirits on Evangelical missionaries from the neighboring village upriver. For they, with their threats of eternal damnation, convinced Grandfather to let them pour kerosene on his batons and burn them, scattering all the spirits corralled within. He blamed Grandfather only for weakness. Valentín, the ill-favored grandson, son of the daughter who married a Waunan man, inherited nothing to speak of, is not literate, and wanted only local, informal power as a community leader. He thought Grandfather was evil. He thought that Grandfather lived still in the underworld with the Chämbëra and that he brought the spirit boat to the village not for cure but because he was greedy for power. A year or two after the fateful song, he said that

Grandfather told him: "This will be all forest around here again, because one by one you will die. After I die you all be finished off by the *hai*."

As Taussig's (1987:159) work with healers and sorcerers in Colombia shows, good and evil shamans, like the Christian God and the Devil, "can stand not merely in opposition, but as a mutually empowering synergism." Even as the healer does good, he or she is empowered by the struggle with evil. The ambivalence of this fact underlies the argument of the cousins about Grandfather and informs their debate over the roles of shamans in the villages. The favored grandson focused on the curing skills of shamans. Along with Emberá representatives in national government, he was all for holding a shamans' convention. He had hopes, in the long run, of incorporating shamans into village and *comarcal* bureaucracies and of using their powers in the management of crime. The ill-favored grandson thought that power itself corrupts. He focused more on how evil shamans must be punished and destroyed. In the negotiation over how shamans will be positioned in the changing social order, the sudden voices of whirling madness that overtook village members continued to be interpreted in relation to this one shaman's historic disappearance.

Tamarinbó

Tamarinbó was the smallest of the three settlements, the most recent to become a village, and hence the most ecologically sound. It was primarily an extended kin group of Emberá with little missionary exposure. It was also the most egalitarian, judging by land use and inheritance practices (see Chap. 9). Evil shamans figured only in the personal histories of villagers: Eva's mother had one or two children killed by a *häïmbaná* when she was a young woman in Colombia. He was caught and burned at the stake by the state, her nephew reported. Zelda, another elder woman, attributed her deafness to the vengeance of a *häïmbaná* whose advances she rebuffed as a young girl in Colombia. There was no shaman, alive or dead, who was associated directly with the settlement and considered to be evil.

There was a power vacuum in the shamanic field, however. The principal shaman and first settler, Eva's father, was inexplicably murdered (see Chap. 3). Although he was a shaman, there was no reason to associate the murder with his ritual practice. Not everyone had good things to say about him when it came to everyday matters, but no one thought him evil, and no one voiced any suspicion of his intent as a shaman who cured. Being hit over the head with a rock was an evil, but not unnatural, act of aggression against him. The unknown assailant was assumed to be a man with a grudge or a debt, but without special power.

Healing responsibilities in the settlement were partially taken over by the deceased's sister-in-law Beatriz. She took a crash course on the song from another brother-in-law who was a shaman in a dispersed site out on the highway not far from Cueva (the same one Joaquín went to for cure after he left home). She was generally considered a not too powerful first line of defense for immediate kin. During my stay, she held a number of songs: one for Carolina's infant with diarrhea who died; one for Eva's infant with bronchitis who made it to the Yaviza hospital and lived; one for a boy who almost died a fire-related death twice on one Easter day; one for her nephew who was going away to school in Yaviza. In some cases, such as Gabriel's, people went to a shaman in a neighboring village, or sought further to find shamans of greater renown, such as the woman in Chucunaque.

Because of the death of the shaman and first settler, this settlement was in transition. Villagers did not perceive a generalized threat emanating from an out-of-balance shamanic field, however. The ritual power of the murdered shaman was perceived to be safely stored in the batons. The social mechanism for passing on the batons to the next generation, much like orchards, was in place. The day I visited the cemetery with Eva, her mother, and her sister-in-law Celestina, we passed the cacao trees on the path and Grandmother said: "This is the chocolate of the old man, the father of Onofre. That one sung too. He passed the baton on to Onofre. He also died. Now Eva has the batons." Grandmother said that Eva had sung once. Miming as she spoke, Grandmother said: "With eyes closed, all *brujos* sing like this with eyes closed." So perhaps someday Eva will activate her inheritance and secure the shamanic field for the healing of the people in her settlement, whose discourse positioned the killing aspect of the shaman outside of their immediate field of social interaction.

Each settlement has a shamanic field that corresponds to it; that is, the social field and shamanic field are in dynamic relation.[17] Incidents of illness and misfortune are interpreted in terms of that dynamic relation. The synergistic opposition between good and evil is worked through in everyday and ritual discourse within the village. Although the struggle to achieve some balance focuses on the local context, problems solved and solutions created are simultaneously part of an expanded political economic field.[18] By means of the social-shamanic dynamic, local culture struggles to impress meaning on changes wrought by transnational forces so that they can be molded to local purpose.

In this expanded context, the particular forms that good and evil assume change with history. In his ethnohistorical study of cases of eighteenth-century shamanic combat that were brought to trial as witch-craft cases in Ecuador and Colombia, Salomon (1983:425) finds that curing and killing were considered to be distinctive, antithetical roles for shamans. He suggests that these roles might be phases in political careers, wherein successful curers who gained power by protecting clients and defeating antagonists came to preeminence with a ready base of support. Later, if their decisions proved harmful to some members of the community, they would come to be seen as killer shamans whose presence demanded a cure. Contemporary cases of Emberá and Waunan shamans lend support to this suggestion, where the shamans are also patriarchs and first settlers, such as the case of El Viejo in Cueva. As the case of the deceased grandfather-shaman in Palo Blanco also suggests, a community might not achieve consensus about where to assign antithetical aspects of curing and killing, and one shaman may be spoken of as either curer or killer depending on the speaker's experience.

In the cases of Cueva and Palo Blanco, where the evil aspect of shamanic power is associated with particular local shamans, it may be no accident that they are also patriarchs who were the first settlers. Respect for their dominion could lead to resentment if they or their well-positioned descendants are ungenerous with resources. These feelings could intensify with village formation as land becomes more limited. However, for lowland shamans practicing in the Emberá and Waunan traditions, I would argue that there is no necessary link between shamanic power and political and economic power. It is the inequalities generated by patriarchy and linear descent (see Chap. 9) that lead to the identification of specific local shamans as evil, whether evil shamans "use another man's wife" or claim more than a fair share of land for themselves and their descendants. The assignment of evil to particular shamans in the local context is not inherent in shamanic practice itself. Although we cannot separate shamans from the social and political context in which they live and work, egalitarian modes of social relationship are nevertheless conducive to the perception of ritual power as curing. Killing, curing's antithetical aspect — however necessary to the logic of cure — may be displaced onto a nonspecifiable person or being outside the realm of everyday social interaction. This is applicable to the case of the murdered grandfather-shaman in Tamarinbó and, indeed, for the several rituals of various shamans that I attended (as far as I could tell, given my reliance on translation from Emberá to Spanish). In these public events, blame for causing illness tends to be assigned with vague or unknown referents— people met on journeys afar, a poisoned drink offered by one of many possible people, an invasion by an otherworld spirit that slipped in through a breach in the boundary. In effect, at this point in history, most real-world encounters that the Emberá and Waunan have with shamans are for the purpose of healing not harming, and the process of healing engenders positive, peaceful relations among family members. Antagonism is continually deflected to realms seen only by those with shamanic power; the everyday consequences of this process is apparent peace.

Among the living Emberá shamans whom I have met with or heard of, ritual practice is not linked to political power in any official or otherwise explicit sense. Consistent with the egalitarian, dispersed, and autonomous organization of traditional Emberá settlement patterns and work organization, the institution of shamanism is nonhierarchical. When not engaged in ritual practice, an Emberá shaman lives, works, and dresses as any other man or woman. As a general rule, they do not use their special powers to control others. In everyday life, they appear indistinguishable from ordinary persons.

But even if all killing shamans are imaginary and all real shamans are curers, the paradoxical power of curing shamans requires analysis. Although they do not cause it, in their struggle against it, curing shamans are nevertheless empowered (and endangered) by illness and misfortune (Taussig 1987:159). The state too, in its best-intentioned offers of development, could also be said to be empowered by illness and misfortune— for example, in fulfilling society's "needs" (coming to aid in natural disaster, punishing crime, etc.). Certainly shamanic and state power are very different, and yet they may share some structural characteristics. Foucault's (1980:98) analyses of state power are also useful in thinking about shamanic power: "Power must be analyzed as something which circulates, or rather as something which always functions in the form of a chain. It is never localized here or there, never in anybody's hands, never appropriated as a commodity or piece of wealth. Power is employed and exercised through a net-like organization. And not only do individuals circulate between its threads; they are always in the position of simultaneously undergoing and exercising this power. They are not only its inert and consenting target; they are always also the elements of its articulation. In other words, individuals are the vehicles of power, not its points of application."

Shamanic power lacks the imposing dominance of state power.[19] It has no military might to back its words with force, no organization to command and channel resources, no modern communication or transport system, no capital to speak of. Instead of relying on the state's imposing dominance, shamans rely on symbolism that is embedded in everyday life. The field of meaning that encodes ritual healing power is produced in conjunction with social relations more generally — shamanism already is where the world system seeks to be; Emberá think and act in its terms; it precedes world system dominance. As a mode of interpretation, shamanism exceeds the practice of specialists; it is an integral part of common survival strategies, as fundamental to daily life as ecology.

As a kind of cultural transformation, the effects of shamanic healing may act in critical counterpoint to state power. By indirectly linking illness and misfortune to social, political, and economic conditions, shamanic interpretation and treatment may lead to solutions not in line with development expertise. The discourse of shamanism, in or out of ritual, may function to resist the power of capitalist efforts at organizing labor, creating consumers, and concentrating settlement. For example, if social conflict and ecological stress are interpreted in terms of shamanic imbalance but cannot be ritually adjusted in song, dispersal of residence is a standard solution. This shamanic solution has undermined attempts of administrators and their appointed indigenous caciques to concentrate villages in Central and South America since colonial times (Salomon 1983:417; Spalding 1974). Dispersal may take place on the level of individual, household, or group, and may do so with or without a shaman's prescription (or threat).[20] Considering that the Emberá have always preferred to live a river bend apart, allowing them enough land for orchards and fields and protecting them from the sight of neighbors (for to see is to have power), it is amazing that the Emberá have adjusted as well as they have to the squeeze of history. For this, shamanism must be credited as well. For while its effects can give form to resistance, like witchcraft and psychoanalysis, shamanism is also a remedial institution (cf. Favret-Saada 1989) that helps people adjust to the range of opportunities and constraints in the transforming social structures of our planet.

Conclusion

As historical actors, shamans can exploit their ritual powers. While there is no contemporary evidence that shamans use ritual power directly to wrest control over resources from others in their communities, their ritual power may lend them a certain advantage, making nonspecialists more afraid of opposing their unfairness, should it occur. As these cases from Darién suggest, the opposing and synergistic logic of the shamanic field is in dynamic relation to the social field, both structured by the paired concepts of good and evil, curing and killing. Where relations among people in a community, including the shaman(s), are basically egalitarian, it seems that attributions of evil intent are displaced onto some distant terrain with unspecifiable actors. Where there is an asymmetric distribution of resources due to a nonegalitarian organization of social relations, as for example, in patriarchy, the attribution of evil may be brought closer to home. If a shaman is a patriarch, or a woman who benefits from patriarchy, and is implicated in asymmetric resource distribution, the evil/killing aspect may be attributed to his or her ritual role by a whole or a part of the community. In that case, the ritual role would assume the character of sorcery in the perceptions of some or all of the community. In contrast, as Mauricio Pardo's (personal communication 1993) experience among the Emberá of the Chocó indicates, given two shamans of equal power (in terms of the number of batons they rule), the person with the smaller base of support from kin is the one who is most likely to be accused of and attacked for sorcery. This suggests that a marginal woman shaman may be more susceptible to accusation than an established patriarch. The dynamics are clearly complex, especially if the circle of accusation widens. In nonegalitarian situations, for example, the charge of sorcery may be applied to male or female actors who benefit from patriarchy but who are not shamans and who may feel that they themselves are victims of the "envious." And these indeed seek out sorcerers to enact either retributory or protective magic for them. In this way, sorcery, the negative cast of shamanism, may become a generalized mode of discourse in certain social and historical contexts.[21] If things get worse in Darién, shamanism could sink further into the discourse of sorcery. But if it is true that the more evil things get, the greater the power of healing, we may take faith in the forces of creative transformation.

In their ritual work, shamans continue to prepare precise points in time and space to link up the everyday world with a circuit of healing power. With song, drink, smoke, and perfume, shamans seduce spirits into the circuit of power and then borrow their otherworld vision. Their seductive lure is made more compelling by the language of capture. The once-worthy traditional metaphor of shamans as hunters winning animals/spirits in battle has nearly been eclipsed by metaphors derived from the Conquest. The better to compel spirit seduction, the lowland tropical forest shamanic bricolage is now accented with signs of colonial power: batons given to indigenous intermediaries by colonial administrators as icons of their apportioned power; the name *patrón* for the foreigner who stole what he wanted and called himself master; coins and printed paper, icons of the abstract power of universal exchange. But it is not for the purpose of multiplying the effects of oppressors that the trappings of power are appropriated as symbolic resources in shamanic ritual. Ritual draws the gestures of oppression out from signs of domination and replaces them with gestures of healing. In this way, the shamans continue to tie their ancient song to the dynamic of history for the good of humankind.

nine

Cosmo-Snake and the Nation-State

The paradoxical dimension of human experience is addressed in the myth of Hëïropoto, a culture hero/antihero whose strange birth and disgusting habits imbue him with the power to battle the cosmo-snake Hëï. Hëï is the serpent of paradox who twists fertility and mortality in its coils; he is the river dragon of whirlpools who generates the waters of life only to devour the humans who drink of them. Hëïropoto succeeds in challenging Hëï because he is made of the same paradoxical stock.

Born from the calf of his mother's leg [*hëïro*], Hëïropoto's birth was his mother's death. Raised by his grandmother, he started questioning as soon as he could speak. He wanted to know why his mother died. He wanted to drink the monthly blood that seeped from women's wombs. He kept asking for it. The women hated him. They sent him off to the edges of the realm, telling him, "The moon [*hëïdeko*] killed your mother." And so he tried to cast the moon down to earth; climbing, climbing, climbing up a bamboo pole, he grabbed the moon badly, and the bamboo broke. Hëïropoto fell like a bird, like the fluff of a balsa flower, like a rock into the other land below where the humanlike beings called the Chämbera live (the same beings who challenged the Grandfather-shaman with a phantom gringo boat, Chap. 8). Doing everything backward, Chämbera sleep in the day and work at night. They cannot eat. They can only inhale smoke from their cooking pots, for they have no anuses, or their anuses have only tiny little holes big enough for cockroach-size turds. So Hëïropoto stayed and cut anuses for them, collecting the blood. And when he returned from the land of the Chämbera, he brought the women fruits that they had never seen before: *hëïa* (pejibaye), *tuétahö* (guava), *nënzaráhö* (star apple). The women were grateful for the gifts. But then he started in again, asking the women if they saved their moon-blood for him. They would tell him that this monster, then that monster, killed his mother, hoping he would die in battle. But he always came back. When he was swallowed by the Hëï, they thought he was surely gone. But he was inside searching for Hëï's heart. When he found it, he cut it with his machete and returned to the women again. He brought the little sons that had been devoured, returning them to their mothers from the belly of the cosmo-snake. And then he asked again: "Women, where is my calabash of moon-blood?" They wanted to kill him. Finally they thought, "We women will have to kill him ourselves." (The men did not disagree.) Then he, in that way of his, changed into mosquitoes and flies, turned into all this piece by piece — horseflies, blackflies, bats punishing our dogs. He's still drinking blood. He did not die. He lives asking. It's still ugly. It's finished already. To here, no more is the story. (T/E)

The myth of Hëïropoto has become central to my understanding of how gender is used in the management of paradox.[1] The short version I tell here is adapted from three tape-recorded versions of Hëïropoto, one told by a man, and two by women. As I interpret it, the myth encodes a series of principles concerning paradox that are fundamental to the organization of Emberá culture and its articulation with the nation-state:

Human existence is founded on paradox: death in life.

There are key symbols that represent paradox in Emberá cosmology. These include the mythical images created in the narrative of Hëï (cosmo-snake) and Hëïropoto (hero and anti-hero). The narrative links its created images to images that exist in nature, that is, moon (whose celestial rotations govern tides, whether its image is present or absent) and moon-blood (a periodic sign of fertile continuity and the absence of conception; from a male's point of view, a wound or matter out of place).[2]

The imageric linkage of mythical elements to natural elements mythologizes the natural world (cf. Lévi-Strauss), such that "Nature" itself becomes a cultural construction.[3]

Of the two natural images representing paradox, only the moon-blood can be humanly controlled — that is, it can be allowed to appear or made to disappear. In moon-blood resides the meaning of paradox *and* the potential for its management.

Paradox can be managed by separating contradictory aspects (e.g., defining sacred and profane, home and otherworld) or by removing signs of paradox from view (absenting moon-blood). But in order for this management strategy to be effective, the work involved must be hidden; for reality to appear, the details of its construction must not be announced.

Although paradox is a source of anxiety that requires management, confrontation with paradox (transgression) is also a potential source of creation and restoration.

Desire to confront paradox can be displaced and fragmented but not destroyed (myth turns nature's parasites into proof of its own eternal cycles).

A Girl's Ritual Training

There is a myth about Young Woman (E. *Awëra*) first recorded among the Chamí of Colombia, an indigenous group culturally related to the Emberá (Chaves 1945:152–53, cited in Vasco 1985:114). During the enclosure ritual of her first menstruation, Young Woman gets extraordinarily fat. As she gets fatter, she gets heavier. Little by little she sinks into the earth until she arrives in the world below. She is the sister of the Mother of Fish and is still down below in the time of now. When she moves, there are tremors on earth.

Quite by accident, I happen upon a girl's first moon-blood ritual in Tamarinbó. There is not much to see. For a week, the girl is made to stay inside a small, leaf-walled enclosure just big enough to lie down in. Her family goes about their affairs, ignoring the enclosure set up on the sleeping platform. She is not permitted to speak. Her mother passes food to her, removes her excrement in a chamber pot, and helps her bathe with clean water every little while throughout day and night. Her brother-in-law explains that it is a time of great danger for her and everyone around her. If her body is not treated in the right manner, she could cause cases of skin eruption (S. *granos*). Like the transition of tree to canoe (see Chap. 5), the danger of life-stage transition is described in the discourse of disease, here magnified by the paradoxical power of moon-blood. When the week of silence and withdrawal is over, the girl-now-woman is available as a sexual partner. She can no longer adorn her body with flowers, perfumed water, and black paint, singing as she crosses the cleared space of the village in preparation for her shaman-grandmother to cure. The 1½' length of *paruma* cloth that encloses her lower torso is replaced with a 3½'-length cloth. Leaving her soon to be milk-laden breasts bare, the woman's *paruma* hides her torso and hampers her stride, making it impossible to run and leap in the forest with the same freedom as boys. She will not (may not?) speak to me of her experience.

The Management and Confrontation of Paradox Is Organized by Gender

Moon-blood is the substance of paradox arising from the female body in the center of the Emberá everyday. The management of moon-blood (and giving birth, the positive aspect of this paradoxical sign) anchors the analogous tasks of separation, withdrawal, and repetition that culture assigns to the female domain (e.g., growing and gathering food, bringing food and fresh water into the home, paring peels off plantains in preparation for cooking, sweeping, carrying out refuse, caring for the dead, making lightweight tools, repairing, curing ailments with plant medicines). Together the performance of these tasks creates a space for life (everyday, home) and pushes back the boundaries of death (illness, otherness, misfortune). This is the symbolic dimension of housework.[4] Training girls to dedicate their bodies to the management of paradox (i.e., the reproduction of life) is fundamental to their constitution as gendered subjects. Women uphold their cosmological role, even though the significance of their actions is hidden by the supreme ordinariness of the tasks involved; even though they have the natural ability to carry out tasks assigned to the masculine role. Unproclaimed, women thus perform the primary acts of culture. In contrast to contemporary theory in psychoanalysis and anthropology, this analysis suggests that culture originates in gesture, not language. What is spoken is contingent on myriad and overlapping motions. The repetition of daily movement creates cultural space.

While both men and women find their center in the home, the cosmological division of labor orients their responsibilities in complementary directions.[5] The male body lacks the capacity to carry out tasks involving the substance of paradox.[6] In contrast to girls, boys are trained to seek new sources of creation by crossing out of the Emberá everyday into the unknown, posting the other pole of paradox in the outside world. This is fundamental to the constitution of male subjectivity. Though centered at home, men's responsibilities are oriented outward toward other races and species. Men have primary responsibility for building the larger structures upon which the everyday depends (the house, canoe, larger wooden processing and cooking tools). In their shared agricultural labor with women, men are responsible for axing down the large trees. Men are trained to travel between home and the outside world to engage in hunting, fishing, adventure, and trade. Male transgressions of cultural boundaries are found acceptable within a range that is negotiated with women. The limits of this range are marked by Hëiropoto, the one who tears the veil between the sense of reality and its manufacture.

Upon this fundamental gendered split in cosmological work, an organization of labor is elaborated that overdetermines the roles of men and women in history. The fairness of this division depends on the continuing presence of the Emberá home as a valued symbol, a source of stability, identity, and shamanic power. If history changes the conditions under which the cosmological underpinnings of the everyday are reproduced—pushing egalitarian relations toward patriarchy and taking authority and control out of the household—it could make dedication to cosmological tasks a burden. Because the mechanism linking housework to the construction of reality is most secret, the guardians of paradox least acknowledged, women (and men who are oriented outward to the upriver forests but not to *kampuniá* towns and *comarca* politics) are most likely to be negatively affected by recent changes accompanying development.

Official Dance

Then: An elder woman in Palo Blanco told me: in the fiestas of old, men and women got drunk and fought. Grabbing each other by the hair, they'd stagger around locked together and sing songs to raise the fighting spirit.

Later: The entourage of officials, uniformed military officers, media, and other guests stand in a circle out in the sun with the rest of the Emberá audience. We watch an old woman lead young girls in dance. Holding hands in a line, black-painted skin set off by bright *parumas,* necklaces of silver coins flashing on their breasts, their gestures signify a series of wild animals—armadillo, parrot, agouti.[7] When the dance is done, the crowd moves over to the open field next to the school. We close our ears to the noise and watch. Mechanical wings whip up the edge of the bush as the minister of government and justice gets back in the helicopter with the Guard and flies off into the sky.

Figure 29. Two cousins in Palo
Blanco dressed for the same
party. Drawing by E. Goitein.

Just a few women remember these dances, once performed by men and
women during nighttime curing songs and celebrations. Finding the old
patterns in her memory, this old woman taught the young ones the dance
so they could perform them at political congresses and international events
of cultural exchange sponsored by the government. In the multiethnic field
of Panamanian politics, Emberá culture = nature; being "natural" is the
trademark of indigenous status, and indigenous status is the basis for rights
to a *comarca*. A few chosen, bare-breasted women miming the gestures of
wild animals enact the emblem of Emberá ethnic identity after the men are
finished negotiating the details of state.[8] The bare-breasted woman and the
suited man is a composite image that encodes indigenous relations to the
kampuniá world (Kane 1986a; Taussig 1993:187–88; see Fig. 29). They

index the way in which men take on the trappings, and may eventually assume the power of the state, within the Emberá household.

The dance is performed at the end of the morning session of the last day of the twenty-ninth annual congress of the Emberá and Waunan held on May 27, 1985, in Lajas Blancas, home village of the second cacique. The morning starts with great expectation, everybody hoping that the new president Barletta would come. In midmorning a motored canoe arrives and a helicopter lands, and several officials take their places on chairs at the front tables in the long open hall constructed for the congress. Bright yellow strips of *horopo* palm and sculpted balsa dolls hang from beams; painted rainbows, fruits and fish, and two large welcome banners complete the decoration. Emberá leaders and government officials face an Emberá and Waunan audience sitting on a series of benches and logs aligned on the ground. (To assure attendance, an ad hoc jail — variant of the stockade mentioned in Chap. 1 — has been built under a house nearby for those men found skipping out on the long hours of log sitting.) All women wear blouses with their finest traditional *parumas* (bright paisleys imported from the Far East by Panama City merchants especially for the Chocó); all the young women are painted with *jagua* (there will be a big dance this evening to mark the end of the congress). The men wear factory-made, imported shorts, pants, and shirts. The major in charge of the Ninth Military Zone of Darién is introduced first. He gets up and says: "We are here in the patio. Whatever uneasiness you have we will send to our command or resolve right here."

Oppression and protection are offered in the same breath. No one forgets that the latter is "civilization's" current cast of the former.

We wonder if one of the officials up there might be President Barletta. But no, the man is introduced as the new minister of government and justice. (The cabinet had been shaken up just a few weeks before this, and its new members knew practically nothing about the *comarca* process. This is the first major *comarca* setback in the series leading up to the U.S. invasion. The annual congress had actually been canceled three times because of government turmoil that delayed funding for food and transport, provoking much argument among the Emberá about dependency.) The minister, an architect, speaks in Spanish: "The first thing I see is a village, pretty and traditional. I have admired your architecture and traditions for a long time. Here in nature you are near the Creator, near the center of being human; you will help us love and defend nature. Thank you."

A series of reports are presented by Emberá men on committees: The

Agriculture and Cattle Committee asks for technical assistance; loans to increase plantain production; positions relating to Emberá development for the many unemployed Emberá with bachelor's degrees in agronomy; expansion of export markets; industrialization of yucca; diversification of cultivars; more jobs; less restrictive regulations concerning hoof-and-mouth disease so that Emberá could own more cows to provide milk for their families; facilitation of transport and sales by, for example, the construction of new ports. The *Health Committee* says it can't proceed because they have no money and not enough staff; mortality and common infectious diseases have increased to alarming rates in the last few years; medical teams from the hospital in Yaviza are supposed to make trips to upriver villages twice a year, but they only come once; wage increases are needed for health assistants who work in the distant zones upriver; aqueducts for the larger villages and wells in the smaller ones are needed to prevent consumption of contaminated river water and the increase in parasitic infection. The *Education Committee* needs a new provincial education director; more Emberá teachers to be named for village positions; resolution of a problem with student scholarships; funds to finish outfitting schools; the beginning of design, production, and distribution of teaching materials (especially for the bilingual Emberá-Spanish education program); agricultural and sports equipment.

After the committee presentations, the minister gets up and says, "The list is so simple yet necessary; it grieves me, it causes me anguish, and I identify with it. All groups in Panama have to unify to progress. We have to unite our wills. He that has, gives, from us as a people, not just from the government; we give you this basketball equipment. . . . As a Panamanian, I am proud to share with you your destiny. We're all together. Our destiny is of all the *pueblos* in Panama." The first cacique gives him a baton that was in the little craft boutique set up for the congress; a girl comes up and gives him a basket for his wife; a woman comes up and gives him a hat that he puts on and gets a laugh. Then they move out to the sun to watch the dance.

Women are not vocal participants in most congressional dialogue (except for one young college-educated woman, who dons the mandatory *paruma* when she comes to the congresses from the city). Many women do not speak and understand Spanish with ease.[9] They are released early from every session to cook and wash for the men whom they accompany from home villages, doing the mundane tasks that make all this play of signs in the field of politics possible.[10]

Cosmological echoes: women's distinctive presence in the official arena is the essential silent embodiment of Emberá identity. "Tradition remains the sacred weapon oppressors repeatedly hold up whenever the need to maintain their privileges, hence to impose the form of the old on the content of the new, arises" (Trinh 1989:106).

Women's Land Rights

The association of women with the home and men with outside adventure is repeated throughout the larger corpus of Emberá myth. With this persistent structure, slanted differently in its tellings, myths have crossed the space and time of history. As the twenty-first century closes in, upriver forest diminishes, and even myth points downriver to a postnuclear otherworld where animals are few, races of *kampuniá* multiply, and devils roam multinational banks and munitions dumps. Emberá are met more often by humans with different modes of reality construction and their own versions of the fantastic. But even as encounters with alternate realities increase, the cosmological dynamic of guardianship — deflection of transgression, otherworld adventure, and gift-bearing return — continues to be played out according to gender. The mythical assignments of the sexes, with its implicit privilege of male freedom of movement over female bonds to home, encodes an unequal structural relation that can be appropriated and emphasized by foreign/nationalized forms of dominance.

Women's guardianship of Emberá ways is a responsibility that has always been accompanied by rights. Cosmology has ordained them, but egalitarian principles of social organization make their acceptance worthwhile. For women to accept the burden of the internal dimension of making the world knowable and to forgo the responsibilities and rights of the external dimension of this process (dealing with other races), the political and economic balance between women and men must be maintained. If power and authority are to be drawn out of the household and in to markets and official meetings, gender assignments also need to be restructured. Unfortunately, women's rights are not always recognized by outside authorities, including scholars and leaders of change — who have been mostly men. Women are being excluded from positions of power made available with integration into the national political economic structure. Their rights are increasingly ignored, yet their obligation to uphold tradition is called upon more and more.

[June 23, 1985, Palo Blanco:] Everybody was happily getting ready to celebrate the first day of the fiesta of San Juan in Palo Blanco. The women
were painting me. It felt nice, gentle, the first time anybody really touched
my body except for Grandmother patting my shoulder in Tamarinbó. They
cut a piece of bamboo with two points. This they dipped into a calabash
holding *jagua,* black dye squeezed from the *Genipa americana* fruit that
they collected from a neighbor's dooryard garden. Then, slowly and carefully, they traced from one ear along my jaw line skipping over my mouth
to the other ear, then two vertical lines from mouth to chin. Using the
double point, they drew cross-hatching lines in the rectangle on the chin,
then filled in solid the bottom of my face from the jaw line down. (I was
still too shy to take off my shirt.) Then they drew double lines around my
upper arms and filled in the rest of my arms solid.

We were talking and laughing when Isadora [the teller of the Antumiá
story, Chap. 5], whose house we were in, came in. She was hopping mad.
She had just found out that her former husband was about to sell the land
that was their farm downriver without saying a word to anyone. He had already sold the house and the orchard and kept all the money when they
split up. She found out about his attempt to sell the rest of the farm only
because she happened to go there. She knows no means of redress.

This is one example of how a man can take advantage of patriarchal
presumptions and ignore a woman's joint rights to land when dealing with
persons who are not a part of the local community. He and Isadora built
the farm together. Were the situation reversed, she would not have been
able to bypass his rights so easily. In contrast to some statements in recent
literature on Emberá land practices in Darién (Faron 1961, 1962; Herlihy
1986), my study of land use and ownership in two villages provides evidence that supports women's rights to own and inherit land.[11] Men in
general do not contest these rights, at least to me. Evidence includes in-
depth interviews with men and women in all the households in Tamarinbó,
Río Tupisa, with twenty households (including four in dispersed sites),
and Palo Blanco, Río Chico, with forty households (dispersed sites not
interviewed). It is supported by maps of all areas under cultivation around
both villages and informal discussions on land use practices.

With systematic certainty I find that women's rights to land do exist,
only to find that they are beginning to be ignored or taken away. Tamarinbó was composed of households that came together into a village five
years before I began fieldwork; Palo Blanco was a village for fifteen years
before. Through comparison, changes wrought by village formation could

be discerned.[12] As expected, with time and population increase, land area under cultivation increases. In Tamarinbó, 35 *kabuyas* (128 acres) of plantain orchard were under cultivation; in Palo Blanco, 75 *kabuyas* (275 acres).[13] Assuming that Tamarinbó represents forms of land practice that are closer to those used in traditional dispersed settlements, the two-village comparison can be used to observe a number of changes that are tied to gender. Intensification of land use with village formation is altering the gender of those who claim ownership. In five-year-old Tamarinbó (population 102), women claimed ownership to 59 percent of the plantain orchards, men 41 percent. In fifteen-year-old Palo Blanco (population 232), the ratio shifts dramatically toward men: women claimed ownership to only 28 percent of plantain orchards, men 72 percent. The decline of women's land claims in Palo Blanco is accompanied by a decline in generalized sharing of land claims among the kindred; that is, the settlers in direct line of descent are keeping a tighter hold on plantain landholdings. In the more established village, there was also an increase in the amount of land claimed on the basis of cash sale (28 percent, compared to 10 percent), rather than inheritance, or owners' own labor clearing and planting. In sum, this comparison suggests the more general hypothesis that with increasing time in nuclear settlement, land use intensification, and incorporation into a cash economy, the ownership rights to plantain orchards are shifting away from women and kindred groups and toward male-oriented groups descended from original settlers.

But claims are not the same thing as rights. Women may have rights to land and men may acknowledge these rights, but when it comes to claiming ownership to male outsiders, women's rights may be glossed over. Telling powerful outsiders what the Emberá think they expect to hear is a common discursive strategy. The Emberá know that a man's word carries more weight than a woman's in the outside world, so his authority, not hers, is used to represent the household's best interest. Some (male) scholars and officials feel justified in making statements that ignore women's rights, because that is probably what they have been told. The process of representation mediates what Emberá do and think in everyday life and what gets communicated to non-Emberá. If the mediating process of representation itself is not problematized in the collection of data about social reality, scholarly and official texts may be skewed; even false representations can seem unquestionably objective.[14]

Male bias in ownership and inheritance practices must be posed as a subject in question, not a given. Except when they have newborns to care for, women work together with men in the orchards and fields — and since when are their complementary labors, whether agricultural or not, accorded less value? There's a split between egalitarian ideals and patriarchal actualities.[15] Why is it growing wider? Naming a tradition of internal patriarchy as origin of present day inequalities does not seem an apt answer, unless we refer to the "tradition" that results from an accommodation to Conquest and colonization. The incorporation of gender asymmetries may have begun between the sixteenth and eighteenth centuries, when Spanish warriors, bureaucrats, and missionaries — unsuccessful in concentrating Indians in mining centers — began assigning Emberá ("Choco") "caciques" and "household heads" to carry work orders to and collect taxes from dispersed settlement sites (cf. Castrillón 1982:128). Today, the intensification of gender asymmetries with integration into a patriarchal nation is not a phenomenon unique to the Emberá.[16] Perhaps the cosmological imperatives that underlie women's insistent pressured labors that re-create tradition and distinctive domesticity are also not unique.

Cosmologically, Women Are Poised at the Site of Historical Contradiction; or, How Gender Bears the Weight of Colonization

Constrained by the symbolic, women continue practicing the roles that tradition assigns them. Yet the pressures to re-create the identity of a people as a distinct group are in contradiction with ever-increasing pressures to leave home, marry *kampuniá,* fight for their own land rights, and handle money. It is this contradictory situation that shapes the way that women think of themselves and how others represent them. Women are now constrained by both cosmology and the new politics to enact a role with minimum decision-making power at the village and *comarca* level, the levels that increasingly condition and redefine their lives. Held back from full participation in the otherworld and foreign, yet responsible for and affected by it, women stand poised at the contradictory site that articulates the Emberá with nation. Their value as identity constructors is unspoken, allowing cultural construction to seem real. Poised at the contradictory site of articulation, women monitor and selectively resist foreign interventions that might weaken their control over households' economies. The monitoring and selection of foreign forms functions politically, not only in the construction of a revised tradition, but, outside the official arena, as a form of active political resistance to foreign intervention. The traditional forms

that we see are not remnants of a precapitalist past; they are symbolic con-
structions designed to work against pressures that are specifically foreign
(the particular combination of quasi-socialism and capitalism that the U.S.-
backed Torrijos/Noriega regimes promulgated as development). Despite
the official silence in which it is submerged, the vitality of women's politics
can be discerned if analysis proceeds on this basis and includes the local
level.

Autonomy and Survival

*It all began that time Agouti was taking care of Uncle Jaguar's babies so his wife could go
out hunting with him in the forest. Besides taking care of the babies, Agouti was supposed
to prepare a meal for her to eat when she returned. When the time came, he had gotten
nothing together with which to make it, so he made a stew out of one of the babies. Each
night he fed her another baby stew. After she ate, she would ask him to bring the babies
down from the rafters, one by one, so that she could suckle them. As there were fewer and
fewer up there, he'd bring the same one down over and over again. She didn't discover this
until the night there was only one left. But Agouti was gone. He escaped through a tunnel
he'd made in the back of the house. That's where it all began.*

from an Emberá folktale

One afternoon in January, an impromptu meeting is called in Tamarinbó
to find out who failed to show up for the group clearing work the day
before. The meeting is held in Carolina's house because school, which oc-
cupies the one public building, is in session. People arrive one by one. Talk
turns to the benefits of cooperation. The discussion is led by Lucinda's
husband, Felipe, the recent arrival from Colombia who is literate and ambitious (but who is forced to leave some months later for lack of food). He
has an idea about how they could buy a chain saw if they worked together,
sell wood to lumber companies, and buy tin to replace thatch for their
roofs. Eva's brother Agouti chimes in on this theme. Inez's husband, Dalas,
brings the conversation around to a more immediate issue. In addition to
clearing paths and plazas in and around the village, they ought to widen
the earthen steps up the river bank port that functions as the village's main
toilet. The house is full by this time. Most of the women arrived after the
men and are grouped around the entrance. The village head, Eva's husband, Rubén, suggests that the men should all work together on each other's orchards. Each person's orchard would get a day of work done by the

189

whole group. Inez, looking into the empty basketball court beyond, mutters something angrily under her breath. I find out later (she is still angry) that she'd said that she doesn't want her husband, Dalas, working on somebody else's orchard.

That evening, I ask Eva if she thinks cooperative labor on the orchards would work. She said when they tried it once before, it failed because of the women. The women tell the men not to work on the orchard of another. "Why, even as it came up today, Inez opposed the idea. She's a bad person," Eva said. I suggested perhaps it isn't that she's bad but that she wants to do things the old way, where each family works for itself alone. Eva agrees that this is true.

Tradition predisposes Tamarinbó's residents to resist cooperative interhousehold work and persist in organizing work independently. Eva may blame the lack of cooperation on women, but I think that it is the women acting as spokespersons for the traditional point of view. There are plenty of men — like Inez's husband, Dalas, and father, Dzoshua — who agree with her. But particularly in the context of official meetings, men are made to feel that if they speak at all, they should identify with the promoters of "progress" — in whatever form that happens to take. But for reasons as vague as mistrust and as specific as past experience of getting taken, in practice the men pay little more than lip service to change when it comes in the form of cooperative effort, continuing on in their own corresponding but separate ways.

Tradition, despite its association with the conservative perspective, includes the possibility of its own transformation (Williams 1977:115–20). Indeed, to continue resembling itself in changing conditions, tradition has to be transformed (Hall 1981). People like Inez, who refuse to reorganize their agricultural work, and her husband, Dalas, who is willing to get involved in small projects basic to village infrastructure like fixing the port but who shares Inez's attitude toward major changes, are not just conforming to habits that are tried and true. Their stance critically assesses current conditions of possibility. In addition to transporting plantains to market, a task that has been cooperatively organized in Tamarinbó only to a limited extent, the biggest task in plantain production is clearing away jungle overgrowth. Most lose some portion of the plantains because they can't keep their orchards all clear. (When it grows well, it's more than you can eat anyway, and it's a long way down to Yaviza to sell.) If such a cooperative plan were to go into effect, something like this would not be an unlikely

Figure 30. Tamarinbó in dry season, with main port in foreground. Photo by L. Stoller.

scenario: men would do the cooperative work, leaving women to maintain the family orchards. In the initial enthusiasm, some people's orchards would get cleared. (Eva's would probably be one of these.) Other contingencies would intervene; some men would stop showing up for cooperative work. Eventually, after discussion and cajoling, everyone would get fed up. The families still waiting their turns would not get the direct benefits of their labor (there might be a later exchange as compensation), and women will have had full responsibility for the family plot. Like Inez says, it seems better for every man to clear as much of his own orchard as possible by working with his wife and extra paid labor if affordable. That way everybody gets food and maybe some money.

Cooperative labor in villages is useful only because it can lead to pooled resources. In this way, money earned might amount to something, like Felipe's chain saw idea. In the larger, more organized villages like Cueva, the village can get a big bank loan for agrotechnology and transport vehicles.[17] While interhousehold capitalist endeavors can work, it is a process that leads families to become dependent on the national economic

Figure 31. Yard in Yaviza.

system at the village level. The Emberá don't like to lose control over their family's labor and resources to state bureaucracies — even when they're supposed to get something good out of it. Some who live in dispersed sites do not willingly deal with the state at all.

Short List of Practical Contradictions

As the world comes increasingly under state control, getting a voice in the politics of state is perhaps the only viable alternative to isolation. But regional development has contradictory effects. A short list relevant to the Emberá of Darién suggests some of these:

In order to hold on to the knowledge and environment needed to live in the traditional way, the Emberá enter more directly into the political economy of the nation-state. In doing so, however, they risk losing autonomy and self-determination at the level of the household — the precise locus of tradition.

Women are raised in complementary equality but marginalized by male-dominated official arenas that, while willing to exploit women's mundane labors, are not the least bit interested in their cosmological significance.

The villages are safer—if someone murders you, your corpse is sure to be discovered fairly soon. But it takes longer and longer to walk between field and canoe carrying sacks of rice and corn on your back.

The bush is being pushed back, opening the land for people to use, but erosion and lack of shade are shallowing out and drying up the rivers. Even if you do have a motor instead of a pole, there are many stretches you have to get out and push the hollowed-out tree loaded with plantains.

You hope that the sardines can process enough human excrement to keep your village's water clean, and you try not to worry about villages downriver and upriver. (In the Nué flood myth, sardines eat the clay foundation under the last little island of land that the people have left to stand on.) Some villages are getting aqueducts that bring clean water from the hills, but the technology usually breaks down.

There are new and different kinds of things to eat and drink (cold coke and beer in town), but food processed with chemicals, packed in tins, and transported costs more in Yaviza than in New York City, where the money comes from. And around the villages, fish, game, and firewood get scarcer.

People don't have to move into villages, but they are constantly pressured to do so. Parents who live too far to send their children to school are threatened by the Guard.

Children learn reading, writing, arithmetic, and Bible studies in school. But most of their teachers are campesinos/as who speak only Spanish and decorate the room with magazine pictures of pale necks wearing diamond necklaces and knotted ties. Then if the children want to go past sixth grade, their parents must have the will and the money to send them to live in town. If they make it through high school and college, they learn that there's nothing in the forest to come back to, so they either join the ranks of young, literate, and ambitious Emberá leaders or slip into the multiethnic ranks of an urban underclass.

Some villages have health posts with basic medicines, but babies still die of diarrhea because the water is bad. Once they are sick, they cannot swallow the replacement fluids made with the electrolyte packet that the health post passes out.

When you go to the hospital, it is so strange—and there is so much that pills cannot cure.

The U.S.-sponsored malaria prevention program systematically sprays DDT on Emberá dwellings, inside and out. This has accomplished a major drop in malaria infection rates in Darién as compared with those on the Colombian side of the border. The DDT kills cats but not rats and cockroaches. It's given out as favors to Emberá who cover their rice with it before planting so they won't have to stand in the fields shooting birds and small mammals while waiting for sprouts. It all eventually flows into the river, where it is eaten by animals higher up the food chain.

In the 1950s, the U.S.-backed hoof-and-mouth disease program (COPFA) killed off all the pigs in the Darién, establishing a "disease free" control zone between North and South America. This was just a precaution: when they did it, there weren't even any cases of hoof-and-mouth disease in Darién. The pig-killings destroyed the Emberá's principal protein base, one that foraged for itself—keeping a pig in a pen (the current regulation) isn't worth the labor invested in feeding it.

Since 1983, when Law 22 was passed, proposing the Emberá *comarca*, it has seemed that the Emberá were well on their way toward being a people with the security of forested land. But then in 1985 one goes to the congress and hears that the *comarca* is still in the "implementation phase," waiting for the government to allocate $60,000 for aerial photographs of proposed boundaries. The neighboring Kuna fought for their *comarca* early and succeeded. But the Guaymi, of land-poor and copper-rich western Panama, have been fighting for a *comarca* for longer than the Emberá but without success. Their case is worrisome, reminding that when politics gets rough, the government has infinite methods of procrastination.

Life goes on this way till 1988, when the whole Torrijos-Noriega government falls.

In 1990, for a 2 percent interest, the Panamanian government sold the gold-mining rights to an area of ninety-five thousand acres in the upper Tupisa and Tuquesa Rivers to Panamanian and Canadian companies.[18] This acreage, according to the government maps of Darién that were available to me in 1985 (see Fig. 3), must be either within the domain of the proposed *comarca* or the proposed wildlife reserve. Gold extraction is carried out by means of placer mines, in which mercury—although illegal in the United States because of severe environmental damage—is typically used in Central and South America. Such actions throw into question the entire premise that zoning and development in Darién is (1) what it purports to be and (2) is for the good of the people.

Sometimes technology and development seem to be as mythical as Ancient Times, a proud and dangerous folly spinning its wheels at the limits of planetary ecology.

Does anyone remember how to prepare curare for hunting with blowguns? Where do those poison-dart frogs live anyway?[19]

Devil-Making: Bush and Noriega

Out of the clashing of cultures and the fires of war, devils arise and assume human image. This is my Emberá-gringa mythico-historical version of events surrounding the U.S. invasion of Panama:

There were two powerful *kampuniá* devils—a Spanish soldier and a gringo politician. They were once colleagues of sorts; like Bush, Noriega snaked his way up government ladders through the CIA (Scranton 1991:13–14). The Spanish soldier became general and ruler of the once-democratic little country of Panama. The gringo politician became president of the United States. They continued their collaboration. The Spanish general worked with the gringo president's Drug Enforcement Agency, trying to put the Medellín cocaine cartel out of business. Being a participant in this same cartel, the Spanish general knew all the ins and outs. He played both sides of every fence, keeping friends in high places within Cuba and Nicaragua too (p. 15). Meanwhile, financial aid from the United States to his little country skyrocketed from $7.4 million in 1983 to $12.0 million in 1984 to $74.5 million in 1985 (p. 78). When he rigged the 1984 national election to put in a president that he and others thought would keep military rule stable for international corporate interests (Barletta), he had to call out his special riot police, the Dobermans, to quell all the protesting demonstrators. The democratic cloak over the Spanish general's violent rule was falling off (La Feber 1989:197). The scam was getting out of control. The gringo president had no choice: the Spanish general had to go. The gringo president used the television, print, and radio to remake the Spanish general into the gringo image of evil: he turned the once-militaristic but benign force of political economic stability into the devil-dictator, the recently budding democracy into the entrenched "narcocracy" (U.S. Government 1989). By mid-March of 1988, the gringo president stopped sending money to the Spanish general. By the end of March, all the nation's teachers stopped getting paid (Scranton 1991:137).[20]

But the Spanish general was also trained to play cunning war games using the media. He remade the gringo president, a once-powerful benefactor, into the image of a devil-imperialist, coming to renege on the last canal treaty the gringo government (under Carter) had made with Panama. The Spanish general called on his special friends. The Medellín cartel and the governments of Cuba, Libya, Mexico, Taiwan, and Japan offered advice and/or cash to help him and his army get through the financial squeeze ruining the rest of the little country (Scranton 1991:15). The gringo president grew impatient for results. In December of 1989, he started a war hunt to capture the Spanish general-devil-dictator in the name of the Panamanian people (most of whom had wished him long gone, even while the gringo president was propping up his power). The gringo president sent word to his general inside the mountain base betwixt Canal Zone and Panama City, central headquarters of the U.S. Southern Command. Acting on the president's orders, the gringo general unleashed his army of tanks, helicopters, and bombs from inside the Zone onto the city of Panama, blowing up the Spanish general's headquarters and hundreds of surrounding residential and commercial buildings. There was no warning to civilians, thousands of whom were left homeless or dropped unceremoniously into mass graves (p. 204; Independent Commission of Inquiry on the U.S. Invasion of Panama 1991; Weeks and Gunson 1991). The gringo people did not learn how devastating the war hunt proved to be for the Panamanian people, but they did find out what the gringo soldiers thought they saw in the Spanish general's desk when they broke into his office: pornography, voodoo paraphernalia, photo of Adolf Hitler, and cocaine (National Public Radio, evening news on December 21, 1989).[21]

The gringo president's army didn't catch the Spanish devil-dictator right away. There was some mishap about gringo tanks forgetting about one of the three main roads that led out of the city (Engelberg 1989). (After all, for the gringo military, it was just a practice run for fighting the war against devil-dictator Saddam Hussein in Iraq, wasn't it?) The Spanish general evaded the overstaffed and overequipped effort of the gringo president's army for five days after they bombed his headquarters. Then on Christmas Eve, the Spanish general went to a Dairy Queen store in his city and telephoned the papal nuncio to ask for sanctuary (Scranton 1991:205–7). He surrendered to the church, hoping that its sacred space might have the power to repel the gringo president-imperialist-devil.[22] Outside the sanctuary gringo soldiers blasted rock music, and Panamanian civilians chopped up and smashed pineapples that reminded them of the Spanish general's face (pp. 205–6, 212). After ten days of this, the gringo president had the Spanish general agree to be taken from the sacred sanctuary in his little country to North America, where he threw him in jail — after all, the Devil made him do it. The Spanish general was tried in the courts of the gringo president. The trial cost millions of dollars. It was admitted that the cocaine in the Spanish general's desk drawer was in fact flour for making tamales (National Public Radio, evening news on April 9, 1992).

To here, no more, is the story.

Humans give devils the lead in scripts of sudden disruption. They call on images of devils when they cannot cope with the thought of their own lying and destructiveness. The clashing of cultures and the fires of war produce leaders whose humanity is ambiguous enough to fit the devils' images, while their subjects play the fools, soldiers, and victims.

Caught, Nearly

Colonial history is full of moments when humanity stops. The following perverted story fragment belongs to Easter, as some *kampuniá* celebrated it in the Putumayo of Colombia during the rubber boom, in the early part of this century. First reported in an Iquitos newspaper called *La Sanción* (The Sanction), it was translated by the gringo adventurer Walter Hardenburg (1912:213–14) and retold by the anthropologist Taussig (1987:3, 21–22) in his study of terror and how it is mediated by narration.

> And they also tortured the Indians with fire, water, and upside-down crucifixion. Company employees cut the Indians to pieces with machetes and dashed out the brains of small children by hurling them against trees and walls. The elderly were killed when they could no longer work, and to amuse themselves company officials practiced their marksmanship using Indians as targets. On special occasions such as Easter Saturday, Saturday of Glory, they shot them down in groups or, in preference, doused them with kerosene and set them on fire to enjoy their agony. (P. 34)

In his own time, Hardenburg's stories brought these events to the attention of people in Great Britain, the United States, and Canada, turning the brutality practiced by this consortium of British and Peruvian interests into a public issue. I repeat it here because I think it conveys something about what gringos mean to the Emberá, even though the Emberá may not be the particular kind of Indian tortured in this reference. The abject attitude of mind demonstrated by these white businessmen, their ritual passions for savagery, has few equals. The Indians may have turned Easter into a drama of rainforest regeneration replete with comedies about getting free money back from the Devil (see Chap. 3), but gringos shall not be easily freed from the legacy of torture. The figure of strange evil has a number of classic variants in Emberá tradition. One is Tuli Vieja, the old *kampuniá* woman with breasts to her knees and a sieve for a face, who is said to steal Emberá children and take them to the rivers upstream (see Chap. 7). The *duende,* a figure who probably arrived from Spain with the Conquest, is another. Dwarfish, ugly, wearing a big hat, and carrying a staff, the *duende* has been reappearing from generation to generation in cultures throughout Central and South America and the Caribbean. He usually is said to have his feet on backward, one to the front and one to the back, as if put on hastily in a rush to step into the everyday world. Like Tuli Vieja, the *duende* is a post-Conquest personage at life's extreme. Ancient and alive, he continues to evoke the horrors of contact. Here is one final story.

When Valentín of Palo Blanco told me about the phantom gringo boat [Chap. 8], he said that his daughter Veronica was one of the prepubescent girls who prepared the ritual in which the tide was created to bring the boat upstream. This was not the only event of her childhood that linked her and her father to encounters with spirits in *kampuniá* form. One day when she was just a little girl, they went across the river to pick bananas. Suddenly a mist lowered and Veronica disappeared. He could barely see the broad green leaves for the haze. He called and called, ran everywhere, home to his wife, back again, calling, calling. . . . (−T/S)

In place of her father, Veronica saw a dwarf with a big hat and a staff in his hand: a *duende.* He grabbed her, and she shouted, "Mamma come! I've been grabbed, Mamma!" She shouted loudly. And then he took her. He grabbed her hand and they went so . . . instantly a path opened up. And then they went, went, went. And then the *duende* said to her, "Go back to your house. He's already after us. There's your father already." And there, right then, he went away saying gruffly, "What are you doing, you? I'm going to where my woman is." And then her father found her. (T/E)

The *duende* comes out of the mist and into the orchard of everyday life seeking a human child to complete a strange nuclear family in minia-

Figure 32. Dooryard garden on Pan-American Highway with coconut, pineapple, and banana.

ture. He threatens with his oddness. Then, joining the other fantastic and incongruous images, he walks abruptly back into the surreal. According to a semiotics of unnatural encounters, the *duende* releases Veronica into the world again to tell her story. So many years later, the child now a mother herself, the colonizer and colonized are still locked in struggle with each others' promises and failures. The story is told anew into my tape recorder: reflections of colonial encounter bouncing across time. I know that to Veronica and her father this gringa-in-the-flesh is more real than a *duende*, but how much more, I cannot tell for sure. To me, her personal-experience narrative is like a collective dream in which I grope for memories of surreal encounters in other times and places, memories of impossible things that make their way into history. And I brood upon the points at which cultural confrontation trains our emotions to fix and hide. Becoming a listener and then a teller in the chain of interpretation through which we all negotiate our differences and desires, our distinctiveness and common humanity is confirmed. Multiplying the possibilities for discourse and imagination may help us come to grips with the politics of war and waste that govern our planet.

A promise of health, wealth, and happiness rides a phantom gringo boat that is always just beyond reach — like progress and development. And you who read this book at night, the colors of your garments illuminated by a soft electric glow, perhaps your sense of identity can be jolted just a bit to incorporate the *duende* and Tuli Vieja into the edges of its frame. From the outside, you know, your reality and your humanity do not appear to be as firmly in place as you may think. Consider the things being done in your name, gringo, and answer: Is it you who challenge the rainforest people with these elusive promises?

Notes

Chapter 1: Contours of Social Space

1. I thank Kristin Koptiuch (1989:54–61) for her persistent reminder that ethnographers are always already in the field. Although this field may be rhetorically constructed as local, it is simultaneously part of global forces, events, and divisions.

2. Ecological and political shifts in regional history are documented in Gordon 1957; West 1957:82–125; Wassén and Holmer 1963:9–39; Shook, Lines, and Olien 1965; Castrillón 1982.

3. See Koster and Sánchez Borbón 1990 for a more critical insiders' appraisal.

4. Between 1972 and 1976, the Panamanian government undertook the largest project it ever carried out. With funding from the World Bank, the Interamerican Development Bank, and a Venezuelan bank, the Bayano Hydroelectric Complex was built in the westernmost edge of Darién Province. The dam flooded thirty-five thousand acres of agricultural land, forcing resettlement of Kuna, Chocó (Emberá and Waunan), and campesinos, in order to create electricity for the metropolitan region of Panama City (Wali 1983:103–27; 1993).

5. Between the sixteenth and eighteenth centuries, the Spanish conquistadores and missionaries tried to get the Emberá and Waunan to live in concentrated

settlements at mining sites. They never succeeded. They did, however, institute a system of tributes and tithes that linked the dispersed settlements to centers of power (Castrillón 1982:129, 156). There is also ethnohistorical and mythological evidence that there were Chocó villages before the Conquest. Dispersion may thus be considered a reaction to Conquest (Kennedy 1972:35).

6. For comparative work on Kuna political organization, see Howe 1986.

7. See Herlihy 1986:161–89 for historical review of village formation, including a more detailed story of Peru (pp. 164–67). I thank Catherine Radford, who passed on pages copied from Peru's astrology notebook that he left in the village of Manené, in the Balsa River of Darién.

8. By 1984, when I went to Panama to do fieldwork for my dissertation, Noriega's drug-trafficking activities were at their peak, and he had just rigged the election that began Barletta's short-lived presidency (Scranton 1991:14, 75).

9. I follow local Darién usage of "ethnic group," restricting it to the context of nation-state politics, and use the interchangeable terms *culture* and *race* in all other discursive contexts. This is consistent with the findings of other researchers (e.g., Adams 1991 and Jackson 1991) who study contemporary indigenous politics in Latin America.

10. I did preliminary research the year before in preparation for the current project. At that time, I had gotten permission from the Emberá who worked in the government Office of Indigenous Affairs (Política Indigenista) in Panama City to return the following year to continue research. I had also obtained permission for future research from the National Institute of Culture, which, from a purely legal standpoint, was sufficient. The then acting subdirector of the National Museum, Pedro Luis Prados, helped me through the impasse I experienced in obtaining Emberá permission upon my return in 1984.

11. I have changed the names of people and their villages to protect their privacy. Exceptions are public figures, scholars, towns, and rivers.

12. Both Tamarinbó and Palo Blanco were relatively unaffected by divisiveness caused by Catholic versus Evangelical loyalties.

13. Noriega's involvement in the cocaine trade was common knowledge in Panama long before the U.S. government decided to take official public notice. Because former president Bush and his staff were implicated in Noriega's illegal dealings, much of the documentation from Noriega's trial was rendered inadmissible.

14. This conceptualization is a variant of Buchler's (1984) definition, drawing on Lévi-Strauss and Lacan, of the mythical. According to this definition, the mythical is that which fills with signs the ontological gap between self and other, event and meaning.

15. Hebdige's definition of politics as the "art of the possible" (1988:201–2) joins these modes of discourse in a refreshing way.

202

16. Raymond Williams (1977:132) writes that in talking about structures of feeling, "We are talking about characteristic elements of impulse, restraint, and tone; specifically affective elements of consciousness and relationships: not feeling against thought, but thought as felt and feeling as thought: practical consciousness of a present kind, in a living and interrelating continuity. We are then defining these elements as a "structure": as a set, with specific internal relations, at once interlocking and in tension. Yet we are also defining social experience which is still *in process*, often indeed not yet recognized as social but taken to be private, idiosyncratic, and even isolating, but which in analysis (though rarely otherwise) has its emergent, connecting, and dominant characteristics, indeed, its specific hierarchies."

Chapter 2: Authentic Discontinuities

1. This analysis draws on Gramsci's (1971) concept of hegemony as being the ways in which social life is practically organized by dominant meanings and values. In this, hegemony is a complex, not totally effective, and not totally conscious interlocking of political, social, and cultural forces that can be distinguished from the more direct coercion of military rule (see also Williams 1977:108–14). It also keys into Foucault's (1980:81–82) concept of subjugated knowledges as both (1) histories that have been disguised by dominant discourses and (2) popular, local knowledges that are incapable of unanimity but that owe their force to the harshness with which they are opposed to everything surrounding them.

2. *Cimarones* is a term that refers to Emberá and Waunan who resisted Spanish oppression by running off into the most inaccessible regions of forest. They are historical actors who have gained mythical stature in the Emberá imagination (see Castrillón 1982:158–64 for a history of *cimaron* movement and Pardo 1984 for mythical texts). Their black counterparts call themselves the Maroons (see Price 1983).

3. *Achira* is a masculine plural greeting.

4. For a compelling analysis of the confrontation between myth and colonial history in Hawaii, see Sahlins 1981.

5. This discussion draws on recent feminist work that conceives of self and subject as multiple and shifting sites of identity and difference, as loci of identity that combine the personal and political in complex and conflicted ways. For explication, see, for example, De Lauretis 1990 and Kondo 1990:3–48.

6. I thank Amy Burce (personal communication 1983), drawing on Renato Rosaldo's Ilongot ethnography, for suggesting to me that Emberá villages might be unformed as easily as they are formed.

Chapter 3: Transformation and Taboo

1. Much of the hilly region along the Darién highway looks like Switzerland—cows and all. But how long before it turns dry and infertile, all the cows gone to Burger King? How long before it will only be the pieces the Emberá, Waunan, and Kuna struggle to preserve that remain forest? The Emberá and Waunan communities along the highway have been struggling to keep their rights to forested land. They are in competition with *colonos* who want to turn the forest to pasture, a strategy that is favored by development officials who believe that uncut forest represents a block to the progress of regional development. Even when official reserve status has been granted to sections of forest along the highway, it is difficult to defend from encroachment in practice. (For discussion of a land dispute between *colonos* and an Emberá and Waunan village located on the highway outside the proposed *comarca,* see Kane 1986b:198–201.) In the westernmost end of Darién, the Emberá have recently won a piece of land in exchange for resettlement resulting from the Bayano hydroelectric dam project. However, the Kuna, who are fighting for a bigger piece, have yet to succeed (Wali 1983, 1993).

2. Wailing is a formal style of expressing grief, a cry composed of variations on a specific melodic pattern in minor key. I heard only women wailing. Eva's mother wailed regularly each dawn and dusk for her recently deceased husband. Holidays and arrival times, when people come together and miss those absent more keenly, are also a context for wailing.

3. In myth, the white-lipped peccary (E. *bidó*) is associated with the beings that live in a backward way beneath the world called the Chämbera (see Chaps. 8, 9).

4. But as Crain (1991) argues for the Quimsa of Ecuador, the use of devil imagery in critiques of inequalities probably precedes the twentieth-century institutionalization of wage labor and proletarianization. The Emberá of Darién are still relatively independent of these processes and yet there is a rich and diverse corpus of devil lore. My guess is that the application of the term *devil* to otherworld animals/spirits began when gold-hungry Spanish began to tell the Indians about Christianity while they simultaneously enslaved, tortured, and killed them.

Chapter 4: The Absent Patriarch

1. Carolina's baby died from diarrhea, for which medical treatment was delayed and complicated by lack of clean water and the distance and cost of reaching either the health post in Tuquesa (six hours' walk through the forest for an adult and not always open) or the hospital in Yaviza (two days' poling downriver). Based on the reproductive histories of all adult women in the village of Tamarinbó ($n = 26$ in the village, with total population of 102), only 70 percent of all

infants born survive past three years. The causes of death cited in order of decreasing frequency are "unknown," diarrhea (with or without vomiting), fever, stillbirth, snakebite, killed by evildoing, and swelling.

2. Maintaining a cemetery to bury the dead is an imported Christian practice. As they did with houses that collapse from age and misuse, the Emberá used to let the graves of their loved ones disappear back into the earth without collective markings.

3. *Vela,* from the Spanish word *velorio,* refers to the practice of inviting family and friends of the deceased to the home for some days to mark a death. The body is covered with a white shroud and surrounded with candles.

Chapter 5: Techno-Magic

1. In addition to my usual role as ethnographer, I am acting as interpreter between an Emberá man and a gringo male friend visiting from the States as they talk about a masculine endeavor.

2. Lévi-Strauss (1966:101) discusses how natural systems of difference carry meanings associated with social difference. Through this symbolic process in which the "natural" organizes the "social," social structures come to seem as if they are indeed natural.

3. For example, there is a taboo against penetrative sex during times of transformation. Some Emberá versions of the flood myth (Noah/Nué) and many folktales associated with Easter time invoke the image of heterosexual couples who have sex inappropriately (e.g., anally) at the wrong cosmic moment and becoming petrified (literally turned to stone while in position; see Chap. 3). These images are structurally related to the folktales about animals who were once people, such as Woodpecker and Horned Lizard, whose axes get frozen on top of their heads when the world changed (see Chap. 2).

4. Nothing but cigarettes and eggs (from women) and meat from the hunt (from men) were available for purchase in the village. In an experimental attempt to make a monetary contribution, I gave the village $100 to buy some goods with which to start a cooperative store. Only later did I find out about the contentious history surrounding previous attempts at starting a store and the conflicts that would be generated as a result of my intervention (see Kane 1986b:176–95).

Chapter 6: Misfortune's Hat

1. See Vasco (1985:115–19) for further discussion of Antumiá.

2. Kinship categories are partially determined by age. While Americans might call Isadora's father's nephew a cousin, she calls him uncle, reflecting the difference in age between them.

3. The black towns of La Palma, where the rivers meet the sea (the regional capital), and El Real, on the major river route to the interior, were the two most important centers of trade in Darién until the highway extension was built, diverting trade to Yaviza.

4. This is before the Emberá had permission to bury the dead in their own upriver settlements (see Chap. 2).

5. Corpses tend to swell in the heat. Swelling, however, is also associated with spirit invasion.

6. Grade school teachers, who, like the *colonos,* come mostly from western Panama, stay upriver for longer periods of time and rely on these government workers for transport.

7. Gathering ipecac, as gathering rubber earlier, was once an important source of income for the Indians in the Chocó. It was reportedly bought by the American company Chicle and used to treat colds and as an emetic.

8. Levels of Spanish competency varied a great deal, with women generally understanding and speaking less Spanish then men, and elders speaking less than youth.

9. For further analysis of how shamanic discourse that is repressed in the official arena of a political congress erupts and expands in the local village context, see "The Sorcerer's Toad" (Kane 1986b:539–50). Aihwa Ong's (1987) ethnography discussing spirit attacks among young Malay women who work in factories is also of comparative relevance here because it explores the phenomenon of multiple spirit attack as a gendered response to new, intrusive forms of authority.

Chapter 7: Scale of Sentient Beings

1. See Chap. 2 n. 2 above about *cimarones.*

2. The Emberá and Waunan replaced the Kuna in Darién, an indigenous people who moved out of the interior to get away from the Spanish between the sixteenth and eighteenth centuries (West 1957:91). Most of the Kuna now live on the San Blas Islands along Panama's Caribbean coast and have their own *comarca,* Kuna Yala.

3. The Emberá make a regular practice of asking black-*kampuniá* whom they know as neighbors, government workers, or store owners to be the godparents of their newborns. As godparents, the black-*kampuniá* help the Emberá families, often paying for such things as the child's books and clothes and letting families from upriver stay on their property when they come through Yaviza to trade. In 1985, however, Catholic priests from Spain took issue with racial asymmetry in choice of *kampuniá* godparents for Indian children. The curates felt that the Emberá have a poor self-image, that they think that the "Indian has no value." They were dismayed to hear that the Emberá think of the church as a *kampuniá* institu-

tion and therefore that they need a *kampuniá* to be baptized. Indeed for some Indians, a *kampuniá's* participation, if he or she can bring a little holy water, may obviate the need for a priest altogether. The priests tried to disallow Yaviza blacks from becoming godparents of Emberá and Waunan children unless they traveled upriver for the baptismal ceremony. This was an impractical requirement; one Yaviza store owner, for example, had over a hundred Emberá godchildren.

4. The census count was Darienitas (blacks of Colombian descent), 52 percent; Emberá, 20 percent; *Chocoanos* (blacks born in Chocó, Colombia), 17.5 percent; *colonos,* 6.5 percent; Waunan (Nonamá), 2 percent; Kuna, 2 percent. Given the extreme difficulties of collecting census information and the dramatic changes occurring in Darién since 1972, when the report was first published, these figures are only a rough approximation biased in favor of town and road (i.e., blacks and *colonos*).

5. The reference to "dispositions and habits" refers to Bourdieu's (1985:72) definition of *habitus:* "The structures constitutive of a particular type of environment (e.g., the material conditions of existence characteristic of a class condition) produce habitus, systems of durable, transposable dispositions, structured structures predisposed to function as structuring structures, that is, as principles of generation and structuring of practices and representations which can be objectively 'regulated' and 'regular' without in any way being a product of obedience to rules, objectively adapted to their goals without presupposing a conscious aiming at ends or an express mastery of the operations necessary to attain them and, being all this, collectively orchestrated without being the product of the orchestrating action of a conductor."

6. See Chap. 3 n. 1 above about land dispute.

7. *Jumarasó,* an Emberá name meaning "all of one heart," was a successful coalition of Emberá and black plantain producers and transporters that threatened to strike if the government-fixed price for plantains was not raised.

8. For example, as per Britt Perez's conversation with an Emberá man, September 11, 1988 (unpublished notes).

9. Enrique García (his real name) influenced my thinking about strategic international interests in Darién. He thinks that the *comarca* is a way of protecting the strategic isthmus, that one road will eventually go through, and that the jungle around it will eventually be settled with obedient Indians to a create a buffer zone.

10. This is not to say that such murders don't occur among the Emberá. In an attempt to dissuade me from walking about the village environs mapping land use with only my dog for company, a black-*kampuniá* man who lived among the Emberá in the village of Palo Blanco told me about three Emberá youths who murdered an old Emberá man outside the village of Palo Blanco because they knew he was carrying cash.

11. Dante is selective about how he engages with Noriega's military. He ben-

efits from this particular transaction with the Guard, yet he continues to resist mounting pressure for him to move into the village. "I don't do anything to prejudice the village by living as I do—I don't cut any of their plantains," he says in a conversation with a black-*kampuniá* about the *comarca*.

12. Requirements of land use and ownership are an important factor governing settlement and migration patterns. For example, the village of Promesa, just downriver from Tamarinbó, was split by religious affiliation. Half the village ended up leaving with an Evangelical missionary to form an independent village in another river. Just as their lands started to look abandoned, however, they all came back and resettled.

13. As La Feber (1989) explains: By the mid-1980s, the debt that Torrijos incurred during his tenure to rebuild the state economy had ballooned to over $4 billion, the largest per capita debt in the hemisphere. By 1987, debt payments ate up half of Panama's national budget (p. 189). Bananas were the single largest export commodity, but the crop was controlled by the U.S.-owned United Brands (p. 191). Only one part of the economy boomed: Panamanians close to the government found ready cash serving as a "drug and chemical transshipment point and money-laundering center for drug money," according to a 1985 report to the U.S. House of Representatives Foreign Affairs Committee (p.192). The Reagan administration did not protest when Noriega fixed the May 1984 elections that put World Bank economist Barletta in power. Nor did it protest when Noriega blatantly removed him from power after Barletta protested the torture and slaying of physician and opposition leader Hugo Spadafora (p. 196). The semblance of democracy that disguised Noriega's dictatorial rule became less and less credible.

14. Rare now, but once common, are breastplates made of coins and beaded skirts for men and boys to wear.

15. Men and women share in most forms of agricultural labor, with men tending to specialize in heavier, more intensive or hazardous labor. For example, men are responsible for felling trees and burning the forest after it is cut and dried, whereas women are responsible for carrying loads back to the house from the fields. After clearing and planting together, women tend to be in charge of rice cultivation, especially rice for home rather than market use. Women also grow their own sugarcane patches and cultivate medicines, spices, flowers, and fruit trees in dooryard gardens. Men do the hunting, although women often accompany them on long forays and occasionally bring home game that their dogs catch while they are out gathering without men. Gathering is primarily a woman's task. Men do most of the fishing. Men do all the spearfishing, but women sometimes fish with baskets. Recently some communities have been fishing with nets to get enough food for large gatherings.

16. See Torrés de Arauz 1972 for more detailed description and analysis of diet.

17. Women do have small businesses selling eggs and cigarettes. In a fair marriage, a woman has considerable authority over the decisions that motivate men's use of money outside the household. And elder women continue to have authority over decisions regarding money, even after it is in the hands of their children.

Chapter 8: Shaman's Song

1. See also Comaroff 1985 for an analysis of how this process occurs in the indigenous ritual practice of a South African people.

2. Not all ethnographers have documented Chocó women shamans. Those that have include Kennedy (1972:14) and Pardo (1987a:14), both of whom worked in the Colombian Chocó.

3. A note on terminology: In this chapter, I use both the Spanish word *brujo* and the Emberá word *häïmbaná* to refer to the shaman, following the way the speaker uses it. Differences in usage do not seem random or simply a matter of translation but, rather, reflective of attitude: *brujos* seem to be run-of-the-mill shamans; *häïmbanás* are much rarer. In fact, I never met a shaman in Panama that was called a *häïmbaná*. That people say most great *häïmbaná* are still in Colombia is an idea that has grown to mythical proportions. However, it seems that most great *häïmbaná* are wherever you are not. Where I am not sure of the term used by the original speaker, and throughout the other chapters, I remain consistent with past literature and use the term *shaman*.

4. For documentation citing a Kuna medicine man talking about the skills of the Chocó in Panama, see Sherzer 1986; in Colombia, see Taussig (1987:175). Of comparative interest is Chapin's (1983) and Sherzer's (1983) work on Kuna medicine. Taussig's (1993) study of mimesis and alterity draws from the entire range of Kuna and Emberá ethnography.

5. The partiality of ethnographic representations in general has become a widely asserted—and resisted—assumption of anthropological practice (Clifford 1986). The limits of and gaps in our knowledge must weigh into our consideration even more when dealing with subjects of secrecy and imagination.

6. Carolina's remarried father was trying to reclaim the orchard lands he had given her and her brother as inheritance when her mother died, even though she, her brother, and her husband had been maintaining and improving them for years.

7. *Chicha* is the Spanish name given to indigenous alcoholic beverages, traditionally brewed of corn, but also referring to store-bought rum (called *seco* in local Spanish). The name *chicha* metonymically refers to the whole ritual in which it is used as a central symbol. *Canto*, the Spanish word for song, is also used to refer to the healing ritual as a whole.

8. In order to maintain a productive relationship with the shaman in Tama-

rinbó, I would bring her special gifts from Panama City, substituting money with bought objects. While I managed to appease her with these gifts, I always had the sense that I was using the wrong currency. From her point of view, she was giving me shamanic knowledge (= power) and therefore expected money in exchange. From my point of view, she was giving me something that was already publicly available; that is, she was not giving me what shamans ordinarily give for money — namely, well-being or the power to effect well-being — and so I could therefore legitimately give her something (a gift) but not what she ordinarily gets (money). Thus we accomplished a not quite satisfactory exchange. In contrast, I did pay for translations, because that required someone to invest work time in a project that I initiated.

9. Thanks to Steve Feld and Charlie Kiel for commenting on this transcript. Throughout, I indicate where Joaquín speaks in Spanish to me and in Emberá to Gabriel. I preserve the original words he uses to distinguish between terms for specialists or specialties: *häïmbaná* (E. shaman), *brujo* (S. shaman, sorcerer), *médico* (S. doctor), *doctor* (S.), *brujería* (S. shamanism, sorcery). Words spoken LOUDLY are written in small caps. Lines are determined by length of pauses. Spirit-talk is talking in a particular speech style, characterized by an imperative, heated tone, faster, tenser, and higher in pitch than normal speech, with some swallowing of parts of words. Two separate varieties of spirit-talk can be distinguished on the recording, but I do not analyze this aspect. Again, line length is not proportional to actual length of spirit-talk. There are variations of two basic melodic forms — one falling or, more rarely, rising in steplike fashion down or up the scale, another falling more dramatically from the upper to lower end of the scale. I do not analyze the variations in song patterns but simply note the presence of song.

10. For review of the interrelationship between different forms of Emberá healing that focus on plant use, see Kane 1989.

11. *Aché* is a term of male address.

12. Vasco (1985:25) participated in a song in the Cauca Valley in which the shaman called various spirits to augment the forces confronting evil, including the *hai* of Simon Bolívar and the *hai* of "doctor" Vasco himself, of the light (camera flash) and the recorder.

13. The Emberá word for heart or intention, *so*, is used to describe a shaman's predisposition for good or evil. It is also used more generally to describe a person's character, as in *so-droma* (one of an angry heart); to name a temporary state of being, as in *tadzi so-pua* (I/we am/are in pain or feel discomfort); and to name the bottom of the work basket *(ë)*, the place from which the strands of vine are first bound together and from whence the rest of the basket grows. Note that in contrast to interpretations of particular cases of illness and misfortune in which intention is discerned, the more pervasive misfortune befalling the Emberá as a race is taken as a perplexing given and narrativized in mocking folk tales in which

God somehow takes umbrage with an Emberá from Ancient Times (e.g., Legio's story of why man has to labor a canoe, Chap. 5, or the Easter stories, Chap. 3).

14. For a description of the land conflicts involving the village of Cueva, see Chap. 3 n. 1.

15. For analysis of the context of the tellings of Bernabe and Valentín, see Kane 1990. For complete transcription of Bernabe's tape-recorded account and Valentín's formal statement concerning the affair, see Kane 1986b:430–92.

16. Following the Popular Memory Group (1982), the discourse about past events concerning the phantom gringo boat is considered here as a "matrix of present possibility" that is produced as a function of the interacting influences that frame and organize it.

17. For analysis of the dynamic and ambiguous relation between curing rituals and social and political process among the Emberá of the Chocó, see Pardo 1987a:85–99, and among the Aguaruna Jívaro of Peru, see Brown 1988.

18. Following Jameson 1981:17–102, the texts of shamanic interpretation are considered here as collective texts of a political unconscious that should be read in a series of broader interpretive horizons.

19. This analysis benefited from discussion with José Limón (personal communication 1986).

20. I heard of one example pertinent to each level in the short time I was in the field. First, there was an Emberá man who lived in a village near the proposed biosphere reserve. He was getting trained as a park guard but felt that he had to leave the area because he feared retribution from those jealous of his position (Richard Weber, personal communication 1985). Second, Larú and Beatriz moved their family back to Tupisa from Tuquesa after their son was killed out of envy and their daughter was killed by a snake (see Chap. 2). At the time, their son had owned a motor, a chain saw, two horses, pigs, and was selling fifteen thousand plantains a week in Yaviza. Third, a small village in the Pirré Mountains of Darién dispersed because of a sequence of two or three accidental deaths (William Harp, personal communication). Pardo (1987a:92–93) discusses the role of shamans in Emberá migration patterns. He and Isacsson (1975:22) and Stipeck (1976:126) document cases in which Emberá temporarily abandoned territory as a result of a shaman's attack.

21. The topography of positive and negative attribution in shamanism as sorcery (or witchcraft) is complexly related to axes of social difference: gender, ethnicity/race, and class. In the French Bocage, for example, Favret-Saada (1989) finds that the "unbewitching" of male farmers, their families and farms, entails ritual changes in lifestyle that reverse gender roles in the household. This helps men overcome their own resistance to distasteful patriarchal practices such as disinheriting their own siblings of land. Unbewitching is directed at neighbors, displacing conflicts within the family onto those who are not too close or too far. The dynamics of evil attribution can be more complex when analysis considers contexts

broader than endogamous communities. In colonial contexts, state formation, which restructures societies along axes of difference, is central to the analysis of shamanism and sorcery. In Ecuador and Colombia, people of Spanish descent in highland economic centers search the lowlands for indigenous shamans to reverse effects of sorcery (Salomon 1983; Taussig 1987). In Indonesia, Tsing (1988) finds that one ethnic group, the Meratus, are cast as perpetrators and curers of the kind of illness-causing sorcery that makes the neighboring ethnic group, the Banjar, most vulnerable. In southeast Cameroon, Geschiere (1988) finds that class differences motivate witchcraft accusations. As the Maka attempt to fit new forms of state power and wealth into local patterns of organization, "revenge" against the state is expressed in the idiom of witchcraft. As intermediaries with the state, local elites hire witches to protect them from accusations.

The directed nature of sorcery charges in these cases may be compared with the ambiguities created in the healing of Gabriel. The young man, cut off from his inheritance, a satellite to his sister's family, a victim of crime when he heads to Panama City, is surely caught up in the problems of the nation-state as they play out differentially according to race, class, and gender. Nevertheless, according to Emberá shamanic practice, the manner of his cure avoids the specificity of blame.

Chapter 9: Cosmo-Snake and the Nation-State

1. Hëïropoto is a foundation myth in the Emberá corpus — everyone has heard it; many can tell it; it is encyclopedic, including many images and episodes that circulate in different myths. For transcription of three versions, which the above account summarizes, see Kane 1986b. For discussion of myth collection as historical encounter in which differences between versions of the Hëïropoto myth I collected are compared with those of missionaries (the latter omitting the menstrual blood motif), see Kane 1988.

At least one of the central motifs of the Hëïropoto myth appears widely in the myths of other indigenous peoples in the north-central Andes and adjacent lowland areas (McDowell 1994:59 n. 34). The motif refers to beings who can only smell their food because they have no anuses and a culture hero who cuts anuses for them. While the Emberá conceptualize these beings as the humanlike Chämbera from the otherworld, the Kamsá of Colombia, as McDowell (1994:59 n. 33) discovers, conceptualize them as lowlanders who are "savage" but human.

2. The withdrawal and empowerment of menstrual blood, its symbolic suspension between heaven and earth, has been a subject of ethnographic inquiry since the early work of Frazer (1981:242–43). Vasco (1985:121–22) finds several words that incorporate the morpheme *hëï* as root (which he, following Spanish, transcribes as *je*). These include the crab *(hëïbé)*, whose moltings convey immortality and the duality of predator/prey; *hëïnene*, the tree from which water bursts

forth upon the earth; *hëïnsra,* the "ant-mother," whose scheming causes Ankore to break open *hëïnene;* and *hëïmeneto* or *hëïmenede,* the name for girl's puberty rites.

3. The correlative of this principle, following Barthes 1972:129f., is that the deconstruction of myth reveals the process by which history (and culture) is transformed into nature.

4. This symbolic analysis of housework is inspired by Bourdieu's (1985) theory of *habitus.* See Chap. 7 n. 5 above.

5. Ethnographic study of how male and (less obvious) female spheres of influence articulate is influenced by Weiner's (1976) pathbreaking work.

6. In some cultures, men mimic female capacity for releasing and controlling menstrual blood in male circumcision rituals (see Trinh 1991:81–105 for analysis and review).

7. Another elder woman was all dressed up too, so I asked her if she was going to dance. It turns out she was Waunan, not Emberá. Before she walked off in a huff, she said: "No, our dance is different." Not only is tradition condensing around the female body, but in the quest for a unified image, variations associated with language difference are suppressed.

8. In addition to meeting with representatives of government agencies, congress work time is used to advance the cause of the *comarca.* Law 22, the original *comarca* legislation, was passed by the National Legislature in 1983. In 1985 the Emberá were in the process of writing an "Organic Charter" (S. *Carta orgánica*) that would contain the rules and regulations of *comarca* governance. At this congress, the Emberá were informed that to implement the *comarca,* aerial photographs of all the boundaries need to be done. The government would have to approve $60,000 for this work. The new president also sent word that he would like the Emberá to establish a new post of governor. This man, who would receive a salary, should be educated and would be the *comarca's* top emissary to the president. The people at this congress voted in the head of the Emberá Teacher's Association as acting governor. A list of government allocations was read. Everyone was quite surprised that the huge sum of $14,000 was authorized for building a cement school building in the tiny village of Tamarinbó. Later, hearing this reported back in the village, Celestina comments wryly that such a building will outlast them all.

9. Although people try to speak Emberá as much as possible, and are reprimanded at times for slipping away from it, there are a number of reasons that a good deal of Spanish is spoken at congresses. For one, it is the dominant language of the state and authorizes speakers accordingly. Second, there are many things pertaining to bureaucracy and development for which there are no words in Emberá. Third, many of the young leaders who actually run the show have been living in the city so long that they are not accustomed to speaking Emberá. Fourth, the congress is also a political body that represents a second linguistic

group, the Waunan, and Spanish is the language they share. (As the minority, however, the Waunan tend to speak and understand Emberá more often than not.) Finally, the congress is a place where representatives of the government and military show themselves to the people; formalities and practical interchanges with them must be carried out in Spanish. In this multilingual setting, a good deal of translation goes on.

10. For comparative analysis of American women's work in the home supporting men's professional work outside, see Smith 1979:168.

11. The ethnographic and geographic literature has been inconsistent in reporting women's rights to land. In a brief summary of scant literature in scattered sites, Stout (1948) reports that women own land; in his broad survey of dispersed sites in the Colombian Chocó, Reichel-Dolmatoff (1960) reports that women own land; in Faron's (1961, 1962) brief study of a village in Río Chico, he reports that women can only work but not own land; Stipeck (1976) finds that both men and women in northwestern Colombia have partial rights to joint property. Kennedy (1972:207) finds that Waunan women in the Chocó attain ownership of land just as men do, but because they initiate fewer activities, and those on a smaller scale, they tend to own less. Herlihy (1986:191), whose fieldwork among the Emberá in the Darién preceded mine by only one year, reports that "agriculture remains an adult male activity," and "agricultural lands of the parent generation are normally passed to the male siblings much as they were in the past. Outside of widows and females with peculiar inheritance situations, females do not, as a general rule, own land." Peculiar inheritance situations, indeed! He does not say on what basis he makes these statements, but he must not have asked (m)any women. That a scholar can state in cavalier fashion what must be the bias of his own male-to-male experience is especially frightening if one considers the paucity of existing "authoritative" documentation on Emberá landownership and inheritance practices. In the construction of what might seem to be traditionally appropriate laws for the proposed *comarca,* people in charge (probably men) might turn to false statements like this, which leave Emberá women with no land rights at all. The myths of the most empirical thinkers must also be subject to scrutiny, even where they serve merely to cover what they consider the gaps in their comprehensive studies. For a more detailed analysis of my study of landownership and inheritance, see Kane 1986b:77–158.

12. The Chico River, site of Palo Blanco, was settled and linked by trade to Yaviza much earlier than the Tupisa, site of Tamarinbó. Besides its relative remoteness, Tamarinbó is comparable to Palo Blanco in terms of language groups (both have Emberá majority with some in-marrying Waunan and Catio) and agricultural practices (both depend on plantains for subsistence and market). Neither village was directly related by kin to *comarca* leadership in 1984–85, nor had social relations in either village been strongly skewed by Catholic and Evangelical missionization.

13. Although plantains are a cash as well as subsistence crop, there was no significant difference between the villages in the average amount of plantain orchard each household had under cultivation (1.8 vs. 1.7 *kabuyas,* or 6.6 vs. 6.2 acres).

14. For critical analysis of data collection as a problem of representation in Emberá myth, see n. 1 above, and in women's medicinal plant expertise, see Kane 1989.

15. The term *egalitarian ideal* refers to the lack of economic stratification, as well as to sexual symmetries in the division of labor, extended family autonomy, equal inheritance among male and female siblings, and joint decision-making powers of male and female household heads.

16. For a comparative case of pressure to shift from egalitarian to patriarchal relations among the Bari of Colombia, see Buenaventura-Posso and Brown 1980:109–33.

17. For example, Cueva, the Emberá and Waunan village on the highway, was able to get a government loan to buy a truck.

18. The source of this information is a book published by Metals Economics Group (Beamish 1992:506–7) that lists as principal owner Minera Remance SA (Apartado Postal #5, Santiago de Veraguas, Panama City, Panama; phone [507] 984–230). The book also noted that the operation was placed on hold in June of 1991 for environmental and economic reasons.

19. For description of blowgun and poisoned-dart hunting practices of the Emberá and Waunan in the Chocó, see Myers, Daly, and Malkin 1978.

20. In real-time, for the Emberá of Darién, this meant that the teachers left, abandoning the schools that were the founding focus of the villages.

21. For photomontage of Noriega's collection of power objects, see Jones 1990:122–30.

22. Stories of people going to hide from the devil in churches are quite popular. In Tamarinbó, Agouti told me the story of King Piroli, for example, who made a contract with the Devil. In exchange for the Devil's money, King Piroli promised to give up his son when he reached age twelve. When the time came, he hid his son in the church and spread holy water around it to stop the Devil from entering. Then he snuck his son out in a wooden coffin with food and set the coffin out at sea. Eventually the coffin found land, and after passing through the land of the giants, the son returned home safely.

Glossary of Emberá Words

(S) indicates Spanish words or Emberá variants of Spanish words.

achiote (S): red fruit used for cooking and painting, *Bixa orellana*
algorobo: fruit with hard exterior and fuzzy meat
ambugé: bench for sitting by hearth, shaman's ritual bench
anhó: wooden tray that holds a sieve for separating liquid from fibers
animalitos (S): little animals/spirits
Ankore: God
Antumiá: demonic messenger of shaman
barra: baton
batea: large wooden tray for winnowing rice or panning gold
baú: catfish, *Rhamdia wagneri*
begí: deer, *Mazama american* (S. venado)
bicho: beast, parasite
bidó: white-lipped peccary, *Tayassu pecari* sp. (S. puerco de monte)
brujería (S): sorcery
brujo (S): shaman, sorcerer
cacique: chief
campesino (S): peasant (S. colono, interiano)
canalete (S): little canoe
cativo: tree, *Prioria copaifera*

chachagaráiri: palm used to make prongs for picking up pots (S. teneza)
chankla: genito-urinary disease
chibigi: turtle
chicha: corn alcohol drink, ritual shamanic song
chicharra: dragonfly
chícharro: catfish
chikwé: crab
chile (S): work basket (E. ë)
Chocoano: black person from the Colombian Chocó
cholo (S): Indian from Colombia
cimaron: Emberá who shuns outside contact, escaped black slave
cocada (S): coconut sweet
colono (S): peasant from western Panama in Darién (S. campesino)
comarca: reserve
compadre (S): godfather
con cabanga (S): disturbed state of mind
creciente (S): rising current, flood
cuipo (S): deciduous tree, *Cavanillesia platanifolia*
Darienita: black person from Darién
daú: eye
daúbaráda: shaman
detripando: taking out the innards
diablito: little devil, spirit
doedá-besia: remained in the river
dogowiru: bird known as the Devil's chicken
dokán: plant used for fish poison, *Clibadium* sp.
doté: canoe pole
dribibidí: ant species
dueño (S): owner
ë: work basket (S. chile)
eba-bákiri: palm used for flooring, *Socratea durissima* (S. jira)
ëräka: wild palm tree with edible seeds
eyábida: indigenous person in marriageable category
gente (S): people
grano (S): skin eruption
gringo: Euramerican, non-Spanish Caucasian
guarapo: alcoholic beverage from sugarcane
guineo: banana variety
hai: spirit(s), devil(s), animal(s), familiar(s)
häïmbaná: shaman (S. brujo)
hamará: basket with straight sides and open mouth
hampá: canoe (S. piragua)

häüre: spirit

hëä: pejibaye palm, *Bactris gasipaes*

hëï: cosmic serpent, whirlpool

hëïbé: crab

hëïmeneto: girl's puberty rites

hëïnene: mythical tree that bursts to form the world's rivers

hëïnsrá-torró: ant-mother, ant-white, *Campenotus* sp.

hermano (S): brother

hirua-numua: caught in the heat of the devil/spirit (an illness)

hoja vijado (S): wide-leafed weed used to cover and wrap

hombre (S): man

huéchichi: nettles

huéporo: rubber tree (S. caucho)

humpé: armored catfish, *Chaetostomus* sp. (S. guacuco)

imamá: jaguar

iña-bákara numua: unable to breathe (an illness)

itarra: hearth

iwá: hallucinogenic vine, *Datura* sp. (S. pindé, pildé)

jagua (S): black dye from *Genipa americana* fruit

kalkolí: wild cashew tree, *Anacardium excelsum,* used for canoes (S. espave/epave)

kamísusú: large wooden stirring paddle

kampuniá: non-Indian, black or Caucasian

kapupudu: ant species

kau: term of address for daughter

kewará: toucan, *Ramphastos swainsonii* (S. pico)

kirrima: large beads

kitatri: jawbone

korogó: snail

koromá: armored catfish, *Plecostomus* sp.

kugurú: giant steel pot

kuriwa: agouti, *Dasyprocta punctata* spp. (S. ñequi)

libre: black person from Panama and Colombia, freed person

machucador (S): pestle

makenke: wood used for firewood and construction

makudo: laundry beater

makwá: vine used for rope, love potion

me: loincloth (S. wayuko)

mohópono: balsa

monte (S): forest, land

monte virgen (S): virgin forest

monteando (S): food acquisition in forest: hunting, gathering, fishing

nënzarahö: star apple, *Chrysophyllum cainito* (S. caimito) *neta:* small beads

nulpa: palm used to make brooms

ochorró: horned lizard, probably *Banisteriopsis banisteriopsis*

opogá imi: iguana eggs

ormiguito (S): little ant

orrekuabua: sides

paisa: Colombian of Spanish descent

pärärä: palm used for decorative braiding and basketry, *Carludovica palmata* (S. joropo)

parata kada: coin necklace

paruma (S): women's wrap-around skirt (E. wa)

paseando (S): hanging out, traveling about, cruising

patákoro: plantain variety

pepena: woven hearth fan

përöwära: paca

petá: oblong basket with lid

pico (S): toucan, *Ramphastos* sp.

pidókera: hardwood used for house posts, *Myroxylon* sp. (S. bálsamo)

pikiwa: vine for making work baskets

pindé (= pildé) (S): hallucinogenic vine, *Datura* sp. (E. iwá)

pino amarillo (S): tree used for making canoes, *Lafoensia p. unicifolia*

platanillo (S): wide-leafed weed, *Heliconia* sp.

primo (S): cousin

raizilla: ipecac root used as emetic, *Ipecacuana harabes*

ranchito (S): little shelter

rastrojo (S): field lying fallow, area cleared of forest

regidor (S): alderman

sambirruka: calabash with holes used as sieve

samó: guan, *Penelope* sp.

säö: calabash (S. totuma)

secreto (S): secret, verbal formula with specific healing function

Semana Santa (S): Easter week

sicatoca (S): disease affecting plantain and banana trees

so: heart, intention, character

so-droma: angry-hearted

sokorro: tinamou, *Tinamus* sp. (S. perdiz)

so-pua: in pain or discomfort

sorré: woodpecker

sukula: sweet plantain drink

tadzi: I/we

tallo (S): orchard

tamarinbó: tamarind

teneza (S): prongs of palm stem for picking up hot pots

tibɨ: firewood

tío (S): uncle

tra: ant species

tuétahö: guava, *Inga* sp. (S. guavo)

tumé: notched log for climbing into house

üchuburrɨ: little baskets with round bottoms and narrowing tops

umatipa: high noon

ürähó: honey

uruta (= trupa): palm fruit that is source of oil

vela (S): funeral wake

wa: wrap-around skirt (S. paruma)

wëra: woman

zorro (S): fox

Bibliography

Abbot, Wills
    1913   *Panama and the Canal in Picture and Prose: A Complete Story of Panama, as well as the History, Purpose, and Promise of Its World-Famous Canal — The Most Gigantic Engineering Undertaking since the Dawn of Time.* New York: Syndicate Publishing.

Adams, Richard N.
    1991   "Strategies of Indian Survival in Central America." In *Nation-States and Indians in Latin America,* ed. Greg Urban and Joel Sherzer, pp. 181–206. Austin: University of Texas Press.

Arocha, Jaime Rodríguez
    1992   "Afro-Colombia Denied." *Report on the Americas* 25 (4): 28–31.

Atkinson, Jane Monnig
    1987   "The Effectiveness of Shamans in an Indonesian Ritual." *American Anthropologist* 89:342–55.

Barthes, Roland
    1972   *Mythologies.* London: Jonathan Cape.

Beamish, Marilyn, ed.
    1992   *Opportunities in Latin American Gold Acquisitions.* May ed. Halifax, N.S.: Metals Economics Group.

Bennett, Charles
1968 "Notes on Choco Ecology in Darién Province, Panama." *Antropológica* 24:26–55.

Bort, John, and Mary Helms, eds.
1983 *Panama in Transition: Local Reactions to Development Policies.* University of Missouri Monographs in Anthropology No. 6. Columbia: University of Missouri–Columbia, Museum of Anthropology.

Bourdieu, Pierre
1985 *Outline of a Theory of Practice.* Cambridge: Cambridge University Press.

Brodzky, Anne, Rose Danesewich, and Nick Johnson, eds.
1977 *Stones, Bones, and Skin: Ritual and Shamanic Art.* Toronto: Society for Art Publications.

Brown, Michael Fobes
1988 "Shamanism and Its Discontents." *Medical Anthropology Quarterly* 2 (2): 102–20.

Buchler, Ira
1984 "Laughing Dogs, Scheming Infants, and the Facts of Life." *Semiotica* 48 (3/4): 319–43.

Buenaventura-Posso, Elisa, and Susan Brown
1980 "Forced Transition from Egalitarian to Male Dominance: The Bari of Colombia." In *Women and Colonization: Anthropological Perspectives,* ed. Mona Etienne and Eleanor Leacock, pp. 109–33. New York: Praeger.

"Carta orgánica"
1970 "Carta orgánica de la comarca Bayano y Darién de los indígenas Nonamá y Chocóe." Unpublished document in possession of Cacique T. Ortega.

Castrillón, Hector
1982 *Choco Indio.* Medellín: Ediciones CPI [Centro Claretiano de Pastoral Indigenista].

Chapin, Macpherson
1983 "Medicine among the San Blas Cuna." Ph.D. diss., University of Arizona.

Chavez, Milcíades
1945 "Mitos, tradiciones, y cuentos de los indios Chamí." *Boletín de Arqueología* (Bogotá) 1 (3): 152–53.

Clifford, James
  1986   "Introduction: Partial Truths." In *Writing Culture: The Poetics and Politics of Ethnography,* ed. James Clifford and George Marcus, pp. 1–26. Berkeley: University of California Press.

Clifford, James, and George Marcus, eds.
  1986   *Writing Culture: The Poetics and Politics of Ethnography.* Berkeley: University of California Press.

Comaroff, Jean
  1985   *Body of Power, Spirit of Resistance: The Culture and History of a South African People.* Chicago: University of Chicago Press.

Covich, Alan, and Norton Nickerson
  1966   "Studies of Cultivated Plants in Choco Dwelling Clearings, Darién, Panama." *Economic Botany* 20 (3): 285–301.

Crain, Mary
  1991   "Poetics and Politics in the Ecuadorian Andes: Women's Narratives of Death and Devil Possession." *American Ethnologist* 18 (1): 67–89.

Croat, Thomas
  1978   *Flora of Barro Colorado Island.* Stanford, Calif.: Stanford University Press.

De Lauretis, Teresa
  1990   "Eccentric Subjects: Feminist Theory and Historical Consciousness." *Feminist Studies* 16 (1): 115–50.

Douglas, Mary
  1966   *Purity and Danger: An Analysis of Concepts of Pollution and Taboo.* Boston: Routledge and Kegan Paul.

Duke, James
  1970   "Ethnobotanical Observations on the Chocó Indians." *Economic Botany* 24 (3): 344–64.
  1986   *Isthmian Ethnobotanical Dictionary.* 3rd ed. Jodhpur, India: Pawan Kumar Scientific Publishers.

Engelberg, Stephen
  1989   "Bush Aides Admit a U.S. Role in Coup and Bad Handling." *New York Times,* October 5, p. 1.

Etienne, Mona, and Eleanor Leacock, eds.
  1980   *Women and Colonization: Anthropological Perspectives.* New York: Praeger.

Fabian, Johannes
  1983   *Time and the Other: How Anthropology Makes Its Object.* New York: Columbia University Press.

Faron, Louis
  1961   "A Reinterpretation of Choco Society." *Southwestern Journal of Anthropology* 17:94–102.
  1962   "Marriage, Residence, and Domestic Groups among the Panamanian Choco." *Ethnology* 1:13–38.

Favret-Saada, Jeanne
  1980   *Deadly Words: Witchcraft in the Bocage.* Cambridge: Cambridge University Press.
  1989   "Unbewitching as Therapy." *American Ethnologist* 16 (1): 40–50.

Foucault, Michel
  1980   *Power/Knowledge: Selected Interviews and Other Writings, 1972–1977.* Ed. Colin Gordon. New York: Pantheon Books.

Frazer, Sir James George
  1911   *The Golden Bough: A Study in Magic and Religion.* 3rd ed. Vol. 1. New York: Macmillan.
  1981   *The Golden Bough: The Roots of Religion and Folklore.* New York: Avenel Books.

Freud, Sigmund
  1913   *The Interpretation of Dreams.* 3rd ed. New York: Macmillan.

Geertz, Clifford
  1973   *Interpretation of Cultures.* New York: Basic Books.

Geschiere, Peter
  1988   "Sorcery and the State: Popular Modes of Action among the Maka of Southeast Cameroon." *Critique of Anthropology* 8 (1): 35–63.

González, Raúl Guzmán
  1966   "Las migraciones Chocóes a la provincia de Darién, Panamá." Trabajo de graduación, Universidad de Panamá.

Gordon, Burton Le Roy
  1957   *Human Geography and Ecology in the Sinú Country of Colombia.* Berkeley: University of California Press.

Gramsci, Antonio
  1971   *Prison Notebooks.* New York: International Publishers.

Greenberg, Joseph
  1956   "Tentative Linguistic Classification of Central and South America." Paper presented at the International Congress of Americanists, September, Philadelphia.

Hall, Stuart
  1981   "Notes on Deconstructing 'The Popular.' " In *People's History and Socialist Theory,* ed. Raphael Samuels, pp. 227–40. Boston: Routledge and Kegan Paul.

Haraway, Donna
 1988 "Situated Knowledge: The Science Question in Feminism and the
        Privilege of Partial Perspective." *Feminist Studies* 14 (3): 575–99.
 1992 "The Promises of Monsters: A Regenerative Politics for
        Inappropriate/d Others." In *Cultural Studies*, ed. Lawrence
        Grossberg, Cary Nelson, and Paula Treichler, pp. 295–337. New
        York: Routledge Press.

Hardenburg, Walter
 1912 *The Putumayo: The Devil's Paradise; Travels in the Peruvian Amazon
        Region and an Account of the Atrocities Committed upon the Indians
        Therein.* London: T. Fisher Unwin.

Hebdige, Dick
 1988 *Hiding in the Light: On Images and Things.* New York: Routledge.

Heckadon, Stanley Moreno, and Alberto McKay, eds.
 1982 *Colonización y destrucción de bosques en Panamá.* Panamá: Asociación
        de Antropología.

Herlihy, Peter
 1985 "Chocó Indian Relocation in Darién, Panama." *Cultural Survival
        Quarterly* 9 (2): 43–45.
 1986 "A Cultural Geography of the Emberá and Wounan (Chocó) Indi-
        ans of Darién, Panama, with Emphasis on Recent Village Forma-
        tion and Economic Diversification." Ph.D. diss., Louisiana State
        University.

Herrera, Francisco
 1971 "Politización en la población indígena de Panamá." In *Actas del II
        Simposium Nacional de Antropología, Arqueología, y Etnohistoria de Pa-
        namá.* Panamá: Universidad de Panamá y el Instituto Nacional de
        Cultural y Deportes.

hooks, bell
 1990 *Yearning: Race, Gender, and Cultural Politics.* Boston: South End
        Press.

Howe, James
 1986 *The Kuna Gathering: Contemporary Village Politics in Panama.* Aus-
        tin: University of Texas Press.

Independent Commission of Inquiry on the U.S. Invasion of Panama
 1991 *The U.S. Invasion of Panama: The Truth behind Operation "Just
        Cause."* Boston: South End Press.

Irigiray, Luce
 1985 "The Power of Discourse and the Subordination of the Feminine."
        In *The Sex Which Is Not One*, pp. 68–85. Ithaca: Cornell University
        Press.

Isacsson, Sven Erik
1975   "Observations on Chocó Slash Mulch Culture." In *Arstrick*. Göteborg: Etnografiska Museet.

Jackson, Jean
1991   "Being and Becoming an Indian in the Vaupés." In *Nation-States and Indians in Latin America,* ed. Greg Urban and Joel Sherzer, pp. 131–55. Austin: University of Texas Press.

Jameson, Fredric
1981   *The Political Unconscious.* Ithaca: Cornell University Press.

Jones, Kenneth
1990   *The Enemy Within: Casting Out Panama's Demons.* Panama City: Focus Publications.

Kane, Stephanie
1986a   "Cultural Representations of Women and the New Politics of the Emberá." Paper presented at the Eighty-fifth Annual Meeting of the American Anthropological Association, November, Philadelphia.
1986b   "Emberá (Chocó) Village Formation: The Politics and Magic of Everyday Life in the Darién Forest." Ph.D. diss., University of Texas at Austin.
1988   "Omission in Emberá (Chocó) Mythography." *Journal of Folklore Research* 25 (3): 155–87.
1989   "Emberá (Chocó) Medicinal Plant Use: Implications for Planning the Biosphere Reserve in Darién, Panama." Unpublished manuscript.
1990   "Shamans Reconsidered: The Emberá (Chocó) of Darién, Panama." In *Class, Politics, and Popular Religion: Religious Change in Mexico and Central America,* ed. Lynn Stephen and James Dow, pp. 167–86. Washington D.C.: Society of Latin American Anthropology and the American Anthropological Association.
1992   "Experience and Myth in a Colombian Chocó Case of Attempted Murder." *Journal of Folklore Research* 29 (3): 269–86. An earlier version of this paper was published in 1990 as "La experiencia contra el mito: Una mujer Emberá (Chocó) y el patriarcado." In *Las culturas nativas latinoamericanas a través de su discurso,* ed. Ellen Basso and Joel Sherzer, pp. 235–56. Cayambe, Ecuador: Ediciones Abya-Yala.

Kennedy, Elizabeth Lapovsky
1972   "The Waunan of the Siguirisua River: A Study of Individual Autonomy and Social Responsibility, with Special Reference to the Economic Aspects." Ph.D. diss., University of Cambridge.

Key, Mary
  1979   "The Grouping of South American Indian Languages." In *Ars Linguistica: Commentationes Analytical et Critical.* Tübingen: Gunter Narr Verlag.

Kondo, Dorinne
  1990   *Crafting Selves: Power, Gender, and Discourses of Identity in a Japanese Workplace.* Chicago: University of Chicago Press.

Koptiuch, Kristin
  1989   "Notes on the Field: Inscription." In "A Poetics of Petty Commodity Production: Traditional Egyptian Craftsmen in the Postmodern Market," pp. 54–61. Ph.D. diss., University of Texas at Austin.

Koster, Richard, and Guillermo Sánchez Borbón
  1990   *In the Time of the Tyrants: Panama, 1968–1990.* New York: W. W. Norton.

La Feber, Walter
  1989   *The Panama Canal: The Crisis in Historical Perspective.* New York: Oxford University Press.

Leach, Edmund
  1964   "Anthropological Aspects of Language: Animal Categories and Verbal Abuse." In *New Directions in the Study of Language,* ed. Eric Lenneberg, pp. 23–63. Cambridge: MIT Press.

Lévi-Strauss, Claude
  1966   *The Savage Mind.* Chicago: University of Chicago Press.
  1967   *Structural Anthropology.* New York: Doubleday.
  1975   *The Raw and the Cooked.* Vol. 1. New York: Harper and Row.

Loewen, Jacob
  1958   "An Introduction to Epera Speech: Sambu Dialect." Ph.D. diss., University of Washington.
  1963a   "Chocó 1: Introduction and Bibliography." *International Journal of American Linguistics* 29 (3): 239–63.
  1963b   "Chocó 2: Phonological Problems." *International Journal of American Linguistics* 29 (4): 357–71.

Loukotka, Cestmir
  1968   *Classification of South American Indian Languages.* Vol. 7. Los Angeles: University of California Press, Latin American Center.

McDowell, John Holmes
  1994   *"So Wise Were Our Elders": Mythic Narratives from the Kamsá.* Lexington: University Press of Kentucky.

Marcus, George, and Michael Fischer, eds.
1986   *Anthropology as Cultural Critique.* Chicago: University of Chicago Press.

Mendez, Teodoro
1979   *El Darién: Imagen y proyecciones.* Panamá: Instituto Nacional de Cultura.

Mouffe, Chantal
1988   "Radical Democracy: Modern or Postmodern"? In *Universal Abandon? The Politics of Postmodernism,* ed. Andrew Ross. Minneapolis: University of Minnesota Press.

Myers, Charles, John Daly, and Borys Malkin
1978   "A Dangerously Toxic New Frog *(Phyllobates)* Used by Emberá Indians of Western Colombia, with Discussion of Blowgun Fabrication and Dart Poisoning." *Bulletin of the American Museum of Natural History* 161 (2): 311–65.

Nash, June
1979   *We Eat the Mines and the Mines Eat Us: Dependency and Exploitation in Bolivian Tin Mines.* New York: Columbia University Press.

Ong, Aihwa
1987   *Spirits of Resistance and Capitalist Discipline: Factory Women in Malaysia.* Albany: State University of New York Press.

Organización de Profesionales Embërä
1984   *Esbozo de gramática de la lengua Embërä (Documento preliminar).* Panamá: Universidad de Panamá (con ICASE).

Organization of American States (OAS; OEA)
1978   *Proyecto de desarrollo integrado de la región oriental de Panamá-Darién.* Washington, D.C.: OEA.
1984   "Estudio de la región del Darién, Panamá." In *Planificación del desarrollo regional integrado: Directrices y estudios de casos extraídos de la experiencia de la OEA,* pp. 101–29. Washington, D.C.: OEA.

Paganini, Louis
1970   "The Agricultural Systems of the Chucunaque-Tuira Basin in the Darien Province, Panama." Ph.D. diss., University of Florida.

Pardo, Mauricio
1981   "Bibliografía sobre indígenas Chocó." *Revista Colombiana de Antropología* 23:465–528.
1987a   *El convite del los espíritus.* Quibdó, Colombia: Ediciones Centro de Pastoral Indigenista.
1987b   "Regionalización de indígenas Chocó: Datos etnohistóricos, lingüísticos, y asentamientos actuales." In *Boletin No. 18.* Bogotá, Colombia: Museo del Oro.

1992   "Ethnic Survival, Economic Change, and Hegemonic Struggle: The Choco of the Western Rainforest in Colombia." Paper presented at the 1992 annual meeting of the American Anthropological Association, December, San Francisco.

————, ed.
1984   *Zröurä Nëburä: Historia de los antiguos literatura oral Emberá según Floresmiro Dogiramá.* Bogotá: Centro Jorge Eliécer Gaitán.

Pavy, Paul
1967   "The Negro in Western Colombia." Ph.D. diss., Tulane University.

Peñaherrera De Costales, Piedad, and Alfredo Costales Samaniego
1968   *Cunas y Chocós.* Llacta 25. Quito: Instituto Ecuatoriano de Antropología y Geografía (IEAG) and Batelle Memorial Institute

Popular Memory Group
1982   "Popular Memory: Theory, Politics, Method." In *Making Histories: Studies in History-Writing and Politics,* by Richard Johnson, Gregor McLennan, Bill Schwarz, and David Sutton, pp. 205–52. London: Hutchinson.

Price, Richard
1983   *First-Time: The Historical Vision of an Afro-American People.* Baltimore: Johns Hopkins University Press.

Price, Thomas
1955   "Saints and Spirits: A Study of Differential Acculturation in Colombian Negro Communities." Ph.D. diss., Northwestern University.

Reclus, Armando
1972   *Exploraciones a los Istmos de Panamá y Darién en 1876, 1877, y 1888.* San José, Costa Rica: Editorial Universitaria Centroamericana (EDUCA).

Reichel-Dolmatoff
1945   "Lingüística del grupo Chocó." *Boletin de Arqueología* 1:625–27.
1960   "Notas etnográficas sobre los indios del Chocó." *Revista Colombiana de Antropología* 9:75–158.
1962   "Contribuciones a la etnografía de los indios del Chocó." *Revista Colombiana de Antropología* 11:171–85.

Rivet, Paul
1943–44   "La lengua Chocó." *Revista del Instituto Etnología Nacional* (Bogotá) 1:131–96 and 2:297–349.

Sahlins, Marshall
1981   *Historical Metaphors and Mythical Realities: Structure in the Early History of the Sandwich Islands Kingdom.* Ann Arbor: University of Michigan Press.

Salomon, Frank
1983   "Shamanism and Politics in Late-Colonial Ecuador." *American Ethnologist* 10 (3): 413–28.

Saussure, Ferdinand de
1960   *Course in General Linguistics.* London: Peter Owen.

Scranton, Margaret
1991   *The Noriega Years: U.S.-Panamanian Relations, 1981–1990.* Boulder, Colo.: Lynne Rienner Publishers.

Sherzer, Joel
1983   "Curing and Magic: Counseling of the Spirits." In *Kuna Ways of Speaking: An Ethnographic Perspective.* Austin: University of Texas Press.
1986   "The Report of a Kuna Curing Specialist: The Poetics and Rhetoric of an Oral Performance." In *Native South American Discourse,* ed. Joel Sherzer and Greg Urban, pp. 169–212. New York: Mouton de Gruyter.

Shook, Edwin, Jorge Lines, and Michael Olien
1965   *Anthropological Bibliography of Aboriginal Panama.* Occasional Paper No. 2. San José, Costa Rica: Tropical Science Center.

Smith, Dorothy E.
1979   "A Sociology for Women." In *The Prism of Sex: Essays in the Sociology of Knowledge,* ed. Julia Sherman and Evelyn Torton Beck, pp. 135–87. Madison: University of Wisconsin Press.

Spalding, Karen
1974   *De indio a campesino: Cambios en la estructura social del Perú colonial.* Lima, Peru: Instituto de Estudios Peruanos.

Steward, Julian, and Louis Faron
1959   "Native Groups and Languages." In *Native Peoples of South America,* pp. 16–30. New York: McGraw Hill.

Stipeck, George
1976   "Sociocultural Responses to Modernization among the Colombian Emberá." Ph.D. diss., SUNY Binghamton.

Stout, David
1948   "The Choco." In *Handbook of South American Indians,* Bureau of American Ethnology Bulletin 143, vol. 4, ed. Julian Steward, pp. 269–76. New York: Cooper Square Publishers.

Taussig, Michael
1980   *The Devil and Commodity Fetishism in South America.* Chapel Hill: University of North Carolina Press.

1987   *Shamanism, Colonialism, and the Wild Man: A Study in Terror and Healing.* Chicago: University of Chicago Press.

1993   *Mimesis and Alterity: A Particular History of the Senses.* New York: Routledge.

Torrés de Arauz, Reina

1958   "Los indios Chocoes de Darién: Algunos aspectos de su cultura." *América Indígena* 18 (3): 167–75.

1962   "El chamanismo entre los indios Chocoes." *Hombre y Cultura* (revista del Centro de Investigaciones Antropológicas de la Universidad Nacional, Panamá) 1 (1): 17–43.

1969   *La cultura Chocó: Estudio etnológico e histórico.* Centro de Investigaciones Antropológicas. Panamá: Universidad de Panamá.

1972   "Hábitos dietarios y dieta quantitiva de los indios Chocóes (Panamá)." *América Indígena* 32 (1): 169–78.

1975   *Darién: Etnoecología de una región histórica.* Panamá: Instituto Nacional de Cultura.

1980   *Panamá indigena.* Panamá: Instituto Nacional de Cultura, Patrimonio Histórico.

Torres de Iannello, Reina

1950   "Los indios Chocóes en Panamá, su actual situación y problemática." Separata del Tomo 2 del Acta 33c, Congreso Internacional de Americanistas, celebrado en San José, Costa Rica, Junio. San José: Editori A Lechman.

Trinh, Minh-ha

1989   *Woman, Native, Other: Writing Postcoloniality and Feminism.* Bloomington: Indiana University Press.

1991   *When the Moon Waxes Red: Representation, Gender, and Cultural Politics.* New York: Routledge.

Tsing, Anna Lowenhaupt

1988   "Healing Boundaries in South Kalimantan." *Social Science and Medicine* 27 (8): 829–39.

U.S. Government

1989   "Hearing: U.S. policy toward Panama in the Aftermath of the May 1, 1989 Elections." Hearing before the Subcommittees on Western Hemisphere Affairs and International Economic Policy and Trade of the Commission on Foreign Affairs, House of Representatives. July 25, 26, 27. Washington, D.C.: U.S. Government Printing Office.

Vasco, Luis G.

1985   *Jaibanás: Los verdaderos hombres.* Bogotá, Colombia: Talleres Gráficos Banco Popular.

Wali, Alaka
  1983   "The Bayano Corporation and Social Change: The Regional Conse-
          quences of Macro Development." In *Panama in Transition: Local Re-
          actions to Development Policies,* University of Missouri Monographs
          in Anthropology No. 6, ed. John Bort and Mary Helms, pp. 103–
          28. Columbia: University of Missouri–Columbia, Department of
          Anthropology.
  1993   "The Transformation of a Frontier: State and Regional Relation-
          ships in Panama, 1972–1990." *Human Organization* 52 (2):
          115–29.

Wassén, Henry, and Nils Holmer
  1963   *Estudios Chocoes.* Etnologiska Studier Series 26. Göteborg: Etno-
          grafiska Museet.

Weber, Richard, and Ramon Alvarado
  1984   *Bibliografía general: Parque nacional Darién, sitio patrimonio mundial
          y reserva de la biosfera.* Documento de Trabajo Preliminar. Panamá:
          UNESCO/MIDA (Proyecto SC. 582.924.3).

Weeks, John, and Phil Gunson
  1991   *Panama: Made in the USA.* London: Latin American Bureau (Re-
          search and Action).

Weiner, Annette
  1976   *Women of Value, Men of Renown.* Austin: University of Texas Press.

West, Robert C.
  1957   *The Pacific Lowlands of Colombia: A Negroid Area of the American Trop-
          ics.* Baton Rouge: Louisiana State University Press.

Whitten, Norman, Jr.
  1974   *Black Frontiersmen: Afro-Hispanic Culture in Ecuador and Colombia.*
          Prospect Heights, Ill.: Waveland.
  1985   *Sicuanga Runa: The Other Side of Development in Amazonian Ecuador.*
          Urbana: University of Illinois Press.

Williams, Raymond
  1977   *Marxism and Literature.* New York: Oxford University Press.

Index

tity and women, 188–89; infant mortality, 204–5*n1;* language, ix–xi; politics, 181–85; and race relations, xv, 107–28, 206–7*n3;* scale of sentient beings, 106*fig20,* 107–8, 113, 137–39; school, 193; social organization, 40–43; social values, 42–43; studies of, xvi; systems of values, 39–43; and technology, 85

Ethnic identity, 107

Ethnographers, 27, 201*n1*

Ethnographic intentions, 12–13

Ethnography, 24; classic, 15, 18–20; and shamanism, 19–20, 90

Euramerican religion and medicine, shamanic rituals and, 143–53

Fabian, Johannes: on ethnographic authority, 18, 24

Families and national economic system, 191–92

Family: claims of land ownership, 39–43; gardens and social history, 37–43

Faron, Louis: on Emberá kinship, xvi; on Emberá language, x; on Emberá women's land rights, 186, 214*n11*

Favret-Saada, Jeanne: on witchcraft and gender, 211*n21;* on witchcraft and positionality, 102; on witchcraft and psychoanalysis, 174

Feeling, structures of, 20, 32, 203*n16*

Fiesta for San Francisco, 114–16

Fishing, 51, 60–63

Floods: in mythology, 33–37, 46; in 1950, 57; in 1961, 36–38

Foucault, Michel: on power/knowledge, 18; on state power, 173; on subjugated knowledges, 203*n1*

Frazier, Sir James George: on fetishes, 47; on menstrual rituals, 212*n2*

Freud, Sigmund: on myth, 202*n14;* on the unconscious, 23

Gambling, 114–16

Garden, family, 37–43

Gender: and management of paradox, 178–79; political economy of, 74–79, 105–10, 137–38, 184 93

Ghosts, 65–68, 107

God, 30, 74–75

Gramsci, Antonio: on hegemony, 203*n1*

Gringo boat, phantom, 1–3, 160, 167–69, 198–200

Gringo *kampuniá,* 124

Hai, 90–98, 103–6, 151, 155, 167–69; attracting, 160–61

Hall, Stuart: on tradition, 190

Haraway, Donna: on her ecocybernetic model, 85; on situated knowledge, 18

Hardenburg, Walter, 197

Health care, Emberá, 193–94

Hëïropoto, myth of, 177, 212*n1*

Herlihy, Peter: on the Emberá *comarca,* 103; on Emberá women's land rights, 186, 214*n11;* on village formation, xvi, 9, 202*n7*

Highway villages, 112–16, 164–67

hooks, bell: on ethnographic authority, 18

Households, 4, 11, 43, 63, 174; autonomy, 88, 189–92; utensils, 130–34

Houses, Emberá, 4, 45*fig12,* 128–33

Housework, symbolic dimensions of, 180

Human identity, Emberá conception of, 23–24, 105–7

Human-technological interface, 85

Identity: cultural, 29, 43, 55, 81, 105, 188, 200, 203*n1;* and discourse, 42–43; ethnic, xvi–xvii, 107; masculine, 74